Buy this book on a Friday, read it over the weekend, and walk into work the next Monday better prepared to deliver value.

■ David Clarke, Sr. VP Case New Holland

This is an extraordinary book that will become a business classic.

■ Ricardo Bolaños, Director de la Incubadora de Empresas Tecnológico de Monterrey

The CEO's initiatives drive the Big Deals. Think Like a CEO will enable you to work with the CEO to create those initiatives and drive sales!

■ Bob Simqu, Director, Strategic Services, Smartops

Think Like a CEO is right down the alley of what we try to do, but with much more concise breakouts of what and why tied to the value proposition. It is absolutely great in terms of laying out strategy, rationalization, and approach to get the deals done.

■ Henri Duhot, Sr. Director, Business Development, DHL

Think Like A CEO is a "must read" for any business executive who wants to sell his ideas to top management or the board. It's a guide that will help open doors to the top decision makers and create value for the business.

■ Ricardo Hirata, CEO, Keisen Consultores, SA de CV

As an engineer, I thought a great product would sell itself. We built a better mousetrap, but the world still beat a path to our competitor. The strategy and sales concepts in Think Like a CEO allow us to make it clear why our prospects need our mousetrap.

■ Doug Brandon, President Brandon Engineering

Think Like a CEO just vaulted to the top of my list of top ten must read business books.

■ Tom Sherman, CEO Growth Dynamics

Think Like a CEO outlines a selling methodology that is brilliant in its simplicity and effectiveness.

■ Doug Mohr, Vice President, Echostar Corporation

Most sales people don't understand the corporate issues that executives are facing. Think Like a CEO will help a sales exec "think outside the box" and get inside the CEO's head to make a deal happen.

■ Simon Jeacock, Senior VP Sales, SAP

At last, a book that outlines practical strategies for real life sales teams. With over 75 cases – and some humorous writing – this is a must read for anyone involved in any type of business development.

■ Ademilson da Silva, Regional Manager, Banco do Brasil

I enjoyed Mark's humor as much as the insight on dissecting a company's strategy and turning that into a sale. Using this approach, I can better understand how my own company operates and what I might do to improve our bottom line.

■ Mark Ferrell, Leader Enterprise Planning, Bell Helicopter Textron

This book is an important new work in the way it teaches my team to sell. It has changed the way we sell and do business.

■ John Rumasuglia, President, Extended Lean Solutions

This book is nothing short of a groundbreaking method to approach sales and is guaranteed to drive results.

■ David Walder, VP Operations, Credit Protection Association

We sell to technical managers, yet Think Like a CEO taught our sales teams to sell more strategically to everyone in our prospect's organization.

■ Doug Taylor, Founder and COO, Webmetrics

Think Like a CEO concisely summarizes key elements in business strategy. It allows readers to leverage the author's twenty years of experience and generate sales – and value – immediately.

■ Dr. Michael Lawless, MBA Professor, INSEAD

We never got financial information on our prospective clients and partners because we never knew how to find it, or what it meant. I gave your book to everyone in my company and we now integrate your tools into our selling methodology.

■ Nader Ayoub, President, Avianco

Think Like a CEO will turn you into that rare breed of sales executive who understands your prospect's business so well that you could run it. They will trust you and buy from you – BIG.

■ Harry Goodnight, Sr. VP Worldwide Sales Consulting, i2 Technologies

I like how you make these concepts easy to understand. Your practical examples simplify challenging business cases and help to set sales strategies that would normally take years of experience to learn.

■ Kathy Pickowitz, Services Area Manager, IBM

Think Like a CEO is a must read business book.

■ Mark Fera, Executive, Supply Chain Management Practice, Accenture

THINK
LIKE A CEO

Remember that no matter
what your position in
your company... you are
always on commission!

THINK
LIKE A CEO

■

Sell to Any Company in Any Industry…
Better and *Faster* than a Harvard MBA

Mark Kuta, Jr.

FLOW PUBLISHING

Flow Publishing LLC

Belvedere Business Book Packagers

10 9 8 7 6 5 4 3 2 1   06 07 08 09 10

Book design by JustYourType.biz

Printed in Canada on acid free paper.

www.thinklikeaceo.com

Library of Congress Cataloging-in-Publication Data

Kuta, Mark
    Think Like a CEO – Sell to Any Company in Any Industry... Better and Faster than a Harvard MBA / Mark Kuta
        p. cm
Includes bibliographical references and index.
ISBN 978-0-971-30312-6
1. Sales
2. Business Strategy

Either you live in the Serengeti and get up every day running, or you live in a pond and survive on algae.

"Will that be steak...or bologna, sir?"

Acknowledgments

VERY FEW WRITERS have bestselling authors edit their work, yet that is what I had with Wade Tabor. Don't start one of his books on a weeknight. My brother, Dane, took time out from his triathlons and marathons to write comments on virtually every page. Dane – I'm still laughing! John Rumasuglia gave me encouragement for the four years it took to write this book. David Glennon is a strategic thinker, who helped prove out these concepts. Justin Doster was a fellow board member who enlisted and fought in Iraq and still found time to read every page. Nader Ayoub, the smartest person I have ever met, did his best to have some of those smarts rub off on me. I met a class act named Henri Duhot at a conference – and he immediately dived into my manuscript and helped me to "paint the picture" with his ideas. Kathy Pickowitz proved to me why IBM clients always ask for her as she performed "surgery" that tightened up the book. James Barry gave me invaluable insight as to how CIO's think. Jim Bret-Harte, who sells into Latin American CEO's - thanks for playing a part in *my* movie. Doug Mohr still has crayon marks on his fingers for explaining many of these concepts to me the first time around, in B-School. Simon Jeacock has closed more software deals than anyone I know and his feedback has always helped put steak on the table. Mark Fera is an Accenture executive who recognized a few of the deals in the book and gave me some executive advice. David Walder is an operations executive with a CPA whose strategic recommendations were on the mark. Bob Simqu (Captain B) has used the concepts in this book to close monster deals at three different companies. Kathy Ault is a wonderful lawyer, proofreader, and sister. Alan Jilka is an entrepreneur whose first love is literature – and he *still* read this book. Doug Brandon runs an engineering company, but his first love is writing, and *he* still read this book. Ademilson da Silva is a Banco do Brasil executive who helped provide insight to the Brazilian market. I never met Dr. Celso Lemme, but he teaches at one of the top B-Schools in Brasil (UFRJ) and gave me some terrific advice. Dr. Michael Lawless is simply the best MBA Prof in the business. Dr. Flavio Cruz and Dr. Celio Freire de Lima are both using this book to help drive research projects that better our world. Harry Goodnight is the perfect executive, helping close deals yet giving the sales team all the credit. Dianne Howie is a book industry pro who unselfishly spent time advising me on this book.

I have been honored to have a number of CEO's review this book. Dr. John Rutledge helped to shape history with his economic ideas advising US Presidents. If you look up *charisma* in the dictionary it will have his picture there, and yes, that first story is about him. While you have the dictionary out, look up the word *class* and you will see a picture of Tom Clevenger. Manufacturing in Mexico is stronger because of Ricardo Hirata, who has personally saved many manufacturing jobs by making Mexican manufacturers World Class. Doug Taylor is a 21st century Rock Star – a guy with a better idea who quit his job and started his own company.

My past clients are still on speaking terms with me and I would like to thank several who provided insight on this book. Ricardo Bolanos advises and finances startups in Mexico, and unselfishly spent time on this manuscript. Tom Sherman is a senior executive who makes it his business to close deals. Mark Ferrell understands operations better than anyone I have ever met. David Clarke is one of the most strategic senior level executives that I have had the pleasure to sell to, works 80 hour weeks and still hits a 2 iron like Tiger Woods.

I cannot tell you how honored I was to have my hero review every manuscript that I wrote. I proudly use the Jr. after my name, hoping to capture some magic of a true American hero and Hall of Fame Great Guy, my father, Mark Kuta. Mom and Dad, although I fall short, I always strive to be like you.

I want to thank my two daughters for always jumping up on my lap and asking me to type their names on the computer. While their names might not show up in the manuscript, believe me when I say that they are there. Sapa, you know I worship the ground you walk on. Cada sapo tem sua sapa. Everything I do is for you. With apologies to the C&W song, Flavia, *you* are the reason God made Brazil. Thank you for your understanding for all the time I was writing this book instead of doing the things I should have been doing.

Even with this supporting cast the quill and scroll was still in my hand, so let's get this out of the way immediately. All mistakes are mine.

Table of Contents

PART TWO – The Wall St. The Wall Street Selling Methodology™

PART THREE–Profit Strategies

PART FOUR–Value Integration

Dr. John Rutledge
Chairman, Rutledge Capital,
President, Mundell International
University of Entrepreneurship
Business School, Beijing

Foreword

IN ECONOMICS, increased productivity attracts capital. It works the same in sales – the most productive sales teams capture the most capital. They close the biggest deals, have the highest ASP (average selling price) and earn the most money. *Think Like a CEO* will allow any company to build an industry-dominant sales organization. In order to close sales with top executives, you must get inside their heads, understanding what they want, and—perhaps most important—what they worry about. And top executives of just about every company worry about Wall Street and the value of their company.

Think Like a CEO outlines the Wall Street Selling Methodology™, putting your sales representatives on the same page as senior executives of your prospects. This is a cutting edge business book, providing unique tools that will drive sales. One of the concepts that I'm sure will resonate with readers of this book is how the complex language of Wall Street is summarized in easy to understand ideas. Within minutes your sales teams can develop a strategy that will align your value proposition to *what* your prospect is focusing on— Wall Street – and *how* he is planning to drive results – his Profit Strategies.

I have extensive background in the competitiveness of nations, and can assure you that the same principles apply to the competitive environment that companies face on a daily basis. In our book, *Rust to Riches: The Coming of the Second Industrial Revolution*, Dr. Deborah Allen and I make the case that the two most important ingredients driving success are having the willingness to work, and having the right tools. *Think Like a CEO* will re-energize your sales team, and provide them with the top sales tools in today's market. If you have it in your hands right now, you have the opportunity to drive economic value in your organization. **Take my advice and do it.**

Finally, *Think Like a CEO* is much too important a book to restrict its use to the sales organization. It will help everyone in your business understand how to create and execute a strategy to give your company lasting value by teaching them, in understandable English, the connection between work and value. It will help you create a coherent, effective organization by teaching everyone why they are doing what they are doing to achieve the firm's objectives. Investors should read it as well to help them identify value winners and losers when picking stocks.

At all costs, however, keep this book out of the hands of your competitors. Best to keep them in the dark.

Dr. John Rutledge

Columbus negotiated a 10% commission on all riches with Queen Isabella prior to setting out on his voyage. One morning he woke up and thinking he was in China, discovered America. While they say it's better to be lucky than good, the real value lies in being a risk taker.

David Clarke

Sr. VP Case New Holland

Introduction

I AM INCREDIBLY EXCITED to write the introduction to this book, because I've seen first hand how the concepts outlined here work, and work well. You see, my company purchased a software package from Mark Kuta, and I was the C-Level executive in charge of the purchase. After reading *Think Like a CEO*, I now clearly see how Mark executed his sales strategy. By the time the project got to me for final approval, everyone on my team was behind it because it was aligned with the overall direction I was driving. Capital investment decisions come to me, and rest assured that when these projects are aligned with my Profit Strategies it makes the decision much easier to make. Too many potential supplier sales representatives are selling what they believe the sale is centered on – the product. Others attempt to sell their products based on the solution sets – which is primarily based, once again, on the attributes of the product. If I were to give advice to the sales teams that call on me – and other C-Level executives – it would be to understand the company's Profit Strategies, and get your product aligned with them. It would also be to read *Think Like a CEO*. The tools outlined in this book make for a powerful presentation, and you will increase your chances of closing the sale. And never forget - you are providing a better service for your customer, as chances are, your product will drive their profitability. By the way, the deal we did with Mark proved of tremendous value to our organization.

As a senior executive of a multinational company, I face challenges every day. It was interesting reading in *Think Like a CEO* about the Fundamental Football Profit Strategy, because this concept is something that I strive to execute to. I drive results by having everyone in my organization understand our strategy, as well as the value that each of them can individually drive within it. Only when we are all on board and looking at the same scorecards can we collectively achieve the ever-higher goals that management hands us. I will use Mark's book as a key resource to organizing and aligning my team for success.

Finally, I believe that after reading *Think Like a CEO*, **you don't have to be in sales** to get tremendous value from this book. I can tell you from experience that in today's global world, many managers have a difficult enough time just keeping up. Ten years ago, a supply chain manager was responsible for buying a commodity of parts, keeping his supplier on schedule, and minimizing the cost of the commodity. Today, with suppliers all over the globe, and companies outsourcing more manufacturing, that supply chain manager must deal with a whole new set of problems. Profitability now lies in the hands of the lowest levels of the organization. That same supply chain manager is the first to develop strategies to increase value and must be able to analyze these strategies, and fight for budget to get them implemented. Losing this internal battle means losing market share, and by the time a senior executive like me recognizes what is happening, well, it may be too late. Someone else sitting across the globe has acted faster and captured the business, the capacity, or the market share. That is something that is absolutely unacceptable to me and my organization.

So, no matter where you work in your organization, buy this book on a Friday, read it over the weekend, and walk into work the next Monday better prepared to deliver value.

David Clarke

"It's not rocket surgery." Remember Van Halen's David Lee Roth's quip when is seems like a problem stumps you.

Mark Kuta, Jr.
Author, *Think Like a CEO*

Preface

STEAK…OR…BOLOGNA. That's the entree choice given by most of the compensation plans that sales people work under. If you are successful and "hit your numbers" you eat steak. If you don't make quota, you eat bologna. This book is focused on helping sales professionals upgrade their menu. The tools and templates of the Wall Street Selling Methodology™ are unique and unlike any other sales method. This is not a book filled with "fluff" or "feel goods" that promise results. It is not a repackaging of personality definitions, and it doesn't walk you through ten or fifteen or twenty yes/no questions to tell your managers that your deal is qualified. This methodology will transform the way you approach your sales tasks, because if you are dealing with senior level executives, you'd better be able to align your product to the strategies that the CEO is pursuing. This book will provide you with a new set of tools to compete – and excel – in this environment. This book will allow you to:

1. *Become fluent in the language of business.*

2. *Gain a unique understanding of a company's strategies and align your value proposition with them.*

3. *Build a clear, concise, compelling C-Level case for change that will help you close sales.*

Sales teams need these tools because comparing today's business environment to the one just two decades prior is like comparing the latest Corvette to a '65 luxury car with torn seats, fading paint, and a faulty fuel pump. If you don't realize it yet, let me be the first to welcome you to the commodity marketplace. In the 1990s, demand was high, and mid-level managers had a budget. Deals could get closed by focusing on feature function. In today's world, it's decision by committee, and nobody cares about features. CEOs focus their daily actions like a laser beam towards one thing – satisfying Wall Street. Your competitors have someone working and focused on the C-Level in your accounts, and unless you can compete – and differentiate – you run the risk of losing market share. (When we mention C-Level in this book, we will generally refer to people with the word Chief in their title - like Chief Executive Officer, Chief Financial Officer - as well as other senior level executives such as President, Division President, etc.)

While an MBA is an excellent way to learn about business principles and hone decision-making skills, *B-School programs don't teach you to uncover Profit Strategies with the objective of closing business.* This book will take your professional sales career to the next level. It will allow you to differentiate yourself from all the other solution/value/target selling people that compete for your prospect's dollar. It will teach you to Think Like the CEO you are targeting, as you integrate your product with the Profit Strategies he is using to satisfy "the Street."

This book is based on a methodology that I developed and practiced in selling large, multimillion dollar software and technology solutions. As I took on management responsibilities, I taught my teams to use these same tools. They developed the confidence to sell high in the organizations they were targeting by *thinking like the CEO's they were selling to.* The result was **increased sales**. By putting my experience into the writing of this book, you won't have to learn the concepts by trial and error and then spend ten years perfecting them. You will be able to implement these concepts immediately, just like my sales teams did.

Organization

While learning about financial statements gets most people about as excited as getting a fruitcake for Christmas, we will focus on giving you an understanding of financial terms. In the first part of this book, called *The Language of Business,* we will teach you to quickly analyze only what you need to in order to Think Like a CEO. I promise to boil down the relatively complex world of business analysis into language and structure that the average non-MBA non-Mensa member can digest.

The second part of the book is called *The Wall Street Selling Methodology*™, the objective of which is to understand your target company, its industry, and how it stacks up to its competitors.

After the first two parts of this book, we will take a look at different business strategies, and how you can uncover them by reading the "numbers." We will look at many samples of different business strategies, and spend a chapter looking at "blue chips," as well as companies that failed miserably.

The final section, *Value Integration*, will teach you how to deal with senior level executives and how to present a compelling value proposition that aligns with the CEO's strategy. We call this value integration, and it is the only way to sell your product today.

Ideal Audience for *Think Like a CEO*

The concepts in this book are applicable to all types of products and services that companies – and individual sales teams – sell. While it is easy to see the importance of these concepts if you are selling capital equipment or software worth hundreds of thousands or millions of dollars, the concepts are just as important if you are a salesperson selling to a small business. For example, let's say that you are responsible for selling products to independent convenience stores. Using the concepts in this book, you can find the financial returns of a publicly traded company in the convenience store industry, and find out how they have performed. Engaging your client around industry metrics and how his are similar will allow you to begin integrating your value proposition to his objectives. By asking a few pertinent questions, you will uncover his Profit Strategies and begin to align your products to them. While this customer might not be a Boeing, you can bet they are focused on the same results as Boeing's CEO.

Now it's time to get down to the very serious task of learning the language of business. While this might sound like your first shot of bad tequila—tough to swallow and almost tear-inducing—I promise to make it more like Cuervo Gold. A nice lubricant to get to the really good stuff that comes afterwards. So hang on.

Mark Kuta, Jr.

PART ONE

The Language of Business

"When your liabilities exceed your assets, your assets in jail."

A Quick Diagnosis Snapshot

I FELT LIKE THE GUY in *Catch Me If You Can*. You know the one, the guy who pretends to be an airline pilot, doctor, and just about anything else that will make him money and give him a little adventure. I was 30,000 feet over the Mohave Desert looking at a stack of reports on a $200 million dollar manufacturer with a full day of meetings set for the following day. I was going to be working with the company's senior management team and the venture capital firm that owned the company. The firm consisted of four Ivy League MBAs and the managing partner, who just happened to be a regular columnist for Forbes, an ex-Reagan administration economic appointee, and if you hadn't guessed by now, intimidating. I was going to the company as an expert in Lean Manufacturing, billing $4,500 per day to those mentioned above for my advice. My true job was software sales, and I knew less about Lean Manufacturing than the guy who starred in that movie, Leonardo DiCaprio.

I delved through the organization charts, sales literature, plant layouts, market analysis, and three years' worth of monthly balance sheets and Profit & Loss (P&L) statements. I don't recall the specifics of the organization's Return on Equity (ROE) or profitability, but I do remember two main issues that I uncovered and brought up the next day. The first was that cash flow had shown little or no growth over the past three years, and in fact the cash cycle had expanded. I knew that the venture capitalists bought companies for one reason, and that was cash. They also expected cash flow to grow based on the expertise they provide. So I assumed that this would get some attention. In addition to the cash cycle, I noted that it took the manufacturing company, on average, about sixty days to manufacture their product, contributing to their 100+ day cash cycle. I had found the need. If I could just validate this as I saw the factory the next day, I would be able to make a case for change.

During our plant tour the next day, I kept in mind the sixty days that the manufacturing cycle took. I took notes of where there were bottlenecks in the process. I looked at where they had stacks of inventory, and took notes of the dates on the work orders attached to the stacks. I talked to the machinists, and asked them how they scheduled their work, and how they expedited "hot" orders. After four hours of plant tour, the VCs were ready to hear my "expert advice" – which I had already formulated the afternoon before on the airplane ride. Leo DiCaprio with his make-believe medical degree.

Standing up in front of the group, with a white board behind me, I began to outline what I'd found. The company's cash cycle required an average cash investment of over $150,000 per day. For each day we could reduce the cash cycle, I pointed out, the manufacturing company could save this amount of investment. I read from the preliminary information, and confirmed from interviewing the VCs that they wanted to grow the business. Growth means cash requirements, so this was only going to get worse as they grew. In fact, if they did nothing, the more successfully they grew, the more cash they would need.

From the manufacturing end of the business, the plant tour showed me that their product could be expedited in about five days. Yet, the average manufacturing time was on the order of sixty days. If we could bring that manufacturing time down closer to five days, we would save about forty-five days of investment, which at $150,000 in working capital per day adds up to just under $7 million.

Although the process of design and engineering is an exact science, building that product and measuring how that product was built, is not. During our debriefing, there was quite a stir when I mentioned that the average manufacturing cycle time was on the order of sixty days. The plant manager began looking at me as if I were his neighbor and had just stepped outside to walk my pit bull. The Wharton trained VC's openly doubted my analysis.

"Impossible," said the plant manager. "I fill orders within one week, and we are on a four week MRP plan."

"Where did you get those numbers?" asked the CFO of the VC firm, who during the day had casually mentioned that he studied at *Harvard*, not Wharton, as I had assumed.

I walked through the analysis, and explained that yes, although they filled some orders in five days, they had plenty of others that probably sat in queue for weeks. I pulled out some sample work orders I'd taken from the floor and showed them that based on their financial returns, they had approximately sixty days of manufacturing cycle time.

The Managing Partner agreed that there actually were sixty days of manufacturing cycle time in the financial numbers, and if they were going to grow the business without significantly increasing the cash requirements, they should listen to what I had to say. I ended up getting the deal.

This section of Think *Like a CEO* will teach you to become fluent in the language of business. The language of business, as spoken by senior officers of corporations, is that of three financial statements:

1. The balance sheet.

2. The P&L statement.

3. The cash flow statement.

The CEO focuses on these because his bankers are forcing him to, and Wall Street reacts to changes in these numbers. We are going to go over these and focus only on those items that will be critical to understand. No matter how many finance and business classes you have had in the past, I recommend that you go through this section of the book as if you were a novice. It will be important to build this knowledge as we move forward to learn about Profit Strategies. If you're not a "numbers guy" by training, I'll take the pain of looking at the numbers out of the process. It's easy and quick to understand once you know what to look for.

When you visit a doctor for an ailment, he or she typically performs a preliminary diagnosis to figure out where the pain resides, and what may be contributing to the pain's severity. All the doctor is attempting to do is narrow the focus of attention to what is important in diagnosing the situation. By assembling a couple of things quickly about how an organization is doing, you can uncover its financial structure, its ability to generate revenue, the organization's operational and financial risk, and even its profitability. You will even be able to quickly tell how profitable a company has been by looking at the balance sheet, and more importantly, read the not-so-evident details a company may be hiding between the lines. This diagnostic snapshot will allow you to make many practical assumptions and begin to understand an organization's business, leading you to craft a plan of attack.

The Balance Sheet Formula

Our first step will be to gain a familiarity and understanding of corporate balance sheets. Accountants typically study a company's financial health by examining its balance sheet, or what they sometimes refer to as a Statement of Condition. Let's forget the name for the moment, and discuss what this is all about. In order to dramatize the importance of a balance sheet, I am going to outline a situation that almost everyone can understand: purchasing your first house.

Most of us never forget the experience of purchasing our first home, a mixed bag of excitement, nervousness, and cautiousness. I remember when I purchased my first house, how nervous I was. Basically, the bank and I were going to own a home together. Actually, I would own it, but the bank would have a claim against most of it because they would contribute a substantial loan needed to complete the transaction, which they expected to be repaid over time with interest. (We are using a very simple example that won't amortize interest, or show points, etc.)

> The key formula we will use for understanding balance sheets is; What you HAVE = What you OWE + What you OWN. If you can understand this basic concept, then you can understand how "the numbers" impact strategy. If you can't understand this concept, well, there's always law school.

In fact, I bought a home for $100,000, and put down 5 percent, or $5,000. I found myself the proud owner of a home with a pretty good-sized mortgage. So how much of my house did I own? My equity in the house was $5,000, and I owed the bank $95,000 on the loan. If you look at it from another way, the $5,000 equity, plus the $95,000 liability represented a balance sheet.

So, based on a simple formula that what you have equals what you own plus what you owe, I was in the following situation with regards to my house:

$$\text{What you HAVE} = \text{What you OWE} + \text{What you OWN}$$
$$\$100,000 \text{ house} = \$95,000 \text{ Loan} + \$5,000 \text{ Equity}$$

This is the basic equation that we will use whenever we look at a current financial situation.

HAVE	=	OWE	+	OWN

So, let's look at what happened with the house over the years. The first year balance sheet looks like the following.

HAVE	=	OWE	+	OWN
$100,000	=	$95,000	+	$5,000

Even without knowing what I came up with for a down payment, I could figure out that I owned $5,000 of that house.

Now, for the second year, the housing market in Denver was pretty good. Housing prices went up 10 percent, and I actually paid off $5,000 of my loan. So here is what we had during the second year.

HAVE	=	OWE	+	OWN
$110,000	=	$90,000	+	?

Based on this scenario, how much of the house did I own? Actually, $20,000 in year two. Remember, what you HAVE must always equal what you OWE plus what you OWN. The increase in the value of the house led to an increase of overall wealth. Remember I owned the house, while the bank owned the loan. Any increase in the house's value benefited me, not the bank.

In the third year the housing market appreciated even more, so that my house was now worth $120,000. I also paid off another $5,000, so the easy part is that I only owe $85,000. How much do I own? The formula looks like this:

HAVE	=	OWE	+	OWN
$120,000	=	$85,000	+	?

So, what we own is…$35,000. Because, once again, what you HAVE must always equal what you OWE plus what you OWN. The next year saw a severe housing slump hit the area, and the value of the house dropped to $75,000. I continued making payments, and so the loan amount was down to $80,000. The question is, how much of the house do I own now? The formula looks like this now:

HAVE	=	OWE	+	OWN
$75,000	=	$80,000	+	$

The answer is…I owned a NEGATIVE $5,000. Why? Because what you HAVE must <u>always</u> equal what you OWE plus what you OWN. This may sound repetitive, but it is the basis of all financial analysis. In the last example, my new financial status is what is commonly referred to as "upside down." The technical term is called insolvency, and we will discuss it at greater length later in this book. But for now, remember the saying,

Based on these examples, just about anyone could understand how to create and analyze a balance sheet. But just when you are getting the hang of things, the accountants come along and complicate it. Rather than use regular terminology, like HAVE, OWE and OWN, they use Assets, Liabilities, and Equity. In fact, they can substitute equity for net worth, owners equity, shareholders equity,or any number of other names. Just remember that in the end, it is what you own. It is all semantics, and it will get even more confusing. Don't let it confuse you. At this juncture just realize that it is what you own. So, by substituting our words with accountant speak, our simple equation still keeps its mathematical principles, but now we'll say:

"When your liabilities exceed your assets, your assets in jail!"

ASSETS = LIABILITIES + EQUITY

This is the basis of a Balance Sheet, or a Statement of Condition. No matter what it might be called, always remember the basic formula. ASSETS = LIABILITIES + EQUITY, which really means HAVE = OWE + OWN. Now, going back to our house example, we can say we have an asset of $100,000, liabilities of $95,000, and net worth of $5,000. Note that we are saying the same thing, but this sounds more "financial."

As you have seen in the above examples, my housing price was subject to market forces and changed frequently. In fact, the housing prices tend to fluctuate over time as they are subject to market and economic forces. The balance sheet that I outlined was what my financial condition was at a single point in time. It is like a snapshot, in that it describes what is going on at that instant. The P&L Statement,

I once had a sharp young salesperson working for me. Brad had a lot on the ball but found it difficult getting over his looks. Although he was in his late twenties, the lucky devil looked like he should be worried about getting a date for prom. I had him focus on a different vocabulary – the true language of business - referring to sales as revenue, quota as budget, money as capital, etc. Executives stopped seeing him as Doogie Howser and began seeing him as a sharp young MBA.

the financial report we will address in the next chapter, will summarize what happened throughout a period of time. Often times, when you order photographs in a picture book, you can begin to see a sequence of events, a story. Similarly, by assimilating several corporate balance sheets in chronological order we can begin to tell a corporate story. Just like our doctor studying a patient, you will be able to assess a company with a quick diagnosis, and then piece together a story based on historical analysis. With the new set of tools we will teach, you will be empowered to quickly look at numerous snapshots and diagnose an organization's viability, overall health, and its Profit Strategies.

Congratulations, you have just learned one of the most important concepts of this book. But here is the best part: you don't need to make it more complex than is actually is. Just understand the situation, and leave it to the accountants to make it more complex.

Introducing the Accountants

You now know the basic formula of balance sheets, and hopefully you realize that it is really not that difficult. When you begin to analyze "the numbers" to uncover strategies, there are times when they will be complex and difficult to understand. That's the bad news. The good news is that this is as complex as you will ever have to remember concerning balance sheets, using the tools outlined in this book. In fact, we are going to make it TWICE as complex. Now we are going to put two categories underneath our balance sheet for each of the components. We'll have two categories under assets, two under liabilities, and two under equity

Assets

For assets, the two categories we are going to study are called current assets and fixed assets. Everything will fall into one of these categories. A current asset is cash and anything that will be turned into cash within one year from the balance sheet. In a personal example, this might include your cash in the bank, the checks that you have in the drawer that you are going to take to the bank tomorrow, etc. If you prepaid some of the expenses on your house, like if you made a lump sum payment of your entire year's homeowner's association fees, this would also be a current asset. In the business world, current assets would include current bank accounts, inventories that will be consumed, or planned to be consumed, within one year, and anything else that will be turned into cash within one year. Likewise, if a business prepays anything that is owed, this prepaid expense, much like the homeowners association dues discussed above, is also a current asset. So, if you run across some category that you don't understand, you don't need to worry. For our analysis, it is either cash, or something that will turn into cash in one year. For our purposes it all means the same thing. In fact, almost all balance sheets already group these into current assets, so you don't even need to worry about making the decision as to whether the asset will be turned into cash within one year of the amount reported on the balance sheet.

The second classification of assets we'll call "fixed assets." We are going to think of fixed assets as land, and anything that wears out. Buildings, cars, office equipment, computers, etc. If it wears out, or is land, it's a fixed asset. These days you will also see other terminology for these classifications. Like the points that we brought out above, as you read balance sheets, you will probably see something that you don't understand classified as a fixed asset. Just remember the definition of a fixed asset, and you will be able to continue on with your analysis and understanding of the organization's current situation. (It is also important to understand that all fixed assets are listed at cost, minus depreciation. Just as your house may have increased from $100,000 to $150,000 in the past ten years, companies with a lot of fixed assets may have these understated on their balance sheets.

So, to review, let's look at how our balance sheet looks now...

Current Assets
Fixed Assets
TOTAL ASSETS

It goes without saying that if you add the current assets and fixed assets together you will get TOTAL ASSETS. Keep this in mind because we will be using this simple concept a bit later.

Liabilities

Just as assets have two classifications, so will liabilities, and we will use the same general idea of classification by starting with current liabilities. If a current asset is cash, or anything that will be turned into cash within one year, a current liability is the opposite. This is anything that you will have to pay within one year from the date of the balance sheet. Short-term (less than one year) lines of credit, credit card expenses, employee expenses, supplier expenses, whatever you will be paying off within one year are current liabilities.

It is important to remember that a current liability is something that you owe for something you have gotten in return. For example, if you employ 100 people, and each person earns $100,000 per year, on your January balance sheet, you wouldn't put down for a current liability of $10 million. Some of these people may leave, get fired, or for other reasons not be working for the company in the future. What you would show in the current liabilities is the amount that you have to pay the employees for the work they have done (probably two weeks worth of work if they are paid every two weeks) and for which you owe them. Let's say you pay them every two weeks. An employee who earns $100,000 a year earns $3,846 every two weeks. If the company pays the employees after they do two weeks of work, the company pays $3,846 to 100 employees for a total of $384,600. That amount that would be a current liability. Again, don't get mixed up with the different names or classifications, just ask yourself if those liabilities (what you OWE) must be paid off within one year. If so, it is a current liability.

Any liability that will be paid off after one year we'll term a Long-Term Liability. It's really simple. Now, let's go back to our house example; we owe $95,000 on a mortgage to the bank. Is this a current liability, or a long-term liability? The amount we have to pay within one year is a current liability, and the rest is a long-term liability. If in my example earlier we say that we pay off approximately $5,000 per year, then the current liability portion would be this $5,000, and the long-term liability would be the remainder, or $90,000 ($95,000 OWE - $5,000 OWE this year.)

So this section of our balance sheet, the OWE, or Liabilities, would look like this:

Current Liabilities
Long Term Liabilities
TOTAL Liabilities

Several years ago, one of my sales people was working a division of a Fortune 100 company who committed to the deal, but insisted on breaking up the Purchase Order into four distinct orders. I became involved to get the client to sign our "paper" – the terms and conditions that formed a legally binding contract. We got the T's and C's signed, and our new client promptly issued a Purchase Order (PO) for the first phase of the program.

A few weeks later, near the end of the quarter, I was looking for ways to book the entire deal in order to make my team's quota. I went back to the executive, this time as a technology partner, and asked for a PO for the entire deal. I explained that since the contract for the project was signed, the entire amount was now a current liability on his balance sheet. It made no difference in his company's – or his personal metrics. His financial situation wasn't impacted, but my team could book the entire deal. I explained this to him and convinced him to go ahead and cut a PO for the entire deal. My team and I made our number, and we built an even better relationship with our customer.

Equity

Finally, just as the HAVE & OWE, or assets & liabilities sections of our balance sheet have two categories, the OWN, or equity section, also has two categories. There are lots of different names for the OWN piece of the balance sheet. It can be referred to as Stockholders equity, net worth, equity, Stock (in some cases) shareholders equity, book value, and even some more. We are going to call it by the term equity because I believe it is inherently easier to understand, although we will use the other terms throughout so that people can get familiar with them.

The two sections that we have here will be Stock, and retained earnings. Stock will be the amount that the company received for selling stock in the enterprise. Just like the Asset and Liability sections discussed above, you will see several different sections in a company's balance sheet that might have titles like "Additional Paid in Capital," or such.

What do you do to uncover the Profit Strategy? Lump it into either stock, or retained earnings and that is about the extent of what you need to understand. The second part of the equity section will be what we call retained earnings, or the amount that the company earns on doing business. A cliché in business is "the bottom line." The true "bottom line" is that section called retained earnings. Take the difference between the totals one year to the next and you get all the profits the company has made.

Retained earnings are also called Profit, Earnings, etc. We are going to call these amounts retained earnings, because this is the amount of money that the company will keep to grow the business. All the profits not paid out as dividends, bonuses, or anything else will be retained in the business. It is going to be important as you look at the equity section of the balance sheet to think how you are going to classify these two items. As we all know, times can sometimes be tough in business, so retained earnings from one year to another can actually decrease. If the company has never made a profit, instead of calling this section retained earnings, we'll call it accumulated deficit. Like the name implies, this is generally not a good thing to see, as it shows the totals of all the losses the business had endured. If we are looking at a Not-For-Profit company (not a company that for whatever reason doesn't make profit, but an IRS approved charity or other non profit oriented company) retained earnings will be called something else. We'll keep calling them retained earnings, because whether the business is for profit, or not for profit, the objective is to make a profit.

So this section of our balance sheet, the OWN, or equity (net worth/owners equity/shareholders equity) will look like this:

Stock
Retained Earnings
TOTAL EQUITY

Bringing this complex balance sheet to what we already understand, let's build it up from the beginning.

HAVE	=	OWE	+	OWN
ASSESTS	=	LIBILITY	+	EQUITY

Assets	Liablilities	Equity
Current Assests	Current Liabilities	Stock
Fixed Assets	LT Liabilities	Retained Earnings
TOTAL ASSETS	**TOTAL LIABILITIES**	**TOTAL EQUITY**

TOTAL ASSETS = TOTAL LIABILITIES + TOTAL EQUITY

Since the accountants get involved, you will find that balance sheets are also presented in a straight fashion, as shown below.

COMPANY XYZ	
As of December 31, 200X	
Assets	
Current Assets	$1,000
Fixed Assets	$500
TOTAL ASSETS	**$1,500**
Liabilities	
Current Liabilities	$500
LT Liabilities	$500
TOTAL LIABILITIES	**$1,000**
Equity	
Stock	$450
Retained Earnings	$50
TOTAL EQUITY	**$500**

There you have it. We will use this complex balance sheet as we begin to do analysis of business strategies, and their impacts to these returns. If you can remember this simple formula, and the make-up of each of the two sections that make up our formula, you are well on your way to understanding what makes the business world tick.

Fast Five Balance Sheet Metrics

Whenever you look at a balance sheet, we want to immediately focus on five key metrics, and how they have changed over the last several years. This initial analysis will allow us to begin to understand the company, and will begin to focus our ideas as to the company's strategies. In a later chapter, we will quantify financial metrics so that we can judge what changes in them mean to the company. For now, we just want to begin looking at the balance sheet in terms of the "Fast Five."

1. *Asset structure* - We want to look at the makeup of the organization's assets to tell us what the business requires to operate. Does the business require a lot of fixed assets to generate its business, or is the majority of assets short term and liquid? What percent of total assets are fixed assets? This will give us some insights as to how the company needs to finance its operations.

2. *Net working capital* – We are interested in the flexibility that substantial liquidity gives a company. Net working capital is defined as current assets minus current liabilities. While this formula will give us a good understanding of the capital the company has, I recommend subtracting cash (and marketable securities) from this number. This will give us an even more accurate idea of how the operations can fund current obligations, and takes out the financing choice of holding cash. If this working capital number declines as the quarters and years go on, the company will have to raise more money to stay in business. If they're unable to do that, they'll change their name to Enron and start dumping their shares.

3. *LT debt* – Also called long term Liabilities, and often abbreviated LT Liabilities. The purpose of finding out how much long term debt a company has on its books is to compare it to the company's equity, and to compare it to the amount in prior years. The more equity versus debt that the company shows, the less risk the company will undertake, and the less interest expense the company will owe. Remember that just as you take on a mortgage to buy a house, companies generally finance fixed assets with long-term debt. If long-term debt increases year over, our goal becomes using it to finance either assets or operations.

4. *Goodwill and intangible assets* – We will address goodwill at length in a later chapter, so for these simple balance sheets this metric will not be applicable. When we see goodwill, it will immediately shed some light on what growth strategies the company is following.

5. *Leverage factor* – We want to take a look at the makeup of the company's equity section, and then compare the total equity to the total assets that a company has. This leverage factor will allow a quick way to see how much risk the company is undertaking via debt leverage. The higher the leverage factor, the higher the risk that the company is undertaking, by showing us how much of their asset base is being financed by debt versus that being financed by the owners. Since risk and reward go hand in hand, we'll see later that the higher this leverage, the higher the return on equity of the business.

Wall Street Selling Implications – The Balance Sheet

Like it or not, if you are dealing with executives you will have to speak their language, and understanding balance sheets is the first place to start. At this point, if you understand the concepts outlined in this chapter, you will be able to grasp the complete, more complex financial statements, because we are going to work on keeping them simple. No matter how much experience you have in business, sales, or reading financial statements, you should not skip the first section of this book. A company's "numbers" must be second nature to you so that you can focus on the important things – what they mean to a company's strategies, and how you can use that to close business. You will not only learn the language of business, but you will be able to present these simple concepts to your prospects, ensuring everyone is on the same page and enhancing your credibility.

Bertrand Russell showed that lab rats studied by Americans find the cheese in the maze by running about with incredible hustle, while lab rats studied by German researchers find the cheese by moving and thinking in a methodical fashion. Expectations affect results, so be sure to raise yours.

"Looks like interest expense is dragging down the bottom line."

Understanding the Operations with the P&L Statement

EARLY IN MY MANAGEMENT CAREER, I inherited a team that had been hitting "their number" while the organization had been losing money on the bottom line. After reviewing the situation, I decided that the answer was a brilliant strategy that would allow the company to save over a million dollars. I proposed consolidating the sales organization to reduce travel and various marketing expenses. When it came time to present my plan, the CEO asked me a simple question.

"Which is a more important focus in your situation, your costs or expenses?"

I had never really thought about it like that before, but he had a reason for bringing up the question. I had not separated the two in my analysis and decision-making, and my solution focused on the expense side of the equation. The answer was in addressing the cost side of the equation. We were not getting the productivity out of the sales team, so I replaced two of the most unproductive players – downsized them - ended up exceeding my budget in the sales expense category – and also the profit. Learning from my experience, you will also learn to look at expenses and costs separately when analyzing the Profit & Loss Statement.

The P&L also goes by the term *income statement*, and even some other terms that accountants can think up, like *statement of operations, results of operations*, and others. We will use the terms P&L and income statement interchangeably throughout this book.

The P&L Formula

Now that we know the current situation of the company, let's look at how a company makes money. That's right, the "bottom line," profits, earnings, or, as we learned in the last chapter, retained earnings. The concept is simple, sales minus costs minus expenses equal earnings. Once accountants got involved, they complicated it further, so like the last chapter, we will focus on learning several key concepts, and with these concepts you will have an understanding of the operations. In later chapters, we will combine these concepts.

Sales – Costs – Expenses = Profit

Now let's look at what these mean. The first number, sales, is also referred to as "revenue," or "top line," because it is the top line on the income statement.

Costs are what the company incurs to generate sales. These will be called Cost of Goods Sold, or abbreviated as COGS. Some examples of COGS would be the raw materials that companies make product out of, or the direct labor running the machines. In the construction industry, COGS would include direct labor, materials, and any subcontractors that are required. Be sure to understand what directs costs are required to drive sales in your prospect's company.

The result of sales minus costs is called gross profit, and is a simple mathematical formula of sales minus costs. (Note that I didn't say "sales minus expenses." We will refer to direct costs as COSTS, not EXPENSES. We'll get into this later. Gross profit as a percentage of sales is what we will call gross margin, and will be expressed as a percentage. So, our first P&L statement looks like this:

	Revenues
Less	COGS
Equals	Gross Profit

Putting some numbers to this, let's say sales are $1,000, and the direct costs associated with generating these sales are $500. Our P&L would look like this:

Revenues	$1,000	
COGS		$ 500
Gross Profit	$ 500	

Now, if you take a percentage of the gross profit as a percentage of sales, it yields some interesting numbers for us. In this case, our gross profit is 50 percent of sales. We would refer to this as a "…50 percent gross profit" or "…gross margins of 50 percent."

Because we are looking at the relationship between sales and gross profit, an increase in the number of widgets sold does not impact this number. We are looking for the ratio of profitability.

By starting to look at the gross profit margin, you can immediately see what is happening to the operations of the business. If the gross margins are increasing, then the company is able to get a better price for its products, or they are getting more efficient in making them. At this point, we are not really worried about what type of company it is, just the relationship between costs and selling price.

Before we look at our "bottom line" there are some other categories that we want to talk about in the P&L Statement. Let's take a look at the next category that we will worry about – overhead. I'll abbreviate this as O/H.

Overhead is all the indirect expenses that we incur to be able to sell our product or service. Anything that is an expense that we incur that is not directly related to the product or service is overhead. For example, a company might have rent expense, or the expenses related to telephones, and lighting, and management salaries. All of these are indirect, and would therefore be termed overhead. You will also see this broken down as SG&A – sales and general administrative expenses. Sometime, you will have G&A and SG&A. Don't worry, you should lump them both together as overhead for purposes of our analysis. If, when you are looking at financial statements, and you are not sure of whether an item should be an expense or a cost of goods, remember to ask if it can be directly related to the product. If not, it is an overhead expense. There are specific items within O/H that we might want to look at, and indeed we will later, but for now, our sample P&L might look like this:

If gross margins change, it is due to:

1. A change in the sales price for the products, or
2. A change in the costs of the products

Draw some conclusions from gross margins. If gross margins are shrinking, the market is getting more competitive, or the company is becoming less productive.

Revenue	$1,000
COGS	$500
Gross Profit	$500
O/H	$300
EBIT	$200

Subtracting overhead from gross profit, we get what we will call operating profit, or EBIT. If you see the term EBIT, this stands for Earnings Before Interest & Taxes, which is how we classify EBIT. We want to look at this number before we take the financing result – interest – out of it, so that it gives us a true picture of how well a company is running its business. In order to get you used to the term EBIT, we will interchange this with operating profit.

If we isolate the EBIT number, we can make some assumptions as to the efficiency of our operations as a whole. Remember, the gross profit number gave us some insight as to the efficiency of the making of the product, or the market for our product, as related in the pricing of it. Throw in the overhead, and now we can look at how efficient our entire operations are. EBIT is often the number used to analyze companies, because the miscellaneous items that we are going to talk about next are not included. Accountants and finance people can oftentimes manipulate the items in the accounts below EBIT, so this is an excellent gauge to see how the operations are doing.

One thing that we do want to keep in this number is depreciation, which is the number that reduces a company's fixed asset. The reason that we want to look at the result of depreciation is that companies use their assets to generate business. In fact, we will look at a measure later that will tell us how effectively companies utilize their assets. Occasionally you will see a measure called EBITDA, which is pronounced "E-bit-Dah" and stands for Earnings Before Interest Taxes and Depreciation. This measure will not give as good of an indication of how a company's operations are performing, but will closely approximate the operating cash flow measure, something we will address in the next chapter.

The final category that we will discuss is miscellaneous +/-. This can be just about anything, from selling a part of the company and getting some money for it, to tax rebates, and just about everything in between. Since we won't address many of these until later, let's just lump them into Misc. +/-. When these are finally subtracted from operating profit, we will have the complete picture, and finally get to net profit.

Now our P&L Statement, or Income Statement, or Result of Operations, look like this:

	Revenue
Less	COGS
Equals	Gross Profit
Less	O/H
Equals	EBIT
Less	Interest Expense
Less or added	Misc. +/-
Equals	Pre Tax Net Profit
Less	Taxes(benefit)
Equals, (finally)	Net Profit

So, at this point, you only need to understand what each of the six categories mean and how to group what you might see but not understand on an Income Statement to one of these categories. If you understand this, and the balance sheet outlined in the previous chapter, you are ready to learn to uncover Profit Strategies for just about any type of business out there.

Sometimes companies will throw in interest expense above the operating profit number. Interest expense is not an impact to operations; it is a decision as to how to finance the company, so we want to look at our operations with this piece taken out of the equation. Later in the book when we begin to look at specific strategies that companies undertake, and their impacts on the financials, we may want to look at a company in several different ways. One strategy we will look at is their capitalization strategy, where we will want to understand how they use debt and equity financing to capitalize the business. We'll also look at some financial metrics in several different ways. Looking at them from a pre

In this world, there are good reds and bad reds. Some examples of good reds are Bordeaux wines, red Corvettes, and Ginger from Gilligan's Island. Bad reds include Carrot Top, sunburns, the Soviet Hockey Team, and any red you find on a P&L Statement. You want to be "in the black[1]."

tax, pre interest operating profit point of view will give us an idea as to how the company operations are doing, and looking at these same metrics from an after tax point of view will tell us how the financial markets are looking at the company. We'll also talk about how the numbers above can be manipulated.

Now that we have an understanding of the P&L statement, let's look at two different companies, and see what theirs tell us. We will assume that two companies are in a similar field, and we want to compare their results of operations. Our sample companies look like this:

Company A		Company B	
Revenues	$1,000	Revenues	$1,000
COGS	$ 500	COGS	$ 400
Gross Profit	$ 500	Gross Profit	$ 600
O/H	$ 300	O/H	$ 400
EBIT	$ 200	EBIT	$ 200

Company A and Company B have the same EBIT, so you might assume that they are pretty much equal. However, when you look at the P&L in the manner that I have outlined, we see that first off, Company B looks like they are more efficient, earning a 60 percent gross profit margin, whereas Company A is only at 50 percent. But the operating profit is the same, due to excessive overhead of Company B. Although at this point it is still too early to make conclusions, you might file away several things for further review as you begin your analysis. Could the result of the efficiency of making the product be the result of more overhead? Maybe they send out more mailings, or have more salespeople on staff, or perhaps a larger R&D department. Any of those reasons could lead the company to more efficient manufacturing, or even a higher sales price for similar products. Or, they

---

1 Thanks to Lionel Bienvenue, Denver Sportscaster, for initially drawing this analogy, or something like it.

could have excessive overhead and with some cutting of the overhead expenses, which could impact operating profit substantially.

What if instead of Company A and Company B, it was Company A year one and year two? Now how would you see this? Which would you prefer?

Company A

Year 1			Year 2	
Revenues	$1,000		Revenues	$1,000
COGS	$ 500		COGS	$ 400
Gross Profit	$ 500		Gross Profit	$ 600
O/H	$ 300		O/H	$ 400
Operating Profit	$ 200		Operating Profit	$ 200

What if it were reversed, and looked like this?

Company A

Year 1			Year 2	
Revenues	$1,000		Revenues	$1,000
COGS	$ 400		COGS	$ 500
Gross Profit	$ 600		Gross Profit	$ 500
O/H	$ 400		O/H	$ 300
Operating Profit	$ 200		Operating Profit	$ 200

The operating profit numbers – and percentages – look the same, but something is happening to the company in Year Two that might be cause for alarm. Certainly, it looks like management is addressing the issue by cutting overhead to keep operating profits the same, but either costs or the price the market is willing to pay has changed.

Fixed Costs vs. Variable Costs

Another way to slice the operations returns is to look at the costs based on whether they are fixed or variable. A fixed cost is an investment that does not increase based on volume, whereas a variable cost increases with volumes. For example, let's look at a company that manufacturers and sells a telephone set that consists of two parts. The plastic cover is manufactured from their plastic extrusion machines, and the electronics of the unit are purchased from another supplier. The plastic extrusion machine can manufacture up to 1,000 phone cases per week. The company pays $36,000 per year to use this machine. This cost is fixed whether the company manufacturers 1,000 phone cases per week or 500 phone cases per week. The cost of the electronic components is a variable cost, as the company must purchase a set of electronics for each phone system it sells. Given that these are the only costs, Figure 2-1 demonstrates how these costs will act as sales first increase and then decrease.

Figure 2.1

Fast Five P&L Metrics

While the P&L statement gives you tremendous information as to the operations of the business, we will want to initially focus on five points. In a later chapter, we will quantify these metrics so that we can judge what changes in them mean to the company. For now, we want to begin our analysis in terms of the "Fast Five."

1. *Top line growth.* - We obviously want to see this trending up. We can use the percentage growth in top line to judge how the rest of the profitability accounts keep up. For instance, if revenue increases 10 percent and gross profit dollars increase less than 10 percent, this tells us that the company is increasing sales by lowering prices.

2. *Gross profit margin* - Another way to quickly see how the company is performing relative to its internal productivity and the market is to look at the gross profit dollars as a percentage of revenue, or gross margin. For example, if this increases from one year to the next, the company is becoming more productive, and given that overhead does not change, we should see this difference in gross profit drop to the bottom line.

3. *Operating profit, or EBIT* - Ideally, this trend should at least match the percentage increase in top line growth. You can also look at the operating profit margin to get a quick view of how the company is performing. For example, if the gross margin is shrinking, but EBIT margin is the same, you can immediately see that the company is addressing the increase in costs via overhead.

4. *Changes in interest expense* – Increasing interest expense puts an additional earnings debt on the company. Companies that incur debt to acquire businesses or invest in businesses need to make sure that these investments return more than the company's cost of capital. While a growing economy may make interest payments seem minor, during recessions, or when the company's top line revenue falls, higher interest expense can strangle a company's prospects. Dividing operating profit, or EBIT, by interest expense gives us a ratio called *times interest earned*, and tells us how many times earnings can fall before the company will have trouble covering interest expenses without liquidating assets.

27

5. *Net profit margin* – Finally, we want to look at the net profit margin. The changes this number shows from EBIT will be due to interest expense, and miscellaneous +/-. We are focusing on the changes in interest expense in the point above, so any significant changes will be, by definition, caused by additional items. The profits that fall to the bottom line are available for reinvestment in the business, or to pay back shareholders as dividends. The difference between after tax net profits and retained earnings, as we have already seen, are these dividend payments.

Wall Street Selling Implications – The P&L

If you are able to understand what to look for in a P&L you will be able to quickly see how the company is operating. Since every sales person must first develop a need, the P&L will let you immediately see how the company is operating, providing you with a roadmap of where to look first. By analyzing the concepts of costs vs. expenses, fixed costs vs. variable costs, and the various measures of profit you can begin to match your product's value proposition to the needs of your prospect. Too often sales teams don't look at what is important to the customer.

I know of one company that used to base its value proposition on how much paper flow it could reduce. If each invoice cost $1.50 to process, and they could show efficiency levels of the payables organization minimizing 100,000 individual payables, they would focus on the value proposition of $150,000. Now, their solution did not result in a reduction of the payable staff, so an executive looking at this just saw "the leaves being blown around." Start focusing your sales team on what is important to the customer, and you will start gaining mindshare and sales.

If you can read what the P&L statement is telling you, you will be able to understand how the company operates.

Every time Charlie Brown lines up to kick that field goal with Lucy holding the ball, he tells himself, "this time it's going to be different." It isn't, and unless you change your tool set, don't expect your results to be any different either.

"Dad, how many times do I have to tell you, Cash is King!"

Introducing the King

A FEW YEARS AGO I was part of a team analyzing a company's factory operations. We were getting a factory tour by a senior operations executive of a major manufacturer of motors and welding equipment. This company had received a good deal of press for a program that they had implemented called "gain sharing." This program paid the highest producers of parts the most money, the idea being to reward the most productive employees with a piece of the "gain" that the company was generating. At first glance that makes perfect sense. Generally, the person who is most productive probably should make the most money. If a plumber can fix five plugged sinks per day, and the others in the company can only fix four per day, well, he is more valuable, and should probably earn more money. The most productive bricklayer is the highest valued laborer for a masonry company, and an airline customer service rep that can handle the most complaints in an allotted time is more valuable to the airline.

The executive was explaining how the system worked, and proudly stated that since they implemented it, in every manufacturing process the measured parts per hour had soared. He began touting the benefits of their plan almost as soon as we stepped onto the factory floor.

"Our factory manager was able to increase his production output with the same labor force, LOOK OUT!" he screamed, just as a forklift loaded with containers of cut steel parts came zooming by. In fact, there were so many material handlers screaming around that plant in their forklifts or large tricycles loaded with parts that I thought it was the NASCAR factory tour.

While we had never seen so many workers that productive, we noticed that

> Equity doesn't let you eat steak, and it won't let you put a C Note on the pass line in Vegas. Neither will profit, for that matter. It's all about cash, so remember, Elvis is dead and Cash is King.

outside of all the machining and subassembly areas, the aisles of the factory were stacked over ten feet high with buckets of parts. We were walking in a giant maze of machined parts, with one particular machining center encircled by metal containers stacked to over ten feet in height. When I asked him how much cost was associated with its contents, the executive said that the amount was in excess of $1,000. I then took the shop order from the container, and pointed out that it was over six months old, which meant that the company had invested in the raw material, the labor, the storage, and the movement of all of those parts, and they still had not been sold to a customer. In an industry that demonstrates significant and numerous design changes the cost of obsolete inventory is also a real cost. By looking at that container and several hundred more just like it right in front of us, we were both looking at a roll of $100 bills that added up to over $200,000. The productivity that the plant had achieved was at a tremendous cost to cash flow. Later, my observations were verified by looking at his inventory balances on the plant financial statements.

Just like in your personal finances, in business there is nothing more important than cash. While I'm sure you like the equity that you have in your house, ask yourself if you would rather have that amount in equity, or would you rather have it in cash? Case closed.

Let's look at an example. Due to tax laws, companies that do more than $10 million in revenue per year must use the accrual method to determine sales and profits. This means that they recognize a sale when they get the order, and ship the product. Let's say that this company's product sells for $1,000, and they have a cost structure that is a 50 percent COGS, and 25 percent overhead. When the company recognizes that $1,000 sale, they immediately show a 25 percent pre tax profit, or $250. If their customer pays them sixty or ninety days later, well, they still have that $250 in profit on their books. If it is income tax time, they have to pay taxes with cash. You will find in a future chapter that this need for cash is acute for companies that are growing. Until the cash from their sales come in, they have to make do with what they have in the bank, or what they can borrow from the bank.

So we are going to learn to read and analyze the cash flow that a business or organization has, and the idea behind the "flow of cash" will be a primary focus on our analysis of strategy and the effectiveness of its execution. Most all sophisticated financial models apply a discount factor against future cash flows, not future profits. So, in order to think like your CEO, you will learn to be focused like a laser beam on the impacts of the organization's cash flows. Interestingly, my experience has been that for the vast majority of investment decisions, the sponsors developing the business case actually look towards its effect on profitability rather than cash. I've gone around and around on this issue with several different companies, and it almost always comes back to an executive somewhere up the line asking his team how much cash those profits are going to bring in. (When we get to the chapter on building a value proposition, we'll walk you through how to create a compelling one, and make sure you avoid the common pitfalls that I've seen with these.)

Operating Cash Flow

The most valuable thing about the cash flow statement is that it gives you a true picture of what the company is doing in its operations. This is borne out in the title of this chapter. The importance of cash brought about an overused cliché that says, "Cash is King!" Every company needs cash to function, invest, and pay back shareholders. Where they get this cash is demonstrated in the cash flow statement. As an individual, you don't work off the gross salary you earn, but off of the net cash you receive. It might be nice if you earn $100,000 per year, but you can only spend this as you get it. Just like you would like to get your $100,000 paycheck on January 1st for the whole year, most businesses will do just about anything to maximize their cash flow, also. Why? Because Cash is King.

How Cash Flow Statements Work

The detail behind the cash flow statement will do two things for you. It will give you one of the truest views of how the business is operating, and it will confuse you. So, in order to understand what this financial return tells us about an organization, we have to understand what we are looking at, and what it means. We'll start by focusing on the three major categories of this statement to give us a quick view of what is happening with the business.

Sample Cash Flow Statement

Like the other financial returns that we discussed, we will begin our understanding of the cash flow by understanding on an intuitive level what the return says, and then using this understanding to focus on a simplified cash flow statement. Think about your own experience with inflows and outflows of cash. Operating cash flow would be your weekly or biweekly paycheck. You get a weekly check, and with that money the first thing you probably do is pay off your bills. If you have a $200 telephone bill, and decide to not pay it off this month but rather pay it off next month, your accounts payable just increased and so did your cash flow. If you paid off that bill this month, and in fact decided to pay off another $100 of it, that $100 becomes a prepaid asset, and your cash flow just went down by $100.

If you want to buy a house or a car, you might put some of that cash flow towards a down payment. When you invest in that house or car, that is reducing your cash flow, unless you happen to sell your old car to help finance the new one, then you have cash flow from your investment, which was a car (or stocks or just about any other asset you might have.)

Unless you were able to save up a good deal of your paychecks, like most people you will probably go to your bank for a loan for that house or car. That is cash flow that we'll call financing cash flow. Let's look at what our yearly cash flow might look like.

Everyman's Cash Flow	
Paychecks	$52,000
Investing (stocks, house, car)	$(25,000)
Financing to pay for house and car	$20,000

Just like this real life example, companies have operating cash flow, investing cash flows, and financing cash flows, and they tell us different things about how the company is performing, and the strategies the company is undertaking.

Company XYZ		
Year ended December 31	200X	
Operating Cash Flow	$150	= Paycheck
Investing Cash Flow	$(50)	= Investing
Financing Cash Flow	$25	= Financing

The first of the three parts is the cash flow from operations. Since it would be impossible to use actual cash flows in and out of the company's checkbook at the bank, we are going to look at the changes in cash flow by comparing the company's accounts from different periods. This will give us the true changes in cash and allow us to see how the company's operations are going.

In the factory example that I discussed above, the workers trying to put out more parts are building up inventory, which decreases cash flow. Cash flow decreases, because anytime inventory increases, the company had to pay for it with cash. If it is work in process (WIP) inventory, not only did the company invest in inventory, but they invested in the labor it took to manufacture it.

If the inventory decreased, that would mean that the company was either selling more of the product, or building less, in either case freeing up cash flow, because if you don't buy inventory, you don't spend money. Remember this easy to understand inventory example when thinking about how the changes in current assets affect the cash flow.

The current liabilities section works just the opposite. Think of accounts payable. These are accounts that will be paid within one year of the date of the balance sheet. If this number goes from $200 to $100, well, we just paid off $100 of what we owe and our cash flow is therefore decreased by $100. If we don't pay off that $200, and actually increase it to $300, we still will owe it, but we now increase our cash flow by the difference, or $100 ($300-$200).

The key here is to remember the examples above. This is the same for any current asset.

Cash Flow Increases if...	Current Assets Decrease	Current Liabilities Increase

And...

Cash Flow Decreases if...	Current Assets Increase	Current Liabilities Decrease

Depreciation is also related to cash as a "non cash item" on the P&L. Here is how it works… Let's say that you own a car, and this car cost $10,000, and every year you will lose $2,000 in depreciation, so that after five years the car is totally depreciated (and let's assume no salvage value). Well, the $2,000 in depreciation expense would be a depreciation expense in the P&L, reducing your profits by $2,000, but you don't actually write a check from your bank account to that great black hole called car depreciation. The cash flow statement will take care of this by putting the net profits first – again, your profit less your $2,000 depreciation – and then add this back into the statement. So our initial understanding of the cash flow statement will look like the following:

Operating Cash Flow	$150
Investing Cash Flow	$50
Financing Cash Flow	$25

The second section of the cash flow statement deals with investing activities. This could be investments in fixed assets (anything that wears out, and land), acquisitions of other businesses, or investments in financial assets. Investments, as you might guess, reduce cash flow. However, just like the personal example we discussed above, if a company sells fixed assets, that will increase their cash flow. So investing cash flow can be shown as a negative or a positive, and looking at it will give you an idea of a company's strategies. If the last several years have shown less and less investment in plants, equipment, etc. you can bet that the company is conserving cash and unless something has drastically changed in their strategies of which markets they are going after, they may need to reinvest in these assets sometime in the future. There are only three ways to pay for investments:

- the company can either use the cash the operations generate
- borrow the cash (debt capital),
- or sell more stock (equity capital.) (Now you can also see why a strong stock price is important to company executives.)

You will also see other interesting points in the financing cash flow section. If the company paid off long-term debt, that would be here. Maybe the company converted long-term debt to short term debt, or did the reverse. This section will give you a good idea of a company's financial strategy.

Another key category that you will find here is the cash payment of dividends to shareholders. You can also get a quick estimate of this number by looking at the net profit after tax, and if the retained earnings don't increase by this amount, something happened in between, and that is going to be dividends paid out. You will get confirmation of this by looking at the financing cash flow section of the cash flow statement. The net increase in retained earnings from one year to the next will be the net profit dollars plus the dividend dollars.

Finally, the statement will put the beginning cash balances, add and or subtract the amounts from our three major categories (operating cash flow, investing cash flow, and financing cash flow) and provide us with the ending cash flow which will match the amount of cash shown in the balance sheet. One nice thing about the cash flow statement is that it will always catch corporate fraud. You see, you can only bluff the numbers for so long, until it shows up in the actual cash balances in the bank, or the lack thereof. Major corporations can complicate this matter by having thousands of different accounts, for each of their factories, facilities, and in different countries, with different currencies, etc. In some organizations, I have seen cash in excess of that required for working capital sent into corporate, and on other occasions, I've seen localized facilities maintain their own significant cash balances, so if you are looking at a cash flow statement that is not consolidated, you will have to check to see where the division's cash is going. The reasoning for this strategy often depends on corporate finance strategy as well as laws and regulations in the various countries that businesses operate in. What this means is that although you may see a cash balance that exceeds the long-term debt balance, a company can't necessarily use the cash to pay off this debt, and in fact may need the debt to cover working capital requirements.

> **Remember Elvis, and try to understand how every decision a company makes impacts its cash flow.**

Once we look at the operating cash flow, we want to take a look at the investing the company is doing and is outlined in the investing cash flow section. If a company is consistently decreasing investment in capital assets, that is a clue that the company is conserving cash at the possible expense of future assets. We will also look for acquisitions here, which is a good indicator of a company's growth strategy.

Sometimes, it is easier to understand what is happening with a company by looking at the cash flow statement. For example, looking at GM's 2003 cash flow statement we see what will probably be a huge future problem in the operating cash flow section. GM contributed over $18 billion – yes, that's with a B – to their pension contributions, which is more than double the rest of the operating cash flow that the company generated. It is difficult to invest in plants, engineering talent, etc. when that kind of cash is being sucked out of the company. Continued cash outflows like that will drive GM to be the USA's largest "pension company" that just happens to manufacture cars to continue to fund this business. In the competitive industry that is automobile manufacturing, they won't be able to make it under those conditions.

Finally, we'll look at the financing cash flow section to see how they are utilizing debt and equity capital, and see how much dividends they are paying out relative to their earnings.

So, putting this all together, we will understand the cash flow statement as outlined below, and always look for the answers to the key questions outlined below.

Operating Cash Flow	$150
Investing Cash Flow	$50
Financing Cash Flow	$25

PP&E and Free Cash Flow

We are going to introduce one other category in the cash flow statement. Property Plant & Equipment, sometimes shown as PP&E, or business investment, is the amount of cash that the company used for repair and maintenance, and new investment in its current assets. For example, if a company wants to expand capacity and purchases new brake presses, this will show up in PP&E. In a later chapter we will discuss how to read the cash flow statement to see if the company acquired another company, but for now we want to concentrate on this Property Plant and Equipment investment. The reason we are going to look at this specifically is that these types of investments are needed to keep the operations running smoothly. It is like oil changes in your car. You can avoid them for a while, but sooner or later you need to change the oil or you will have big problems with your car. Fixed assets by and large are the same for companies, so we can almost consider this type of investment a "fixed investment."

The Issue: The cash flow statement can provide you with a wealth of information about how the company is operating.

The Work Involved: The information is in one of three summary columns in the cash flow statement.

The Bottom Line: Although each section is important in the cash flow, you should circle the net operating cash flow number, and look for the trend versus the year before. What we are looking for here is an increase in operating cash flow, which tells us the company is generating cash rather than using cash.

If we accept this concept, then the cash generated from operations is not truly available for unlimited investment in the business. Some of it must go to PP&E. Subtracting the investment in PP&E from operating cash flow will yield what we will call "free cash flow." Free cash flow is the cash that the business can use for anything from paying dividends, to acquiring other companies, and is an extremely important concept that we will continue to focus on.

The cash flow statement we now see will have PP&E in the investing cash flow section. It will be shown as indented so that you can immediately see that it is not a total, but rather makes up part of the section that it is in.

Operating Cash Flow	$150
PP&E	$50
Investing Cash Flow	$50
Financing Cash Flow	$25

Financing Cash Flow

We are going to introduce two different types of financing that we will see in the cash flow statement. Companies can either take on debt, or sell stock. They take on debt by borrowing from banks, or issuing IOU's to the market. They sell stock by issuing a stock offering to the market. Note that if they issue more stock, it dilutes the earnings power of the stock they currently have in the market, as the net income, or earnings, will be spread over more shares.

The simple cash flow statements that we will learn from for now will look like the following.

Operating Cash Flow	$150
PP&E	$50
Investing Cash Flow	$50
Issuance LT Debt	$20
Issuance Stock	$5
Financing Cash Flow	$25

Fast Five – Cash Flow Metrics

When we look at a cash flow statement, we will immediately focus on the following five key points. In a later chapter, we will quantify these metrics so that we can judge what changes in them mean to the company. For now, we just want to begin looking at the financial returns in terms of these "Fast Five."

1. *Operating cash flow* - This immediately tells us how business operations can finance the everyday operations of the business. If this is decreasing, or negative, the company will have to raise funds by cutting back on investment in the business, or increasing financing. An increasing trend in operating cash flow is better than a decreasing one. If the operating cash flow is decreasing, that will force the company to either not invest as much or raise money – debt or equity – to pay for its investments. Remember: Cash is King.

2. *Free Cash Flow* - And no, it isn't free. This is operating cash flow less cash invested in capital expenditures. Capital expenditures are defined as current property, plant, and equipment that the company has. This measure is important because once this investment in fixed assets is made, the remainder of cash can be used for other investments, such as acquisitions, etc. If free cash flow increases substantially, only two things can be happening. Operating cash flow can be increasing, or the company can be investing less in their fixed assets, or PP&E. If this happens, this could be a signal that the company is reducing capital investment to preserve cash. If this number is significant, or this trend continues for several years, this could affect the company's productivity moving forward.

3. *Sales and acquisitions of businesses* - Under the investment cash flow, we want to see how much the company is spending on new businesses. If they

spent $200 for $100 of net assets, they will have to put $100 on the balance sheet as goodwill. (The notes to the financial statements will outline the acquired net assets and amount of goodwill to be carried.) Likewise, we want to see how much cash the company is raising by divesting some of its assets. When a company divests what it considers an underperforming business, it often refers to it as "killing a dog," a most unsavory term for me, a lover of German shepherd dogs.

> You can also look at **EBITDA** as a rough-cut cash flow. Remember that **EBIT** is operating profit, and as such includes depreciation. Taking this depreciation out of EBIT will give you **EBITDA** - an estimate cash flow, and can be utilized in your analysis if you don't have access to a cash flow statement.

4. *Financing debt capital* - If companies are not raising enough cash through the operating cash flow to cover their investments, they will have to go to financing. We want to see if they are raising this capital through debt or equity. If they increase debt capital, they will increase the interest expense on the P&L and lower net after tax earnings.

5. *Financing equity capital* – Another way that companies can raise cash flow is to go to the capital markets. If they are raising capital this way, they will not pay the additional interest expense that they would through debt capital, but they will spread their net income across more shares of stock, thereby lowering their EPS.

Wall Street Selling Implications – The Cash Flow Statement

Understanding the cash flow statement will allow you to dig a level deeper in your prospect's organization. It will also provide you with answers to some of the questions that the balance sheet or P&L may have raised. And our value proposition will always be focused to cash.

I once was in a sales cycle for a software solution that was focused almost entirely towards overhead reduction. While the software did an outstanding job of managing files and paperwork, the client we were dealing with gave us the sales equivalent of a big yawn. We turned the sales cycle away from the value proposition focused to overhead reduction and began addressing the ability of the filing software to shorten the time it took to create and send invoices. With the promise of quicker receipt of cash – which was the company's urgent need – we got the deal.

If you can drive your value proposition to the impacts it has on your prospect's cash flow, you will get management attention and drive greater sales.

The father of the H-bomb was once asked where the best place to be when one of those things went off. His answer: "Standing next to somebody who says, 'What's that?'" Keep your answers simple, too.

"Another aud lang sale!"

Happy New Year! Now What?

IT WAS THE BUSINESS EQUIVALENT of deciding if I should put the wire cutters on the blue wire or the red one. My ears were ringing and the sound of "TICK… TICK… TICK" was exploding from the imaginary clock that has been in all the movies. Here I was, giving a seminar on bidding out construction contracts, applying both overhead and profits to multimillion dollar commercial construction bids. I didn't know the difference between a "takeoff" and an estimate, yet here I was in front of thirty construction estimators and owners, all of them experts in bidding. I was trying to teach them a class in how to bid construction projects.

Things were going OK until a fifty-five year old owner of a $150 million dollar office building contractor - who was paying $1,495 for my advice - needed some of his own for his estimators back at the office who were putting the finishing touches on a major bid due the next day.

Most top-flight graduate business programs teach courses based on the case method of learning. Individuals, or small teams, are given a business problem and must solve it using the information that is in the case, assumptions, and business tools. The building of the case is where most of the learning takes place, and that which isn't learned is surely taught when the other students, or the teacher who has seen this case year after year, competitively engage in the case discussion. The process is stimulating. Hook up with the right consulting company, and you are making these business-impacting decisions for real on a daily basis. Now it was my turn, only the stakes were a bit higher now.

"Mark, we have had a good year thus far, and have actually paid off all of our overhead commitments for the remainder of the year. Do we still have to apply overhead for this upcoming bid?"

All eyes were on me, as I was the one holding those wire cutters I mentioned above. And to complicate things, I suddenly had to use the men's room.

The question arose out of a discussion of how we recommend allocating overhead to construction jobs. Thinking back to Managerial Economics 6500, economic theory states that to maximize profits, marginal costs should equal marginal revenues. Marginal revenue for a construction company is a variable cost, or the direct cost of the job. Therefore, the answer was yes, academically. However, the construction industry is known for projects being stretched out, as well as unknowns presenting themselves during the project. It is also known for a high degree of competitiveness, and a difficulty in differentiating quality in construction. (After all, when the owner flips the switch, the lights go on either way.) If the inspectors make sure the work is done to code, where does the quality come in?

I didn't know the answer at that point, so I started reaching in front of the group.

"How long is the project for?" I asked.

I was giving the seminar in July, so there were only five months left in the year. The answer I got back didn't help much; it was an intensive three-month project, and had a hard time schedule due to some government involvement. That meant that the job would be over by the time the New Year started. The job was also just about the size of the average job the contractor's company was doing, was in the same town right down from another job that was finishing up, and had standard contract provisions. This meant less cost involved in gearing up for the job.

The answer that I finally gave was the right one for the real world. They should bid the job with their overhead percentage added to it. You see, the end of year is simply a chosen date to end a period, and it has nothing magical about it. And in the construction industry, jobs can be delayed. If you bid the job without your overhead, you could end up losing money on the job. The real world executives that were in one of the most competitive industries out there agreed. Even though I had on a suit and Italian shoes, at that minute I became a contractor.

The accounting rules that businesses follow don't change for the end of a period, except for things such as taxes, etc. For the focus of understanding the concepts of what happens at the end of a period, we'll use the end of year approach.

Balance Sheet Impacts

Let's look at a company's balance sheet that is dated the last day in December. For this example, we will assume that there are no taxes involved. We'll address this as well as other complexities in a later chapter. The key right now is to understand the concepts presented.

Company ABC		Company ABC	
Balance Sheet		P&L Statement	
As of Dec. 31 2005		Year Ended Dec. 31 2005	
	2005		
Assets			
Current Assets	$1,000	Sales	$500
Fixed Assets	$500	COGS	$300
TOTAL ASSETS	$1,500	Gross Profit	$200
Liabilities		O/H	$100
Current Liabilities	$500	Operating Profit	$100
LT Liabilities	$500		
TOTAL LIABILITIES	$1,000	Interest	$
Equity		Net Profit	$100
Retained Earnings	$50		
Stock	$450		
TOTAL EQUITY	$500		

As you can see the company assets equal its liabilities plus capital. We will also present the company's 2005 P&L Statement next to it, where you see that the company made $100 during the year.

Let's do our balance sheet check and we see that everything is in order.

Have	=	Owe	+	Own	
Assets	=	**Liabilities**	+	**Equity**	
$1,500	=	$1,000	+	$500	

Now the year changes from 2005 to 2006, and the $100 that is shown as net profit immediately transfers to retained earnings in the equity section of the balance sheet. Let's do our balance sheet check again and see what it looks like.

Have	=	Owe	+	Own	
Assets	=	Liabilities	+	Equity	
$1,500	=	$1,000	+	$600	

We see right away that something is wrong, as the equation is out of order. What we have to do now is to put it back in balance. The act of doing this is called *financial management*. Let's do the easiest thing and put our balance sheet back in balance by moving these profits into the current account. That would put the $100 into either cash or something that will be turned into cash within one year. This would make our balance sheet look like the following.

Company ABC		Company ABC
Balance Sheet		Balance Sheet
As of Dec. 31		As of January 1
		Option #1 placing $100 of retained earnings in current assets
	2005	2006
Assets		
Current Assets	$1,000	$1,100
Fixed Assets	$ 500	$500
TOTAL ASSETS	$1,500	$1,600
Liabilities		
Current Liabilities	$500	$500
LT Liabilities	$500	$500
TOTAL LIABILITIES	$1,000	$1,000
Equity		
Retained Earnings	$50	$150
Stock	$450	$450
TOTAL EQUITY	$500	$600

Notice that by looking only at the balance sheet you can see the net income that the company earned the prior year. We will be addressing this point when we begin to look at analyzing financial statements. If a company loses money year over year, you will see the amount of retained earnings diminish. If the company has lost more money than it has earned, you will see retained earnings called accumulated deficit. Whenever you see retained earnings called accumulated deficit in a balance sheet, you should know right away that the company is – at the date of the balance sheet – a money-losing venture.

Let's do our balance sheet check and see if we are in balance now after our financial decision to put the 2005 profits into current assets.

Option #1 placing $100 of retained earnings in current assets			
Have	**=**	**Owe** +	**Own**
Assets	**=**	**Liabilities** +	**Equity**
$1,600	=	$1,000 +	$600

We could also take that $100 and put it elsewhere. Let's say that we will put it in our LT liabilities, lowering by $100 the debts that we will have to pay off beyond twelve months from the date of the balance sheet. Let's see how our balance sheet looks if we place the $100 in this account.

Company ABC	**Company ABC**	
Balance Sheet	Balance Sheet	
As of Dec. 31	As of January 1	
	Option #1 placing $100 of retained earnings in current assets	Option #2 placing $100 of retained earnings LT liabilities
	2005	2006	2006
Assets			
Current Assets	$1,000	$1,100	$1,000
Fixed Assets	$500	$500	$500
TOTAL ASSETS	$1,500	$1,600	$1,500
Liabilities			

Current Liabilities	$500	$500	$500
LT Liabilities	$500	$500	$400
TOTAL LIABILITIES	$1,000	$1,000	$900
Equity			
Stock	$450	$450	$450
Retained Earnings	$50	$150	$150
TOTAL EQUITY	$500	$600	$600

Let's do our balance sheet check and see how our balance sheet looks now.

Option #2 placing $100 of retained earnings in LT Liabilities					
Have	=	Owe	+	Own
Assets	=	Liabilities	+	Equity
$1,500	=	$900	+	$600

We see that we are in balance also, but that the numbers look different. In the first case, assets increased from $1,500 to $1,600, almost a 7 percent increase. Although the profit was the same in both instances, financial strategies allowed for a final end result in the balance sheet. Keep this in mind as we begin to look at more balance sheets. It is imperative for executive management to best use the profits generated by the company to achieve the objectives laid out by the shareholders, or the representatives of the shareholders, the board of directors. Also keep in mind that you are seeing an example of how managers can manipulate their financials. It is possible for executives to manipulate the balance sheet and P&L Statements through financial management decisions. If their bonuses were tied to these results, it may mean additional personal income to them in the form of bonuses, stock awards, etc. (This is why it is important to be able to look at a company's numbers and understand what's happening. Only through due diligence and constant visibility can this be addressed.)

Just like differences in the balance sheet with the end of a year, the P&L statement has some key things that you must keep in mind. To understand, let's look at our sample P&L statement.

Company ABC	
P&L Statement	
Year Ended Dec. 31 2005	
Sales	$500
COGS	$300
Gross Profit	$200
O/H	$100
Operating Profit	$100
Interest	
Misc. +/-	
Net Profit	<u>$100</u>

The key point that we want to keep in mind about the year-end of the income statement is the determination of COGS, or cost of goods sold. The formula to determine COGS is shown below.

Beginning Inventory	$350
+ Purchases	$200
<u>- Ending Inventory</u>	<u>$250</u>
Equals COGS	$300

What we see is that if ending inventory increases, the company becomes more profitable, and likewise, if ending inventory decreases, the COGS will increase, driving profitability down. While accounting rules state that inventory valuations must be consistent so managers don't have the ability to place different values on inventory to achieve either their profitability or tax strategy, there are ways managers can manipulate these numbers, based on acquisitions, or declaring inventory obsolete. Whenever this happens, you will be able to find out how they did this from the notes to the financial statements.

In most companies, the Cost of Goods Sold is the product itself that is sold. If the company manufactures the product, the COGS will be raw materials as well as direct labor costs. While most of your analysis of Profit Strategies will not require you to do this mathematical formula, work with private companies, or analysis on an individual facility level, may.

A good understanding of this can greatly assist your sales cycles, as I found out as I was driving a large technology sale to a $600 million division of a Fortune 500 company. I began by selling an individual factory on a lean manufacturing program, focusing on the cash flow benefits that lean would drive. As you now know, driving down inventory can have a short-term effect on profitability. I found out that the General Manager was compensated on the profitability of his six factories, so to him, this initiative was about as good a match as Bobby Brown and Whitney Houston.

I used this leverage to get to the General Manager and later the Chief Operating Officer, who changed the GM's compensation plan and gave me an order for the rest of the division. He understood that Elvis was dead, and with his increase in inventories eating up his cash flow, his company may soon be too. For him, cash was king.

You will have the opportunity to utilize this formula working with individual divisions of large companies, closely held businesses, just about any type of small business, and anytime one has to make a decision on the cost of sales. Putting this into our P&L statement it now looks like this.

Company ABC	
P&L Statement	
Year Ended Dec. 31 2005	
Sales	$500
Beginning Inventory	$350
+ Purchases	$200
- Ending Inventory	$250
COGS	$300
Gross Profit	$200
O/H	$100
Operating Profit	$100
Interest	
Misc. +/-	
Net Profit	$100

Now let's look at what happens with COGS, and therefore gross profit, as the inventory accounts change. Like the balance sheet example from above, we can decide to manipulate the inventory numbers and see what effect it has on our income statement.

Let's say that we as a company feel that we can capture more market share by shortening the time it takes to satisfy our customer's orders. We have two alternatives as to how we can address this. The first alternative has us providing more product in our distribution channel, both at our central warehouse as well as our distribution sites. I order to do this, we run the factory on overtime, building up more inventory so that we can place it in the proper place, so that when a customer order comes in, we can fill it quickly.

At this point, you may be wondering if Dr. Kevorkian had a hand in developing what I've called the "language of business." While the chapters in this section are a lengthy chunk of hard-core business-speak, with these concepts as a base you're now ready to learn how to use them to start closing deals.

The second alternative is to focus on the manufacturing cycle itself, implementing Lean Manufacturing. Lean manufacturing is a method of manufacturing that has its roots in the Toyota Production System. If we provide parts on a Just-In-Time basis, the factory will only build only what is ordered. Since they don't have to build the other products that are taking up capacity, they don't put as much into inventory, resulting in less inventory in the system. This provides us an excellent example of what happens to the P&L when a company implements this type of manufacturing strategy.

Based on the P&L alone, one might assume that the most financially viable strategy to increase market share in our example would be to produce more product. More product means more profit, because the inventory goes up driving gross profits up. However, while a change in inventory does not change the totals in the current asset columns, it does affect the current assets in a key way. Remember what a current asset is defined as: cash and whatever will be turned into cash within twelve months from the date on the balance sheet. Looking at the impacts to the cash flow of the company will let us assume that each dollar of inventory takes a dollar of cash flow out of the company.

Increasing production will also drive up costs of sales, requiring cash investments, and when teamed with the increase in current assets outlined above, this Profit Strategy will require a large cash investment. Thinking of our problem like this, we now have a better understanding of the impacts to our business, and the simple conclusion of placing more inventory into our channel may not be the easy answer.

Company ABC		Company ABC	Company ABC
P&L Statement		P&L Statement	P&L Statement
Year Ended Dec. 31 2005		Year Ended Dec. 31 2005	Year Ended Dec. 31 2005
		Option #1 Build up inventory	Option #2 J-I-T manufacturing
Sales	$500	$500	$500
Beginning Inventory	$350	$350	$350
+ Purchases	$200	$200	$200
- Ending Inventory	$250	$300	$200
COGS	$300	$250	$350
Gross Profit	$200	$250	$150
O/H	$100	$100	$100
Operating Profit	$100	$150	$50
Interest			
Misc. +/-			
Net Profit	$100	$150	$50

A Note about Formats

As you begin to understand a company's strategy, you are going to focus on specific numbers. From now on, the samples will focus on the key parts that we are discussing by calling them out. Before long, you will be able to look at the most complex financial returns and immediately do the same.

The New Year

The calendar can help you book sales. Companies make decisions based on annual capital and operating budgets. As the year (or quarter) winds down, they may find available budget, or find themselves in the position of having to spend that budget. This is not the most efficient use of either funds or budgeting, so as you can guess, this "use it or lose it" mentality is rampant throughout government and government contracting. The government is on a fiscal year that goes from October 1 to September 30. I have closed deals in September by offering software to ensure that my prospects divisional budget would not run the risk of being cut the next year.

It is important to note that in some organizational structures, such as Subchapter S Corporations or Limited Liability Companies (LLC), the end of year can have tax consequences to the shareholders. In both Sub S corporations and LLC's the company's profits go to the bottom line of the shareholders' Income Tax Return. If you are dealing with these types of companies, you can use the January House Payment Close. Here is how it works.

If you own your home and pay a mortgage the first of every month, you should pay your January 1 mortgage payment on December 31st of the year prior. (That's one day earlier for you math challenged sales people.) The reason you want to do this is that it provides you with 13 months of interest deduction in that year. Keep paying that January mortgage on December 31st so that you have 12 payments for each future year, and that extra month of interest expense is an interest free loan from the government for the duration of your mortgage term. This is something every homeowner should do, but my suspicion is that far fewer actually do it. Once you explain the significance to a company, it makes a compelling case for closing the deal in December, if the company is going to spend the money anyway.

I used this to my advantage when I was selling to Tom, a CEO of a closely held company that was organized as an S Corporation. Although Tom was the CEO, all of the company shares were owned by another shareholder.

After six months of selling, Tom gave me an early Christmas present on the day before Thanksgiving by committing to move forward – sometime in Q1. While that was certainly good news and indicated that Tom was indeed sold, I still had to pay for Christmas presents, so I gave Tom a deal he could hardly refuse. I framed this deal around my explanation as to why I pay my January mortgage payment in December, and suggested that he do the same with the project that I was trying to sell to Tom.

Without discounting the price, I told Tom that we could arrange the deal so that the owner of Tom's company could save 36 percent. We just needed to sign a contract whereby we kicked off the project before the end of the year. Sounding too good to be true, I recommended Tom check with his accountant. After hanging up the phone, he made two calls. One was to his CPA, and the other was back to me. We had a deal.

Tom saved the shareholder 36 percent as he was able claim the entire $200,000 as a business expense in that year, thereby saving $72,000 on his taxes.

While most companies understand the importance of the end of the year, you will see in a future chapter why although 2002 was a good year for Merlot, it looked like a bad year for Robert Mondavi, Inc.

PART TWO

The Wall St. Selling Methodology™

"Nice fish. I am a fisherman too. Where do you fish? Did you catch him yourself?"

The Wall Street Selling Methodology™

TACTICAL SALES PROCESSES can help organize the sales cycle, but these methodologies can be limited in their effectiveness, as many experienced salespeople frequently execute these steps quite naturally. One of the companies that I worked for invested a ton of money on a new CRM (Customer Relationship Management) system which was going to do two things:

1. Help the sales team organize their sales processes, thereby (by osmosis, I guess) helping us to sell more.
2. Ensure that the sales managers could track each and every deal in detail, eliminating sandbagging and increasing their management skills (while turning the weekly headache of forecasting into a full blown, mind- numbing migraine.)

The defined process helped the less experienced sales people and presales consultants organize their sales strategy, but it also sparked plenty of debates about what constituted a goal or an objective, as well as value added discussions around whether something was a tactic or a strategy. And when it came to helping you develop a stratcgy for meeting and selling C – Level executives, it proved about as useful as a man purse for a bull rider.

The Wall Street Selling Methodology™ is different in that it provides a step-by-step process that prepares the sales team to completely understand the Profit Strategies of their prospective client. Sitting on top of the execution system, it will prepare the team to meet senior level executives and speak their language.

This is critical if they are going to be holding meetings with senior executives. Without this knowledge, the sales team runs the risk of presenting their value proposition in a vacuum. If your sales process can't align and integrate the value of your product or service with the Profit Strategies of the prospective client, you are simply not going to develop a compelling message. Chances are, you will "show up and throw up." And you won't get the deal. The Wall Street Selling Methodology™ puts a Colt .45 in that man purse your company may be forcing you to use.

Many sales teams may spend most of their time selling to people several steps removed from the CEO. If this is the situation you are facing, it is even more important for you to position your value proposition in alignment with the CEO's Profit Strategies. Educate your sponsor on what is important to his executives and you will stand a much better chance of getting the deal.

This methodology will give you a complete understanding of what you need to do to accomplish this.

Channel Partners

Many companies utilize partners to sell their product or service. Often times aligned for specific industries, applications, or prospects, this "distributed sales team has many challenges, not the least of which companies often spend more time focusing on their direct sales channel.

I have been involved from both ends of the sales channel, and believe that there is a tremendous opportunity to provide some true value to your channel partners. When I was actively involved managing my company's channel partners, I was able to exceed my group's quota – and the company's expectations – by providing the tools outlined in this book to my partners. I worked with their sales organizations to instill the Wall Street Selling Methodology™ with the objective of providing a consistent message and process that gave us the best chance to win the deals. Since it was impossible to have my team accompany them during every sales call, we had to ensure that our message was getting through in the right way to our prospect's senior executives. By implementing the Wall Street Selling Methodology™ we were able to position our solution in a more strategic way, and our average selling prices (ASP's) increased substantially.

> "Channel Sales Management" for many companies consists of providing their channel partners with a brochure, a map with colored states on it, and a quota.

An interesting by-product of my work was the increased interest the partner's sales organization showed in our solutions. Our partners were not exclusive to our product line, and could go into accounts positioning other solutions. Working with them to utilize the Wall Street Selling Methodology™ differentiated the services that my team was providing to them. We motivated them to look for a fit with our solutions first. The tools helped them to qualify their prospects, so they didn't waste time on accounts that wouldn't close.

> **Most sales methods tell you what you need to do, but don't provide you the tools to get it done. They are kind of like listening to Pele describe how he plays soccer, "I do deese, deese, deese, deese, GOAL!"**

Simply teaching your partners your value proposition and expecting that to move business to closure is about as likely as the average reader of this book getting a job with Death Row Records. Utilize the tools and templates of the methodology and help your channel partners to drive your top line revenue.

Sell Through

Another way that you can utilize the tools of the Wall Street Selling Methodology™ is to use it to "sell through" your prospects. In addition to understanding your target company's business environment and Profit Strategies, show them that you understand their customers' business.

For instance, if you are selling parts or capital equipment to McDATA, a manufacturer of storage devices, you want to help them understand their customers. Consider the following taken from their 10-K report:

> *Our three major storage OEMs- EMC, IBM and Hitachi Data Systems (HDS)- are significant providers of enterprise storage systems. For the fiscal year ending January 31, 2006, EMC accounted for approximately 31% (47% in fiscal 2004), IBM accounted for approximately 26%, (25% in fiscal 2004), and HDS accounted for approximately 9% (9% in fiscal 2004) of our total revenue. McDATA solutions are offered and sold by other major storage and system vendors, including Dell, HP, and Sun. In addition to our storage and system vendors, we have relationships with resellers, distributors, and systems integrators worldwide.*

If you are calling on a C-Level contact within McDATA, you will gain a great deal of credibility and an edge in positioning if you discuss the Profit Strategies that EMC, IBM, and HDS are pursuing. Bring this into your value integration and you will build an even more comprehensive case for purchasing your parts and equipment.

Government & Not for Profit

Selling to Not for Profit and government entities can be a challenge, but today's focus on efficiency works in your favor. Many of these organizations have their own financial statements, so you can judge the effectiveness of their Profit Strategies. Senior executives in these organizations will be just as interested in understanding how their key metrics have performed, and what that means to their ability to achieve their objectives. Revenue per employee, gross margin, and financial structure are key issues for these organizations. Never forget that without profit, these organizations cannot do their job. I am on the board of a non profit organization, and you know what a key driver of our organization is? Profits! Without profits, we can't serve our members. Not for Profit and government agencies that are professionally run will focus on their financial results in order to expand their product offerings, meet additional market needs, and provide stability and growth for their employees. Only then can they achieve their mission.

In many instances you may be able to compare similar organizations' returns to see what the level of efficiency the government agency you are selling to is achieving. You can bet that senior managers in the US Postal Service are interested in how they stack up with FedEx, UPS, or maybe even Deutsche Post. Keep the discussion focused on Profit Strategies and you will achieve the same results working with your government clients.

Wall Street Selling Methodology™

The methodology that utilizes the tools outlined in this book is called the Wall Street Selling Methodology™, and is shown below. This structure fits in well with whatever sales execution process your company is using, because in order to sell to a CEO, you have to understand his issues, and the requirements around which he is driving strategy in his business. Using this process will also ensure that you do not leave any bases uncovered, so that you can extract the most value out of your executive meetings. Figure 5-1 shows the steps in the Wall Street Selling Methodology™.

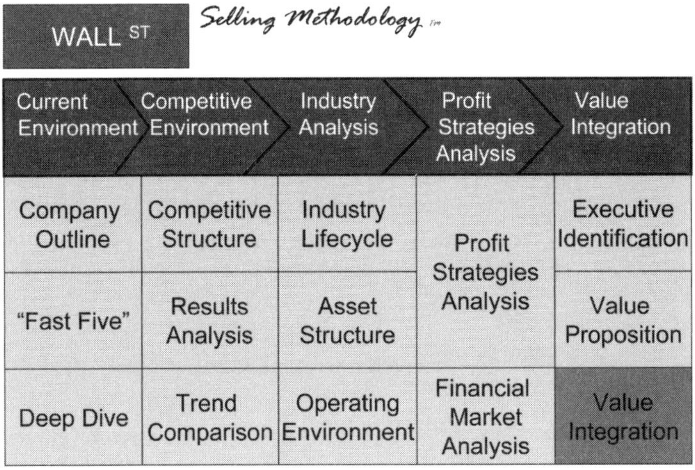

WALL ST *Selling Methodology* ™

Current Environment	Competitive Environment	Industry Analysis	Profit Strategies Analysis	Value Integration
Company Outline	Competitive Structure	Industry Lifecycle	Profit Strategies Analysis	Executive Identification
"Fast Five"	Results Analysis	Asset Structure		Value Proposition
Deep Dive	Trend Comparison	Operating Environment	Financial Market Analysis	Value Integration

Figure 5.1

We will now take a look at each of the major sections that make up the methodology.

Current Environment

The first thing that we need to understand is how the company is operating in its current environment. While you will never get as complete an understanding of how the company is operating from the outside, this method will be the optimum way for you to draw some conclusions that you can then validate through questions.

The Issue: Information overload when all you are trying to do is to develop a sales strategy.

The Work Involved: Read this book, and learn the concepts involved in thinking like a CEO.

The Bottom Line: Follow the Wall Street Selling Methodology™ through each step and you will end up with a value proposition integrated with your client's business.

Company Outline

There are many different ways CEO's employ to organize their companies. Some are focused by industry, or product line, while others may be organized geographically. Once you understand the specifics of the individual division, you will then be able to understand their Profit Strategies by looking at their financials, or by estimating these financial metrics using the industry knowledge that you have. While this should be the first analysis that you do, you may find that these executives are more influencers than decision makers.

You may be able to generate some financial estimates by asking questions of some operations personnel. Often times, you can get basic information such as number of employees, growth in overtime, or number or orders, etc. Line of business managers (LOB managers) will often share information on their areas of pain, be that inventory balances or loan losses. This is one reason why it is important to have a good understanding of the metrics of other companies in their industry.

You must also understand how the decision making process is organized. If the budget will come out of a different organization, you must understand this group as well. Informal divisions are what happen when spheres of influence are not defined in a company's financial statement.

Fast Five

It is important to get a complete understanding of the financial metrics under which the company is operating. If your initial analysis shows that you are going to be working a division of a company, then we want to look at both the division's metrics, as well as the overall corporate metrics. Just as "poop and 'atta boys' flow downhill" the financial strategies of a corporation have a huge influence on the division. A division that has net operating profit margin significantly less than the organization's as a whole will be focused like a laser beam on increasing that metric. Some companies will not be willing to provide specific division financial metrics. In this case, one of the ways to understand their business is to pull the financials of other industry players with whom they compete. For example, Allen Bradley has a division that manufactures motors, the old Reliance Electric. Pulling the financials of Baldor Electric, which manufactures motors, will provide a good starting point for financial analysis. We will address specifics that you should look at in the chapter on industry analysis.

The objective of this financial analysis is to do as much of the *Fast Five* analysis as possible, because this quick overview will generally provide us with all the information that we will need to understand the company and its Profit Strategies.

Deep Dive

A more complete financial analysis may be appropriate prior to your meetings. We are terming this the Deep Dive, and will provide ideas on how to do this once you master the *Fast Five* analysis.

Competitive Environment

Understanding the competitive environment of the company you are analyzing will allow you to try to understand the possible challenges that the executive is facing. It is important to look beyond the current operating challenges and try to broaden the scope of what the executive could be facing. Meeting with division presidents, I would sometimes summarize the strategies that the corporation's CEO is taking. Since these will drive investment and performance measures, the message is: either start looking at these now, or before long you are going to be seeing the focus on these issues.

Competitive Structure

Once you have identified the specific industry, you want to understand the competitors that the division faces in that industry. The information that you can gather from publicly traded companies allows you to map several competitors to investigate. It is important to understand how specific companies line up in the competitive space as well as on a corporate level. For example, let's say that you are targeting GE's Aircraft Engines division. Aircraft Engines competes directly with Rolls Royce and Pratt & Whitney, so you would want to investigate the financials and strategies those companies are undertaking in their aircraft divisions.

Publicly traded companies compete with one another in the equities market. Companies who are in the same sector, or who are perceived in the same manner (such as industrial conglomerates) compete even more fiercely. For example, GE competes not only with UTC's Pratt & Whitney aircraft engine division, but also with similar conglomerates such as Siemens and Emerson Electric. If the senior executives of GE are keeping their eyes on their complete range of competitors, you should too.

Results Comparison

One way that we will quickly be able to see how companies are competing in the same markets is to do a results comparison. Understanding how companies stack up will give you an understanding of areas to investigate and weaknesses to exploit in your sales cycles.

Trend Analysis

It may be appropriate to look at the individual operating trends of the competitors in the industry. Oftentimes, poor performing markets cut across the competitive landscape, hurting all of the companies competing. Likewise, increasing markets help all the players. While generally true, this is not always the case, and there is significant value in finding out how companies have addressed the challenges posed by the market. More successful strategies can be a difference maker among the competitive group. Just like that blue dress did for dry-cleaning, this section will bring that to the forefront.

Industry Analysis

Since any company you will be calling on operates in a competitive environment, we will want to understand as much about the industry as possible. Some of this analysis we will get from the Form 10-K that all public companies file with the Securities and Exchange Commission (SEC), and some will come from the financial statements of the industry players you identify.

Industry Lifecycle

We want to draw some conclusions as to where the industry is in the lifecycle model. We can gather this information in the 10-K reports, as the report discusses the company's strategy and the competitive nature of the industry. A company's strategy will vary differently if its product becomes obsolete quickly versus one that shows years of product lifecycle. A scissors manufacturer won't have the same inventory risk that a computer manufacturer will, because new styles of scissors aren't introduced as quickly as new microprocessors. Likewise, if the industry is a new growing industry, the players may find themselves in a "land grab" focused on top line revenue versus profits. When Amazon.com entered the E-retailing industry, profits didn't come until years later, and neither Amazon.com nor Wall Street minded much. The name of the game was market share, and that is what the market rewarded. There may be many different and unique metrics that companies face based on their lifecycle, and the lifecycle of the industry they are in.

Asset Structure

We are going to look at the asset structure of the industry players to draw some conclusions as to industry requirements. For example, your local electric utility has a much different asset structure than the construction company that built that plant. Chances are the other electricity providers will have an asset structure much more like your utility than that construction company. Certain industries and markets require a certain asset mix, and you will be able to get an excellent idea of operating requirements by looking at several industry competitors' asset structures.

Operating Environment

We also want to compare the operating environment of the competitors in an industry. If four of the five competitors in an industry are showing gross profit margins of over 50 percent, and the final competitor is showing gross profits of half of that, then we will be able to make some assumptions on both the industry and that individual company. In my research and experience, I've found that most of the time, competing players in an industry will have similar operating environments.

Profit Strategies

Profit Strategies Analysis

To call on the CEO, you have to understand his organization and the challenges that he is facing. If you are working with a division, most division executives will drive their organization to be in line with the CEO's vision. Understanding a company's Profit Strategies will allow you to do both of these.

Financial Market Analysis

It is important to look at how the financial market is valuing the industry players. Looking at several metrics can tell you quickly how Wall Street investors feel about industries in general, as well as individual companies within these industries. We will also get an understanding of the recent stock valuations, market capitalization, and future outlook. While some will contend that the market is perfectly efficient and its intentions should be trusted, we will look at these financial market metrics as a piece of our overall analysis.

I was once working with the motors division of a large industrial manufacturer to implement J-I-T and flow manufacturing in their manufacturing operations. While they were very profitable, the division had grown dramatically over the previous several years, requiring a substantial investment in cash from the parent corporation. Unwilling to compromise the market opportunity, this division had its capital budget approved by HQ. Its parent organization was pursuing a strategy of growth by acquisition, which required significant amounts of cash flow. I made the cash flow benefits of the flow- manufacturing project the key point in the sales process. Focusing on the cash returns that the project would bring, the division president sponsored us up to his Executive VP, who saw a fit with the overall company strategy. We ended up expanding what started out as a divisional initiative into a companywide focus on flow manufacturing.

Value Integration

Executive Identification

Anytime you are meeting with an executive level person, you need to understand his background. Prior to the internet, I always used to look up the executive in Who's Who. While internet technology makes it easier to get information on your contact, don't rely only on an internet search. Many executives serve as board members on publicly traded companies. Board members stock transactions and option grants are on file with the Securities and Exchange Commission. Searching these filings will let you know what board seats the executive has.

Value Proposition

You should have a good understanding of the value that your product or service will bring to the purchaser. We will not address your specific value buckets, but we will introduce specific methods to present your value proposition. It's amazing how few people discount their value proposition to bring it to a single number that compares to a company's hurdle rate. We will teach several fundamental ways to present a value proposition to a CEO.

Value Integration

You know value selling is dead if you have ever been interrupted over dinner by a telemarketer promising you savings on your heating bill. You just need to increase your insulation. Even though I used to work in the industry and can vouch for the value proposition, our family has not invested in additional insulation. And I'll bet yours hasn't either. I can guarantee that it is the same in your industry, whether you sell capital equipment, major bonding deals, or software.

> **Value selling is deader than disco. In today's environment, you must align your value proposition to the executive's Profit Strategy in order to close business.**

You must demonstrate that you understand the specific strategies the company is focusing on so that your product or service is seen as integral to achieving this strategy. Doing this increases the odds that you will close the deal.

Now that we have given you an overview of Wall Street Sales Methodology™, we will examine where you can look to gather the information that we've discussed. Using this information, and building on the knowledge that you gained in the first section of this book, you will learn to analyze any company quicker and more in depth than just about anyone you will meet – or compete with. And in the end, that's really what sales is all about. You beating your competitor and getting the deal. It isn't enough to simply ask for the business and "sell the value" anymore. Everyone in your field is doing that. You have to have an edge, an advantage, over the other guy, which is what this book gives you. Unless the other guy bought this book too. Which he probably has. So hedge your bets and buy two copies, read 'em both and get ready to cash the commission checks. (You could also just read this copy twice, but I get a royalty on each copy sold, and remember what we learned above: Elvis is dead, Cash is King.)

Wall Street Selling Implications – The Methodology

The value in the concepts discussed in this book is utilizing them in an overall program, working in concert with the sales process you use to move opportunities to deals. The Wall Street Selling Methodology™ is not just a way to understand C-Level executives, but should be the overall strategic method of breaking into companies. The methodology is laid out in a way that has proven to be effective as you use it for a roadmap, ensuring that nothing falls through the cracks as you build your sales strategy. While not a black box, the Wall Street Selling Methodology™ will allow you to understand how CEO's think. Once you have a grasp of their business issues and challenges – and how your product aligns and integrates with that – you utilize the tools outlined to close more business.

The tools outlined in this book should allow you to drive significant revenue for your company, whether you utilize a direct sales method, or sell through channel partners. Provide your partner with real value and you will become their best friend. Everyone in your distribution and sales channel will increased their profitability

Finally, the concepts of "sell through" will provide you with the tools far beyond what your competitors are working with. Since the C-Level executives you are calling on are thinking about this complete environment, an understanding of his customers Profit Strategies will allow you to truly become a trusted partner.

For those times when you can't refer to the book to help, we have developed the Wall Street Selling Methodology™ "Cheat Sheet" that is in the back of this book. It is intended for you to carry in your briefcase, or in your coat pocket, so that you can quickly and easily use the tools that we are discussing.

Remember what the MGM executive said after Fred Astaire's screen test. "Can't sing. Can't act. Can dance a little." Always believe in yourself and don't necessarily trust the "expert's" opinion.

"That's it! I'm looking at the directions!"

Roadmap to the Information Superhighway

WHILE THE REQUIREMENTS of my job lead me to read several hundred financial statements in the course of a normal year, that didn't prepare me for the research that I put into this book. To research companies and uncover strategies I ordered over 2,000 annual reports. I still remember the phone call I got at work from my wife one day.

"Tell them to stop!" she breathed frantically.

For the third day in a row, the UPS driver had dropped off three boxes – no check that, heavy boxes – at our doorstep. He was nice enough to bring them downstairs to my office, and my wife was nice enough to give him a $20 tip. In the end, I had over fifteen boxes of annual reports that I would look through every evening, researching the Profit Strategies section of this book. You don't have to do that type of research, but to be successful selling to C-Level executives you need to understand the competitive environment in which companies are operating.

The best way for you to understand business strategies and incorporate the tools of this book into your business lives is to read lots of annual reports. Put them by your bed. Next to the toilet. In your gym bag. As you are watching late night curling or bad amateur singers, open the reports and figure our their Profit Strategies. Read through the papers, magazines, etc. and when you hear about a company's story, go get their financials and see if you agree with what the conclusions are. If you are looking to send your hard-earned dollars off to purchase shares, compare them to their competitors in their industry. Companies that either have failed or achieved fantastic results make great learning cases.

The remainder of this chapter will provide you with some ideas as to where you might find information that you can use to understand a company's competitive environment.

SIC Codes

The US Government classifies all businesses by a Standard Industrial Classification, called an SIC code. The SIC code is a four number code that classifies companies by the industries that the companies compete in, and was last updated in the late 1980's. While I'm sure that as you read this someone is in development of the industry equivalent of the Dewey Decimal System, since the Security and Exchange Commission (SEC) uses the SIC code, this is the one you should focus on.

US Securities and Exchange Commission

My favorite bookmark is www.sec.gov. Since May of 1996, all SEC listed companies have had to file their annual and quarterly reports electronically. The SEC requires a great deal of information from publicly traded companies, ranging from stock sales, to employee benefit plans, to registration of new securities. This site is often referred to as EDGAR, a name that the SEC owns the trademark to. There are also businesses that are using technology tools to allow downloads from these electronic filings right into Excel Spreadsheets. www.freeedgar.com and www.edgaronline.com are two sites that can help you do this. As a caution, they are for profit companies, so you can expect to pay for this convenience. You might check out www.edgarscan.pwcglobal.com as another alternative that will allow you to download a company's financial reports into an Excel format. It is free, but doesn't have all of the filers like Edgar online or the SEC site. To simplify your search, here are the main documents that I believe that you will find useful.

> Ever since Al Gore invented the internet, you can gather the background you need on companies in less time than it takes to make a cup of coffee. Any time you are going to call on a senior level executive, or even make a call into a company, pull down their latest 10-Q's. Hit a finance site and read their latest headlines, and you won't be hit with any surprises.

10-K – This is the annual report that the SEC requires all companies to file. The financial statements will match exactly with the annual report that is sent out to shareholders, although this document is usually much more in depth, and much more useful. You will also find the board of directors and executive officers, along with background information on them.

The 10-K is divided into four parts. The first part provides information about the business such as business strategy, competition, and a complete discussion of the organization, and the location and types of assets that the organization holds. If you are looking to find out where the company has offices or factories, or maybe want to understand their distribution channel, this is the place to find it. This section is required reading and will help you gain an understanding of the organization's business environment.

The second part of the 10-K addresses the organization's stock, providing its latest two years' quarterly prices at the beginning and end of the quarter. You will also see some selected financial data, which is where you will generally find the financial information broken out by product line, geography, division, etc. There is another requirement in this section called the "management's discussion and analysis of financial condition and results of operations." This is an in depth report by the management that seeks to outline the financial changes between the years, and is another outstanding way to gain a good insight as to what is happening in the company's environment.

The third part provides information on the directors and executive officers of the company, including executive compensation and board compensation. There is a specific report that deals with executive compensation that comes with the annual report, and is filed at about the same time as the 10-K. This report, the Schedule 14A, will additionally demonstrate the 5 year return of the stock compared to industry averages such as the DJIA, the S&P 500, as well as a basket of their competitors.

The final section of the 10-K is the consolidated results, exhibits, and the notes to the financial statements. This is where you will find the audited financial statements and notes to the financial statements.

10Q – This is the filing that companies provide outlining the results of operations, and the current balance sheet. Generally these quarterly statements will include year to date numbers, so if you are at the second quarter, this report may also provide the numbers for the six month period. Remember if you are

> **The Issue:** When companies are getting over twenty calls per week from salespeople, you must differentiate yourself immediately to keep them on the phone.
>
> **The Work Involved:** Five minutes of prep time using the tools available and outlined here.
>
> **The Bottom Line:** If you can't quickly and concisely demonstrate to your prospect an understanding of his current situation, you are one of twenty. Those aren't good odds.

using the quarterly financial numbers you need to annualize the P&L statement to provide an accurate analysis, as discussed in our earlier chapters. The balance sheet doesn't need to be annualized because it is a snapshot in time.

Schedule 14A – This is also called the prospectus, and is sent out to all shareholders every year with the annual report. Like the 10-K, it provides a list and background of the board of directors. You can find out who is on the board, their background, and what other boards they serve on. The 14A also shows a comparison of how the company's stock has done compared to a market index like the S&P 500, as well as an index of stocks made up of their competitors. This is done in both a table and a graph. Finally, the report also discusses how much compensation the executive officers earned, broken out by salary, bonus, and stock options. These numbers are provided for the past three years, and are always interesting when compared to the chart described above, of how the stock has performed. Unfortunately you probably won't find much of a correlation between the two.

20F – This is the foreign equivalent of the 10-K that is filed by foreign companies that are traded on US stock exchanges. These reports require the filers to utilize US accounting rules.

In addition to these reports, you will be able to get all types of additional information such as executive compensation plans. I used the SEC filings to help close a deal with an Ingersoll Rand executive after reading about his personal compensation plan, and focusing my sales efforts towards that.

TO: VICE PRESIDENT AND/OR GROUP PRESIDENT

SUBJECT: BONUS CONTRACT FOR 1998

The bonus plan applying to you for 1998 is outlined below:

1. Should your operating group attain worldwide operating income of $_____, you will receive a bonus of   % of your annual salary rate in effect on December 31, 1998.

2. For each $_____ by which your worldwide operating income   exceeds $_____ up to $_____, you will receive __%   of your salary. For each $_____ over $_____ _____, you   will receive _____% of your salary.

3. If you achieve a productivity improvement of ___%, you will receive an additional _% of your salary.

4. If you attain _____% accounts receivable and inventory as a percent of sales, you will receive _% of your salary. For each ___% reduction thereafter, you will receive an additional _% of your salary.

Internet Sites

Some of the sites below offer extensive financial information that can provide, within a couple of clicks, just about everything we've discussed in this book.

www.thinklikeaceo.com - This website will provide support for practitioners of the Wall Street Selling Methodology™, additional information on sales methods, data on a software package built on the technology, and much more. It is also, of course, a good place to buy additional copies of the book.

http://finance.yahoo.com/ – Great content covering everything from reported financials to insider stock trading activity. This information will turn up in the Edgar reports discussed above, but you can get quick insight to them from this site.

www.finance.google.com – A great site in the Google tradition, that also has some information on closely held companies.

www.bigcharts.com – Everyone likes charts. This site will provide just about any chart you would like to see. Remember the Wall Street adage, "The trend is your friend."

www.ADR.com and *www.bony.com* – You can use both of these sites to gather information on foreign companies. Many foreign financial markets also require companies to provide financial information on an electronic basis, so if you know which foreign exchanges the stock is listing on, you can often find that data there, too.

Brokerage houses – I like being able to utilize stock screening data, not just for figuring out which stocks I would like to invest in, but also for quickly comparing financial measurements between companies. Some of these provide the additional benefit of allowing you to read analyst's reports on companies. Of course, after reading this book, you will always look at those very same numbers yourself before you either believe what that analyst is saying, or buy into it.

Barclays Global Investors iShares.com – Getting information on specific industries can be difficult, but by looking at industry stock funds, you will be able to quickly determine who the players are in the industry, and how their performance has been on an aggregate level. Go to www.ishares.com to find out more.

Foreign Stock Exchanges – Many foreign stock exchanges have adapted the electronic requirements that the SEC has pioneered, and as a result, you can often find financial information on companies immediately. I have not found any stock exchange with the readily accessible, easy to use features of our own, the Securities Exchange Commission, at www.sec.gov. For example, the Bolsa do Brasil, also known as BOVESPA, www.bovespa.com.br gives you the ability to download financial information of all companies listed on their exchange. The Portuguese language tapes you will have to find elsewhere.

Standard and Poor's – This debt rating agency offers a great website that allows you to get, among other things, debt ratings for commercial paper. The website address is www.standardandpoors.com.

Banking Industry Sites

Government agencies that have oversight responsibility have also been very good about providing financial information over the web. For the banking industry, you can find financial information on any bank or credit union in the United States, by going to the government sites that regulate them.

www.fdic.gov – This provides information for all banks regulated by the Federal Deposit Insurance Corporation (FDIC.) You can look up their financials on a quarterly and annual basis, and find information broken down by the parent company as well as each of their individual branches.

www.ncua.gov - This site will provide you with the financial information on your credit union. This site is similar to its sister site, fdic.gov, which provides information on the banking sector.

Not for Profit Sites

Creating value does not stop at for profit organizations. What you have learned in this book can be – and should be – applied to organizations in the not for-profit sector. I have served on several Not for Profit boards, and can guarantee you that executives and board members of these types of organizations are putting a major focus on…profit. Without profit – and cash – the charity cannot fulfill its mission.

The IRS provides tax-free status to any charity that it defines as a 501 (c). In addition to the financial statements that you will find on this site, you will also find images of the IRS returns filed by the organizations, and you can easily see which ones are spending money on board members and overhead rather than on their mission. Prior to giving money to any organization, always ask to see a copy of audited financials, or pull them up on one of the sites noted here.

www.guidestar.org

www.grantsmart.org

Interested in that charity that you always hear your local sports celebrity – or his agent – talk about? Try pulling it up on www.guidestar.org. I've seen some good ones, and some that have led me to question why they even bother. If you want to see a superstar who has an outstanding charity, go to Jim Kelley's Hunter's Hope Foundation, Inc. Likewise, some companies have foundations funded by their employees.

> I have also used these websites to advance sales cycles. Many C-Level executives sit on non-profit boards, like the Division President that I was targeting in 2002. I queried his name on guidestar.org and found that he was on the board of a certain charity. I pulled down the IRS 990's and found that the organization had done quite well, and had some interesting strategic initiatives. This served as an excellent icebreaker and allowed me to capture and advance my sales cycle. Throughout the whole meeting with him I recall a certain look of puzzlement in his eyes. He was probably wondering just how I got all that information.

Periodicals

The business press can provide for industry insights, as well as that nugget that will lead you to look up and analyze so that you can draw your own conclusions. Here are some gems that will help provide continued insight to how strategy and value impacts a company's financials.

CFO – Much like the magazine, today's CFO is much less of a "bean counter" and much more of an executive looking beyond the accounting function to bring value to an organization. This magazine does an excellent job of covering issues related to this. There is a cost to subscribe, but the magazine also provides complimentary subscriptions to qualified recipients. Contact them at www.cfo.com.

Chief Executive – As the title suggests, you will find executive specific articles at executive length (read: short) that will provide insight to strategic issues.

The "Big Three" Forbes, Fortune, Business Week – "The Big Three" in business magazines. They are each a little bit different, but any of them will provide good coverage of emerging trends and business news. Once you read about the company, go to www.sec.gov and make your own decisions as to the company's Profit Strategies.

Wall Street Journal – This newspaper provides probably the best business coverage you can find. Daily happenings are reported on as well as in depth articles uncovering everything from investigative reporting to case studies.

Barons – Primarily focused to the stock market, this periodical has been challenged by the emergence of the internet to provide more than just basic financial measures. It has succeeded well and is a good source for industry trends.

"Industry Rags" – All industries have their own industry specific magazines. This is an excellent place to learn about the industry you are selling into.

> I was once on a board retreat in Washington DC when I hit the sec.gov site in preparation of a phone call the next day with one of my sales team's accounts. I saw that the company had made an acquisition play for one of its competitors. They were executing a Buy the Business Strategy that is called The Horizontal Bop. I immediately rearranged my conference call for an on site meeting, and flew cross-country to the West Coast the next day. I was able to align my value proposition with the Profit Strategy of the company, and by the time the acquisition had closed, we had executed a deal for over half a million dollars.

Now that we know where to get the information, the next section will provide a step-by-step method of what you do with it.

Wall Street Selling Implications – The Information Super Highway

Using the information discussed in this chapter will allow you to uncover information on just about any company that you will need. Doing this before you speak to anyone within that company will differentiate you from all the calls senior level executives are inundated with on a daily basis. (Think dinner time around your house.)

You can utilize the other, non-financial information that the 10-K's have in them to greatly assist your sales cycles. I was once going up against several competitors for a pricing optimization software solution. The prospect would not tell me who the specific competitors were, so I pulled up the 10-K's of one of the competitors. Since this report has a section on competition, I uncovered the names of several of their competitors. I then pulled up their 10-K's, getting some additional competitive names. This yielded a group of 5 key competitors in the market, not including us. Three of these competitors were publicly traded companies, whose stock was uniformly down. I pulled the financials from each of these competitors, and then compared their poor performance in a chart.

Since two of the companies in the mix were privately held, I used some assumptions for the industry (we will go over these in a later chapter on analyzing the industry) and then compared this to my company, which was fortunate enough to have been on a good two year run, showing significantly better top line growth. This initial research allowed me to effectively put my competitors in a box, and they were not able to effectively compete in the deal. Throughout the process, we were referred to as the "high growth" vendor, and we ended up getting the deal.

Whatever you do, give other people a chance to review your strategy, unlike CBS President Bob Wood when presented in 1970 with the opportunity to air Monday Night Football. "Pre-empt Doris Day? Are you out of your mind?"

"If you don't pay attention to these five, I'm coming back tomorrow with ten!

Fundamental Football with the *Fast Five*

I WAS ON A PLANT TOUR at a large automotive subassembly plant in Canada. Built only several years before I was there, the plant was light years from some of the decades-old automotive plants I had seen before. Rather than large, dark rooms of like machines clanging out metal parts that would be ferried around by forklifts back and forth throughout the factory, this factory had linked conveyors. Each process fed into the other, and material movement was kept to a minimum. Bright lights reflected off the shine of the floors, and work teams concentrated on implementing Kaizen, or continuous improvement, to squeeze out even more efficiency.

It was a world-class manufacturing plant, and the supervisor taking me on the tour was rightly proud of what he was showing me. He was feeling better than I, because we both knew that in less than an hour, he and I were both going to be involved in a meeting with his executives to discuss J-I-T manufacturing software. He didn't think he needed it, and at this point, I didn't see a lot of opportunity either. Yet I knew that my software had provided value at other similar clients, so I just had to uncover a need. In addition to being proud about his accomplishments, he had experience dealing with sales people, and was not going to give me any of the information that I needed.

"So," he said as he paused, forming a smile on this face. "What do you think so far?"

I whistled and followed it up with a pause too, as much for theatrics as for giving my mind time to race ahead.

"Lots of inventory around here," I stated softly, yet with a degree of confidence that I didn't really feel.

"Excuse me?" replied my tour guide. "We get our raw materials every morning, and by the close of the third shift, our parts are put on the loading dock and the customer takes delivery of them. They are off of our books. Where do you see the excessive inventory?"

I didn't, but what I did need was some ammunition, anything, to get the plant manager listening to me during my presentation that was meant to sell him J-I-T software and services. So I began to point at the factory line, anywhere where there was a part not moving.

"Right there, for instance," I said as I pointed out a small carton of parts waiting to be put on the line. I looked down the line from where we were, at the processes that would consume the inventory I was pointing out.

"And over there - that inventory is just sitting, and when it sits, it's non-value added." He was beginning to get the message.

"How many people work in the company here?" I asked.

After some quick adding in his head he said, "About 500."

We continued on the tour, and I was beginning to sweat. If what I was seeing was their entire operations, I might as well punt. Since my company had already sprung for my plane ticket, I thought I'd probe some more.

"How much inventory did you say you try to keep on the books," I asked.

"Well, it fluctuates, but I believe the last report was under $6 million."

I did some quick math in my head. I looked at the parent company's 10-K report, and had their overall employee productivity numbers, so I multiplied 500 employees by $600,000 per employee, figuring sales of about $300 million. Using a gross profit of about 40 percent gave a cost of goods of about $180 million. Keeping the numbers simple, I assumed 'under $6 million' could mean $5 million in inventory. Since this inventory number went into the $180 million in costs about thirty times, I guessed that inventory days had to be between ten and twelve, for a process that had, according to my guide, less than three hours of work content in it. It didn't look like they had much raw material or finished goods, since their deliveries took care of that, so there had to be more work-in-process than what I was seeing. Even half of the inventory in WIP, five days, would be too much for a product that should take less than one shift to manufacture. I had found the compelling reason.

"OK," I said. "I've seen enough. Let's have the meeting."

The first time I mentioned that there was a lot of opportunity at the plant, my sanity was immediately questioned.

"Lars, you're the controller. Can you get your financial statements and let's see if they show us any opportunity? I've been in a lot of automotive plants, and from my experience I see the opportunity, but let's see what they say."

He went to his office to gather them up, and only then did the plant manager speak up and say that yes, he was being pressured to take working capital out of the operations and that there was some opportunity.

When the controller got back, my estimate was only slightly off. I ended up getting the deal, and that plant is even more "world class" than it was before.

I was able to get that deal because of my familiarity with how the financials reflect business operations. This chapter is going to begin teaching you how to get the information you need, either by looking at a company's numbers, or by asking a few key questions.

For most of your sales efforts, this will be the only analysis that you will need. You now are fluent in the language of business. We will now focus on the metrics that C-Level executives are concerned with. They are concerned with these metrics because in no small part, banks and shareholders, the people providing the financing to that CEO, are focused on it. You should be focused on these too - unless your tastes run to processed meats.

Look at the following covenants written for Morrison Knudson, one of the top commercial contractors in the country when I pulled this report. (I hope these worked for the bankers, because we are going to analyze Morrison Knudson in our chapter called *Profits in the Rear View Mirror*.)

It's common for banks to loan money to companies and require covenants based on ratios. The loan officer figures that monitoring a company's ratios will lower the risk the bank takes on the loan, while the executive figures it is just another way for a risk adverse banker to keep his fingers in the business. If you are going to sell to a CEO, you had better think like he does.

CONSOLIDATED CURRENT RATIO
Maintain a ratio of consolidated current assets to consolidated current liabilities of not less than 1.15 to 1

TANGIBLE NET WORTH
Maintain a consolidated tangible net worth equal to at least the sum of (a) $300 million and (b) 40% of the cumulative consolidated net earnings since 1/1/92.

INTEREST COVERAGE
Maintain coverage of not less than 1.5 to 1 of the sum of consolidated operating income, interest expense and income taxes to interest expense

If a company's working capital is dropping, you can be assured that your prospect's executives are focused like a laser beam on changing that trend.

The Sharpness of the Pencil

As we do our analysis, we are not going to put too much emphasis on the number of decimal places our ratios go to. We'll keep many of the metrics to whole numbers, and round a few to the tenth. The reason that we will do this is twofold. First of all, to get the absolute most accurate number in many of the formulas, one should use averages rather than the absolute numbers from the same year's financial return. For example, if your metric includes inventory as one of the numbers, one should ideally take several inventory readings, average them, and then use this number. One could add up the quarterly inventory numbers, and divide by four, or even use the beginning and ending inventory numbers and divide by two.

The Issue: Information overload when all you are trying to do is to develop a sales strategy.

The Work Involved: Memorize the formula's, or take the handy travel card that comes as part of the dust cover with you.

The Bottom Line: The Fast Five metrics will provide you with 95 percent of all the information you will need to understand any business.

Another reason that a quicker analysis will work just as well is that all financial statements can be impacted by individual decisions, either by executives or in the course of doing business. For example, a large order that comes in from a customer on December 31st and is shipped on January 2nd will be in the January sales, not the December sales. A large manufacturing order that takes several times as long as the other orders can skew the inventory metrics that we'll be looking at. We will focus on analyzing numerous metrics and looking at both the absolute numbers as well as trends, but we won't want to focus on any single metric for too much of our analysis.

> Early in their medical school careers, medical students learn a simple but important concept: "When you hear hooves, think horses, not zebras."

Another by-product of keeping this analysis at a higher level is that it will allow us to do it fast. I've found that developing the skill to analyze a company and its strategy quickly is imperative as you start to use this new set of tools in your daily business.

Following along with these ideas of developing your speed of analysis, and utilizing the sharpness of the pencil theory stated above, we are going to be utilizing single points of analysis for our balance sheet formulas. For example, the formula for inventory turns is COGS (Cost of Goods Sold) divided by inventory. The most accurate way to find the answer for inventory turns is to add the inventory values from the last four quarters, divide by four, and use this as your inventory number. You would then divide this number into COGS. If you are looking at two annual reports, you would add the ending inventory balance on both of them, and then divide this number by two for our average inventory. When looking at balance sheets, in most of the instances your numbers will not be that far off if you use the ending inventory number. If you see a great difference in the values of inventory from one year to the next, be sure to take an average. Remember that our main driving force will be speed with "good enough" numbers to develop our understanding of your target's Profit Strategies.

How to Look at the Metrics

When we look at the following metrics, we are going to look at two basics. First of all, we are going to look at the trend in the individual company's ratios. One year of metrics simply won't provide the information that the trend of several years will. Secondly, we will compare our target company's trends with those of their competitors. Trends going in opposite directions, or with significant results, will provide excellent information. While we will learn more about how to analyze an industry in a later chapter, the Fast Five ratios that we are going to learn below can be done on the target company, as well as their competitors.

The Fundamentals

The basic analysis that we will do is an extension of the *Fast Five* metrics that we outlined in the initial chapters of this book. We will look at each of the three financial statements, as well as develop a *Fast Five* for inter-statement analysis.

Fast Five Balance Sheet Metrics

---

1. *Asset structure* – The asset structure tells us what assets the business needs – or is using – to operate. This will give us some insights as to how the company operates, and how they finance their operations. A high percentage of fixed assets means the business has significantly larger fixed costs, and will be more of a volume sensitive business. A higher fixed asset percent will generally require more debt, and will probably have greater interest expense.

We will express the fixed asset percent as a whole number, for example, 35 percent. The formula we will use for fixed asset percent is shown below.

Fixed asset % = (Total fixed assets / total assets) * 100

- Importance - This provides us with a quick look at what type of business the company is in. A higher fixed asset % will generally require more debt. This means more of a company's cash sucked up by interest payments.

- Movement up means – The company is either losing working capital, or investing in assets to drive business. Keep an eye out for additional interest expense if the company uses LT debt to finance its assets.

- Movement down means – The company may be divesting itself from asset intensive businesses, or is increasing its current assets by putting its retained earnings in cash.

- Why this is important to a C-Level executive – Fixed assets mean overhead expenses. They get depreciated, they require costs for upkeep, and they had better drive revenue.

2. *Net working capital* – Working capital is the "grease that keeps the wheels of the organization turning." Almost universally, companies that are in trouble will "bleed" working capital. While many finance texts simply look at current assets less current liabilities as a measurement of working capital, we will subtract cash out of this equation. Cash is a financial decision, and by subtracting it from the current assets, it gives us a better idea of how the operations are financing themselves. This will give you a truer picture of a company's working capital, particularly if that company has a financial strategy of holding a lot of cash.

For example, looking at the Novellus Systems, Inc. financial reports for 2004, the traditional measurement of net working capital, current assets less current liabilities, shows us that working capital reduced by over 300 million, falling to $1.045 billion versus $1.350 billion in 2003. Falling working capital is a sign of a company in trouble, and this number could be cause for concern. However, taking cash out of the picture changes the calculus. (Okay, I know it really *isn't* calculus, that's just an expression.) Now, net working capital actually increases from approximately $345 million to just under $458 million.

Novellus Systems	2004	2003
Current assets	$1,369	$1,571
Current liabilities	$324	$221
Traditional working capital measurement	$1,045	$1,350
Cash	$587	$1,005
Net working capital	$458	$345

Net working capital is an absolute number, for example, $12,500.

Net working capital = (Current assets − cash) − current liabilities

---

•   Importance - Net working capital is the grease that keeps the wheels of business going.

- Movement up means – The company is generating more working capital than it is consuming.

- Movement down means – Movement down will always be a "red flag" that we will investigate.

- Why this is important to a C-Level executive – The CEO either has some bank covenants covering his working capital, or Wall Street Analysts are looking at it. Either way, if it's dropping, someone is going to be asking him questions about it.

Remember that utilizing the most accurate measure of this would have you adding current assets from the beginning and ending periods, and dividing by two and using this number as your current asset base number.

3. *LT debt* – This metric will show us how the company is utilizing long-term debt to finance its objectives, and give us an idea about the risk profile of its CEO. Remember that an industry that requires heavy investment in fixed assets to generate sales (we looked at the fixed asset % ratio above) will likely have a greater need for LT debt. However, the old adage about guns and butter holds true also. Companies may incur long-term debt for acquisitions, to pay for pension plans, or any number of reasons. So you can't always equate long-term debt to fixed assets.

The formula for change in long-term debt is shown below, and will be shown as an absolute number, such as $250 million.

Change in LT Debt = LT debt year 2 – LT debt in year 1

- Importance – This gives an indication of the CEO's risk profile.

- Movement up means – The company is raising more cash, so we want to make sure we understand how they are investing that cash. Are they acquiring businesses, investing in fixed assets, or borrowing to cover working capital requirements?

- Movement down means – The company is paying off long-term debt to increase its future flexibility. We want to find out what is driving this.

- Why this is important to a C-Level executive – Taking on debt better result in better financial performance. The less LT debt that a company holds, the more future flexibility it will have.

4. *Goodwill and intangible assets* – This account will immediately shed some light on what growth strategies the company is following. If the account does not show much growth year over, and the company is growing sales, then we can draw some conclusions that the internal growth strategies are very effective, and/or the company is doing an outstanding job finding acquisition targets. In any event, if the goodwill account is small, we know that there is not too much of a chance of the company shocking us with large losses due to write-offs of these overpaid acquisitions.

Change in Goodwill = Change in goodwill & intangible asset year 2 – goodwill and intangible assets year 1

- Importance – This will provide a quick look at how the company is using acquisition to drive growth.

- Movement up means – The company is growing through acquisition, and probably overpaying.

- Movement down means – The company may have written off the goodwill, taking this out of the company's book value. Little goodwill means the company either wrote it off, or is a well run business that is growing through organic growth.

- Why this is important to a C-Level executive – Most CEO's don't spend too much time worrying about goodwill, unless they have to write it off and impact their earnings.

5. *Leverage Factor* - The leverage factor is another way to check financial risk. Just like your mortgage, this metric shows how much of the company the shareholders own versus the creditors. The higher the leverage factor, the higher the risk that the company is undertaking, but the higher the Return on Equity (ROE) will be also. Leverage factor is one of the formulas for ROE. Leverage factor will be expressed as a number to one decimal level, such as 5.6.

Leverage factor = Total assets / Total equity

- Importance – This helps you answer the question about who is taking on the risk in the business, the owners or the creditors. Remember, the higher the risk, the higher the reward.

- Movement up means – The company is taking on more debt, or its equity is not keeping up with its growth in assets.

- Movement down means – The company is becoming more conservative, and taking on less risk.

- Why this is important to a C-Level executive – Banks and analysts are watching this, and their influence will make sure the CEO keeps an eye on this metric.

Fast Five P&L Metrics

1. *The trend in top line growth* –We obviously want to see this trending up. We can use the percentage growth in the top line to judge how the rest of the profitability accounts keep up. For instance, if revenue increases 10 percent and gross profit dollars increase less than 10 percent, this tells us that the company is increasing sales by lowering prices. What you want to look at here is the rate of growth of the company versus its main competitors. If it is growing faster than the market as a whole, it is capturing market share, which is good. Later in the book, we will look at how those additional sales were won. We will express revenue growth as a number rounded to the tenth, ex 16.8 percent.

> **Revenue Growth Rate = ((Year 2 revenue / year 1 revenue) -1) * 100**

- Importance – This gives a view as to how successful the organization is at generating sales, the lifeblood of every business.

- Movement up means – The company is booking business. Be sure to check the goodwill account to see if they are buying it.

- Movement down means – It is never good when sales go down. Compare this drop to the industry to get an idea of how bad this can be.

- Why this is important to a C-Level executive – Any salesperson reading this book knows that most all CEO's watch the sales numbers closely. Some even think that they *are* salespeople (at least during your account reviews.) The fact of the matter is, many Wall Street analysts look for growth on the "top line" as much as they do on the bottom line.

Always make note of revenue per employee, gross margin, and asset TO. If you know these, you can then quickly compare your prospect's efficiency to their competitors, and draw conclusions as to industry metrics. You can use this knowledge with private companies, or as a line of questioning on a sales call.

2. *The trend in gross profit margin* – Another way to quickly see how the company is performing relative to its internal productivity and the market is to look at the gross profit dollars as a percentage of revenue, or gross margin. For example, if this increases from one year to the next, the company is becoming more productive, and given that overhead does not change, you should see this difference in gross profit drop to the bottom line.

This provides the quickest look at what is happening to the company in the market. Changes in gross margin are caused by only two things: a change in productivity within the company or a change in selling price. (There could be an impact to the sales mix, but this does get back to sales price increases. If a company sells product A that sells for more than Product B, this is still an increase in sales price.) We will express gross margin as a number rounded to the tenth, ex. 56.8%.

Gross Margin = (Gross profit / revenue) * 100

If you don't have the gross profit number broken out, you can back into this by the following formula:

Gross Margin = 1-((cogs/revenue)*100)

- Importance – This will give us information on both the market and the internal productivity of the organization.

- Movement up means – The market is growing, or the company is getting more productive.

- Movement down means – The market is slowing down, the company is executing a penetration strategy to get the business, or the company is becoming more inefficient in its production.

- Why this is important to a C-Level executive – This gives the CEO – just like it does you, now – a quick look at the competitiveness of the market.

3. *The trend in operating profit or EBIT* – Ideally, this trend should at least match the percentage increase in top line growth. You can also look at the operating profit margin to get a quick view of how the company is performing. For example, if the gross margin is shrinking, but EBIT margin is the same, you can immediately see that the company is addressing the increase in costs via overhead. While the gross margin number tells us market conditions and the direct labor productivity of the company, the operating margin tells us the general overhead productivity of the company. Organizations require different amounts of overhead to support the operations and sales functions. Companies that can compete effectively while minimizing this are more profitable. When using operating margin to analyze the business, we have to compare its increase or decrease to the gross margin. A company that shows increasing operating margins might be seeing that purely based on the strong gross profits achieved. Generally speaking, increasing operating margin is good, decreasing operating margin is bad. We will express operating margin as a number rounded to the tenth, ex 45.7%.

Operating Margin = (Operating profit / revenue) * 100

- Importance – This is the best "bottom line" number to summarize the operations of the company.

- Movement up means – This is good. If the movement is equal to gross margin, the company is efficient in its management in addition to its production.

- Movement down means – This is bad. Compare this to the gross margin to see if overhead is the culprit.

- Why this is important to a C-Level executive – Anyone who wants a quick look at how the business is operating will look at operating margin, and the change in operating margin.

4. *Changes in interest expense* – Increasing interest expense puts an additional earnings debt on the company. Companies that incur debt to acquire businesses or invest in businesses need to make sure that these investments return more than the company's cost of capital. While a growing economy may make interest payments seem minor, during recessions, or when the company's top line revenue falls, higher interest expense can strangle a company's prospects. Dividing operating profit, or EBIT, by interest expense gives us a ratio called times interest earned, and tells us how many times earnings can fall before the company will have trouble covering interest expenses without liquidating assets.

We are going to look at the absolute amount that companies pay in interest expense. This one is easy to understand. This number increasing is worse than the number decreasing. However, we also need to look at the relationship between interest and the amount of operating profit that the company earns. For example, if a company takes on significant debt to acquire another company, both interest expense as well as net profits may increase. This number is shown in absolute dollars, such as $ 450,000.

Change in Interest expense = Interest expense year two – interest expense year one

---

- Importance – This gives us an idea of how much debt financing is impacting the profits of the company.

- Movement up means - If this goes up, the company is taking on more debt. The objective is to find out why they are raising the money.

- Movement down means – The company is using less debt, and they can use this additional cash to grow the business.

- Why this is important to a C-Level executive – Interest requires cash. Most CEO's look at this number to see how it impacts their ability to spend their cash, on acquisitions, investments, or dividends.

Times Interest Earned

This will demonstrate how much interest expense the company is paying to cover its debt, as well as how many times profit can fall before it will begin to put the interest obligations at risk. For example, if the times interest earned number is 5X, then the company's earnings can fall five times before they can't make the debt payments. This ratio is even more important in industries that have higher earnings risk, such as the construction industry. This is expressed in a number taken to the tenths, such as 3.2.

> **Times Interest Earned = Operating profit / interest expense**

- Importance – This gives us a quick look at how much the net income of a company can drop before they can't make their debt obligations.

- Movement up means – This is good. The higher this number is, the more the company's profits can drop without having its debt shut it down.

- Movement down means – This is bad. Find out if it is a question of earnings or interest expense increasing.

- Why this is important to a C-Level executive – Anyone who is providing financing to the company is looking at this. Therefore, the CEO is too.

5. *Change in net profit margin-* Like the discussion above, net margin needs to be analyzed within the confines of the entire business. For example, if operating margins – EBIT stay the same year over year, but net profit margin increases, something happened inbetween that needs to be analyzed. Perhaps the company sold off a division, etc.

We will express net profit margin as a number rounded to one decimal place Ex. 35.6%.

> **Net profit margin = (Net profit / total revenue) * 100**

- Importance – This is the "bottom line" of the company, the percent of the sales dollar that the company gets to keep. We want to compare this to operating profit margin, (EBIT margin) to see how non-operating factors influenced the company.

- Movement up means – The company is more profitable.

- Movement down means – The company is less profitable.

- Why this is important to a C-Level executive – Earnings, earnings, earnings. While CEO's are probably more concerned with actual net profit, and how that has changed over the same quarter the year before, looking at the margin will provide you with that information, and more.

Fast Five Cash Flow

1. *Operating cash flow* - This immediately tells us how business operations can finance the everyday functioning of the business. If this is decreasing, or negative, the company will have to raise funds by cutting back on investment in the business, or increasing financing. An increasing trend in operating cash flow is better than a decreasing one. If the operating cash flow is decreasing, that will force the company to either not invest as much or raise money – debt or equity – to pay for its investments.

   This gives an absolute answer as to how the operations of the organizations are generating cash. The higher this number the better the cash situation of the company. Change in operating cash flow is an absolute number, such as $125 million.

Change in operating cash flow = Current year operating cash flow – prior year operating cash flow.

- Importance – This metric shows us how much gross cash the business is generating.

- Movement up means – Movement up means that the business is generating more cash.

- Movement down means – We will treat movement down as a red flag and investigate why operating cash flow dropped.

- Why this is important to a C-Level executive – Most of the sharper analysts and bankers will be focused on this number. Remember that growth takes cash, and the only way to get it is to borrow it from a bank, sell stock to get it, or generate it from operations.

2. *Free Cash Flow* - This metric gives us an idea of how much cash the company is generating. It is termed "free" because some of the company's cash must be used for upkeep of fixed assets. Free cash flow should move in concert with operating cash flow, and differences in either are a cause for investigation. We will only concern ourselves with investments in capital expenditures rather than other investments that a company can make that may include business acquisitions, investments in securities, etc.

> **Free cash flow = Operating cash flow - Capital Expenditures**

- Importance – This metric is similar to operating cash flow, but shows us how much cash the company actually has to invest in dividends and business growth and acquisition.

- Movement up means – This is good, although we want to make sure that the organization is not driving this cash flow by reducing its investment in its fixed assets.

- Movement down means – We will treat movement down as a red flag and investigate why operating cash flow dropped.

- Why this is important to a C-Level executive – This is the cash left over from what operations generated. Watch out for the CEO's who may manipulate this by under-investing in fixed assets if that means more cash to spend on acquisitions.

3. *Sales and acquisitions of businesses* - Under the investment cash flow, we want to see how much the company is spending on new businesses. If they spent $200 for $100 of net assets, they will have to put $100 on the balance sheet as goodwill. (The notes to the financial statements will outline the acquired net assets and amount of goodwill to be carried.) Likewise, we want to see how much cash the company is raising by selling off assets. We will refer to a strategy of selling assets as the Kill the Dogs Strategy. This, and more, will be discussed in the *Profit Strategies* chapter.

> **Sales & acquisitions of business = (Sales of business- acquisition of business) year two – (Sales of business- acquisition of business) year one**

- Importance – This metric will show us how the company is managing its portfolio of assets.

- Movement up means – The company is divesting more businesses than it is acquiring. We want to investigate why they are raising this cash, and if possible find out at what discount (loss) the company is selling these assets.

- Movement down means - Movement down means that the company is acquiring more businesses than they are selling.

- Why this is important to a C-Level executive – Okay, chances are he isn't looking at this anymore than your teenager is looking at his bank account. But you need to look at it to see how much cash the company is investing in the Buy the Business Profit Strategy.

4. *Financing debt capital* - If companies are not raising enough cash through the operating cash flow to cover their investments, they will have to go to financing. We want to see if they are raising this capital through debt or equity. If they increase debt capital, they will increase the interest expense on the P&L and lower net after tax earnings.

> **Debt capital financing = (debt raised – debt retired) year two - (debt raised – debt retired) year one**

- Importance – This metric will show us how much capital the company is raising from debt.

- Movement up means – Anytime a company raises debt capital we want to investigate why they are doing this, and make sure they are utilizing this as investment.

- Movement down means – We will prefer to see companies raising less debt capital year over year.

- Why this is important to a C-Level executive – CEO's are primarily interested in the available interest that they will have to spend. This gives them flexibility. This metric cuts down on that flexibility.

5. *Financing equity capital* – Another way that companies can raise cash flow is to go to the capital markets. If they are raising capital this way, they will not pay the additional interest expense that they would through debt capital, but they will spread their net income across more shares of stock, thereby lowering their EPS.

Equity capital financing = (equity raised – equity retired) year two - (equity raised – equity retired) year one

---

- Importance – This shows us how eager company management is to use its stock as currency.

- Movement up means – The company is selling stock to raise capital. We want to make sure that they are investing this cash prudently. We also want to investigate the impact to current shareholders as their shares are diluted.

- Movement down means – If this metric moves down, this demonstrates that the company is raising cash in another manner.

- Why this is important to a C-Level executive – The currency that CEO's use is their stock. This metric tells you how much they are using. The main concern CEO's have with this metric is how this financing will dilute Earnings Per Share, or (EPS.)

Fast Five Key Metrics

Finally, while we have the aforementioned returns out we are going to look at a series of metrics that utilize both the balance sheet and the P&L statement to provide some information to us. The *Fast Five* Key Metric will utilize the following metrics.

1. *Asset TO* – This tells us how effective the company is in utilizing its assets to generate sales revenue. We want to look at the trend that the company has in this regard, as well as how its competitors are doing generating sales with their assets. This is a key number in the formula to generate Return On Net Assets, or RONA. This is expressed as a number that we will carry to two decimal places, ex 1.33.

Asset TO = Revenue / total assets

- Importance – This is an important productivity measure for us. A higher asset turnover demonstrates that the company is efficiently using its assets.

- Movement up means – Movement up demonstrates that the company is becoming more efficient.

- Movement down means – Movement down means the company is becoming less efficient.

- Why this is important to a C-Level executive – Every asset a company owns should drive sales. CEO's are interested in sales, so they want to see how many sales their assets are generating.

2. *Return On Net Assets (RONA)* - This is the return generated by the total assets of the organization. Similar to asset turnover (which in fact is part of the formula for RONA) this will give us an idea of how effective management is in utilizing their asset base. This shows how effective the organization is utilizing its assets by quantifying the total return of these assets. This number is expressed as a percentage that we will carry to one decimal level, such as 12.5%

RONA = Asset TO * Net profit margin

Note that you can also get this number by dividing net profit by total assets, but this does not give you nearly all the information on how a company is conducting itself strategically as the formula above. For example, take two companies with the same RONA, of 15 percent. By computing RONA by multiplying the asset turnover by the profit margin, we can see that Company A has much higher profit margins, but Company B has a much better utilization of its assets, utilizing two different strategies to attain the same RONA.

Company A		Company B	
RONA = 15%		RONA = 15%	
Asset TO =	1.37	Asset TO =	2.5
Net Profit Margin =	11%	Net Profit Margin =	6%
RONA	1.37 X 11 = 15%	RONA	2.5 X 6% = 15%

- Importance – This metric will allow us to compare the net return that the assets of the organization are generating. The higher return the assets can generate, the more efficient the company is. This is one of the key measures for financial institutions like banks, credit unions, etc.
- Movement up means – RONA increasing is good. We will note if the increase is due to increases in asset efficiency or profitability.
- Movement down means – Movement down in RONA will be investigated. We want to investigate which of the factors is driving the downward trend.
- Why this is important to a C-Level executive – Take those sales that each asset is generating and multiply it by the profit that each dollar makes, and you have RONA. Many CEO's use this as a shortcut to how well they are managing their company.

3. *Return On Equity (ROE)* - This is the return generated by the total equity of the organization. Several of the formulas describing effective usage of assets are included in this ROE number. This number demonstrates how effective the organization is in utilizing its equity capital. This number is expressed as a percentage that we will carry to one decimal place, such as 25.8%.

$$\text{ROE} = \text{RONA} * \text{Leverage Factor}$$

This metric can also be arrived by dividing net profit by equity, but similar to the argument above, does not allow us to make the same inferences that this manner of computing this number does. Therefore, we will use this formula to look at the ROE metric.

- Importance – This demonstrates the returns the organization's equity is driving. Note that this is NOT return to the company's shareholders, which is gauged by stock price.
- Movement up means – Movement up is positive. We want to look at the factors driving this to see the underlying causes.
- Movement down means – Movement down is a red flag and will be investigated. We want to look at the underlying factors that make up ROE for a better understanding.

- Why this is important to a C-Level executive – The CEO's bosses, his board of directors and shareholders, often times look at this metric as a shortcut as to how well their company – and their stock in that company – is doing.

4. *Cash2Cash Cycle* - The Cash2Cash Cycle will tell us how long a company takes to turn its goods or services into cash.

The best way to begin to understand the Cash2Cash Cycle is to think about how a company does business. First of all, they purchase parts, material, and maybe some subassemblies from their suppliers. This material, which we call raw material inventory, arrives and then sits in a warehouse for some amount of time until the company schedules it to start on the manufacturing floor. Once the manufacturing process starts, the raw material becomes work in process (WIP) and takes some time on the factory floor until the parts become the final product. When the product is finished, it is moved to a warehouse and ready for shipping to customers. At this point it is called finished goods inventory, or FGI. Once a customer purchases the product, it is shipped out to the customer along with an invoice. The customer receives the invoice and puts the payment record into their accounting system to pay the company, and once a check is cut the manufacturer receives it and puts it in the bank. Prior to this point, it is his money that is financing all of the process, except for the time that his company takes to pay the supplier. We can summarize this by looking at each individual component of the process as shown in Figure 7-1. Note that we will look at the raw, WIP and FGI inventories together as the time it takes the company to turn its parts into product.

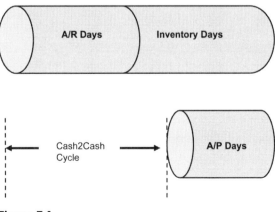

Figure 7.1

To bring our understanding to a defined metric that will tell us how the company has been doing in collecting its cash, we will look at both the balance sheet and the income statement, and turn the key metric into time. We'll look at the time it takes to turn the parts into products - emphasizing the manufacturing efficiencies - sell the product and then collect the cash from sales. We'll subtract from this the time the company is aging its suppliers, and the difference is the time that the company must finance its operations.

Note that the formulas below state "Days in Period." This allows you to do these calculations with statements that are not annual. When dealing with quarterly statements, you can either annualize the P&L statement – as stated previously, there's no need to annualize the balance sheet because it is a snapshot in time – or use the number of days in the period.

Cash2Cash Cycle = DSO + Inventory DSO's – A/P Days

- Days Sales Outstanding (DSO's) = (A/R / Sales) * Days in Period

- Inventory DSO's = (Inventory/COGS) * Days in Period

- A/P Days = (Accounts Payable / COGS) * Days in Period

- Meaning – This will tell you how many days it takes the company to turn its operations into cash. Remember that Cash is King.

- Movement up means – This is bad, because it indicates that the company is taking longer to generate cash.

- Movement down means – This is good. The shorter the Cash2Cash cycle, the faster the company is earning cash.

- Why this is important to a C-Level executive – Keeping in mind the irony we spoke about in the last chapter, I call this the "Meat Loaf Maxim." (Sharing the irony that the singer, not the dish, is actually vegetarian.) While CEO's understand the concepts behind cash flow, they don't understand the specifics behind the Cash2Cash Cycle. This makes this metric one of the most valuable you can use.

Once you get the Cash2Cash cycle, you can quantify this amount by dividing COGS by the number of days in the period, and then multiplying this number by the Cash2Cash Cycle. For example, let's say a company has $365 million in

COGS for a year. That equates to $1 million per day ($365 million / 365 days in the period.) For each day the company can reduce its Cash2Cash cycle, the company can save $1 million of financing.

5. *Revenue per Employee* - A company's revenue per employee is an excellent means to uncover its core productivity. The higher the sales per employee, the more productive – in general – the company is. It is important to note that sales per employee is relative based on industry, so comparing Microsoft's revenue per employee of $647,000 to Proctor & Gamble's $467,000 says much more about their respective industries than it does about the individual companies. Looking at P&G's efficiency as compared to Colgate ($294,000), Gillette ($365,000 based on December 31st numbers, when they were still independent) and Clorox ($509,000) provides a much greater view of how efficient they are. Comparing similar companies, as well as a trend analysis for the individual company over time, will yield some important insights.

> **Revenue per employee = Total revenue / total employees**

- Importance – This is an excellent productivity metric. Different industries have different measures, so you have to check the company's metric against others in the industry.

- Movement up means – The company is becoming more productive, overall.

- Movement down means – The company is becoming less productive.

- Why this is important to a C-Level executive – This metric is the executive equivalent of "mine is bigger." My productivity, that is. If theirs doesn't measure up, look for an implementation of The Right Sizing Strategy, something we will discuss in the *Profit Strategies* chapter.

In the next chapter we will teach you how to read and understand complex, confusing financial statements, and then we will introduce some methods for you to find something to hang your value proposition on.

Wall Street Selling Implications – The Fast Five

The tools laid out in this chapter will provide you with the analysis you will need to cover 95 percent of the cases you find yourself in front of. These are the financial metrics that you should know like the back of your hand. The attached "Cheat Sheet" outlines these metrics, and is made for you to carry with you so that you will always have the ability to utilize this analysis.

Remember that with these Fast Five Metrics you will be focusing on what your C-Level prospect worries about every single day. Frame your discussions around your understanding of these, and you become a "trusted advisor" rather than just a sales person.

I once had a sales cycle that was stopped due to a change in organization at the Division President level. After six months of working the phones and my internal sponsors (yeah, sales sure is glamorous) I finally arranged a meeting with the executive. The morning prior to the meeting I hit the company website where they provided a more thorough financial breakdown of their divisions than what they published in their 10-K. Five minutes of analysis allowed me to carry on a conversation with him revolving around his specific challenges.

Rather than a line of questioning that every other sales person he met with probably used, I immediately put myself on his level. Rather than ask, "How has your division's quarter gone with respect to last years?" I was able to take a more focused view, establishing immediate credibility.

"It looks like your penetration strategy has yielded solid results. How are you dealing with the challenges of your top line increasing 36 percent year over, while gross margins tighten?"

The meeting went well and I used the credibility with him to put my deal back on track.

As you do the *Fast Five* Analysis on your target company, the information you gather will give you an early indication of how you will want to align your value proposition. Doing the same analysis on their competitors will open up even more opportunities for you to focus your message. The upcoming chapters will allow you to focus your message like a laser beam.

"Why didn't he just say it was going to rain?"

Seeing Through the Fog

THERE ARE TOO MANY THINGS in this world that are tough for the Average Joe to understand. What's the difference between a Triple Lutz and a Triple Sal Chow anyway? Or - how about trying to explain the infield fly rule from baseball? This chapter will help you to grow your understanding of just about anything that you will see when you look at a company's "numbers." While we will show many different examples, we'll always bring them back to what we have learned in the first part of the book. In fact, when you are confused you can just lump the account into the groupings that we have outlined and look for the definition in the notes. Chances are, it won't significantly impact your analysis. As Warren Buffett said at the 2003 Berkshire Hathaway Annual Meeting, "If I can't understand it, the management probably doesn't want me to understand it. And if management doesn't want me to understand it, there is probably something wrong going on."

While you will probably not have 100% understanding of each and every line item in an annual report, let's not lose sight of the goal: to uncover corporate strategy and impacts of strategic directives in order to integrate your value proposition with the CEO's Profit Strategies.

Pro Forma versus GAAP

You will invariably see many returns outlined as pro forma financial returns. Pro forma returns simply mean financial returns that are estimated or forecasted. GAAP stands for Generally Accepted Accounting Standards. These standards may be mandated by law. Since we are not taking a CPA exam in this work, the key point to keep in mind is that the numbers you want to focus on are the GAAP numbers rather than the pro forma numbers.

Advanced Definitions

While we won't concern ourselves with too many of the advanced accounts that you will find in financial returns, I do want to address the different looks that you might see as you go through your analysis.

Bonds & Commercial Paper

Bonds and commercial paper refer to unsecured debt obligations that a company has issued – in effect, a "corporate IOU." Bonds are debt instruments generally issued by companies, municipalities, and governments. For our view, they will be classified as LT debt on the part of the company that issues them. Commercial paper is generally short term, and bonds are generally long term instruments.

Deferred Taxes

In fact, most of the time these are created due to differences in operating financial statements and tax policies. For many companies, these may not ever come due.

Goodwill

We want to keep an eye on the goodwill account in the balance sheets that we analyze, because it can be a liability to both earnings and book value. It will also give us an idea as to how aggressive the growth strategies that a company is employing are. A company executing an aggressive buy the business strategy – which we will discuss in the Profit Strategies section of the book – will be less likely to negotiate good deals for its acquisitions. So the goodwill account can tell us how well the company is negotiating its acquisitions, because anything above book value falls into this account. A closer look at the specifics of how Blue Coat acquired Cerberian in 2005 for $19,325 shows why they had to account for over $17 million in goodwill. (The numbers below are shown in thousands.)

> Goodwill is an asset account that is in effect an "ESP" account, ESP meaning, "error some place."

Prior to 2003 (and still in effect in many companies traded on foreign exchanges) this amount of goodwill was amortized over some time frame. If Blue Coat was capitalizing this goodwill over twenty years, they would write off $872,500 per year. This write-off reduces income – and therefore taxes – but since it was a non-cash charge, we would put it back in the cash flow statement. Every year that the company wrote off the $872,500 they would decrease the goodwill account by this amount.

Fair value of Blue Coat common stock given up	$17,357
Direct transaction costs	$437
Fair value of assumed Cerberian options	$497
Promissory notes from Cerberian to Blue Coat	$1,034
Total purchase price	$19,325
Allocation of purchase price:	
Cash and cash equivalents	$2
Accounts receivable	$588
Other current assets	$66
Fixed assets	$184
Other assets	$21
Liabilities assumed	$(2,033)
Deferred stock compensation	$17
Identifiable intangible assets	$3,030
Goodwill	$17,450
Total purchase price	**$19,325**

In the US, companies are not required to amortize goodwill on a yearly basis, but rather they now look at their goodwill yearly and test for "impairment." If there is no impairment, then the goodwill stays on the balance sheet, and everyone is happy. If some amount of goodwill is judged impaired by the company's auditors, the company will write this amount off all at once. This does not make the shareholders happy.

As an example, take a look at Time Warner's financial returns that they filed in 2002.[1]

From this return, things look terrible as net profit is a negative $98 billion! However, when you look EBIT, or operating profit, you see that although 2002 was certainly a more difficult year something other than operations caused this huge loss.

---

1 These numbers are taken from Time Warner's 2002 10-K filings. They have since restated these numbers, so although the actual numbers shown here are not, now, entirely accurate, this example of how goodwill write offs affect the financial returns is still accurate.

Time Warner		
year ended 12/312	2002	2001
Sales	$40,961	$37,166
COGS	$24,315	$20,533
Gross Profit	$16,646	$16,633
O/H	$9,916	$9,079
EBIT	$6,730	$7,554
Interest Expense	$1,738	$1,353
Misc. +/-	$ (103,550)	$(10,996)
Pre Tax Net Profit	$(98,558)	$(4,795)
Taxes(benefit)	$140	$139
Net Profit	$(98,698)	$(4,934)

Time Warner as of 12/31	2002	2001
Assets		
Total Current Assets	$11,155	$10,251
Goodwill	$36,986	$127,420
Total Fixed Assets	$104,295	$198,253
TOTAL ASSETS	$115,450	$208,504
Liabilities		
Total Current Liabilities	$13,359	$12,976
Total LT Liabilities	$49,274	$43,501
TOTAL LIABILITIES	$62,633	$56,477
Equity		
Stock	$154,751	$155,265
Retained Earnings	$(101,934)	$(3,238)
TOTAL EQUITY	$52,817	$152,027

The loss in goodwill devastated the book value, or shareholders' equity as is shown in the Time Warner balance sheet. The good news shows up in the cash flow statement, where all that goodwill and intangible asset write off gets added back in. The net operating cash flow actually increased from 2001 to 2002!

Time Warner year ended 12/31		
Operating Cash Flow		
Net Loss	$(98,696)	
Accounting change	$54,235	
Impairment of goodwill	$45,538	
TOTAL OPERATING CASH FLOW	$7,032	$5,281
Investing Cash Flow		
TOTAL INVESTING CASH FLOW	$(10,460)	$(5,257)
Financing Cash Flow		
TOTAL FINANCING CASH FLOW	$4,439	$(1,915)

Intangible Assets

While not technically goodwill, another account that acts in a similar manner is the one called intangible assets. We will look at these intangible assets as the same as goodwill, because like goodwill, they can suddenly be written off, destroying book value of the company.

For example, Clear Channel took a $4.9 billion dollar charge in its 2004 Q4 by writing off the value of its FCC licenses and outdoor permits that were carried on its books in excess of fair value. Here is how the Clear Channel financial returns looked both before and after this goodwill charge.

A big write-off drops net after tax profit to negative $4 billion.

Clear Channel year ended 12/312		
	2004	2003
Sales	$9,418	$8,930
COGS	$6,850	$6,488
Gross Profit	$2,568	$2,442
O/H	$888	$845
EBIT	$1,680	$1,597
Interest Expense	$367	$388
Misc. +/-	$(5,016)	$424
Pre Tax Net Profit	$(3,703)	$ 1,633
Taxes(benefit)	$334	$246
Net Profit	$(4,037)	$1,387

This write off knocks about a third off of book value, or equity of the company.

Clear Channel		
as of 12/31	**2004**	**2003**
Assets		
Total Current Assets	$2,269	$2,185
Intangible assets	$5,163	$12,938
Goodwill	$7,220	$7,306
Total Fixed Assets	$17,658	$26,167
TOTAL ASSETS	**$19,927**	**$28,352**
Liabilities		
Total Current Liabilities	$ 2,184	$ 1,892
Total LT Liabilities	$ 8,255	$ 10,907
TOTAL LIABILITIES	**$10,439**	**$12,799**
Equity		
Stock	$29,421	$31,183
Retained Earnings	$(19,933)	$(15,630)
TOTAL EQUITY	**$9,488**	**$15,553**

Added back into cash flow, you can see that the effect is minimal on the actual operations of the company. This is a good example, because if you look at the goodwill section of the balance sheet, they have over $7 billion in the account. This effectively brings the adjusted book value of the company down to under $3 billion.

Clear Channel year ended 12/31		
	2004	**2003**
Operating Cash Flow		
Net Loss	$(4,038)	
Accounting change	$4,883	
TOTAL OPERATING CASH FLOW	**$1,815**	**$1,677**
Investing Cash Flow		
TOTAL INVESTING CASH FLOW	**$7,487**	**$(93,256)**
Financing Cash Flow		
TOTAL FINANCING CASH FLOW	**$(1,803)**	**$(1,630)**

Par Value Stock

Par value is for all practical purposes meaningless. If a company issues 1,000 shares of stock with a $.10 par value, and sold this stock for $10, they would raise a total of $10,000, which in the equity section of the balance sheet would show $1,000 as stock, and $9,000 as additional paid in capital. *The net impact for our purposes is that the company raised $10,000 in stock, which is exactly how we will treat this in our analysis.*

Treasury Stock

This is simply the stock that a company has issued, and then repurchased. They may have repurchased it to use as compensation for the employees, or because they believe that it is undervalued in the stock market. When a company purchases additional shares of its stock on the open market, its earnings are spread over fewer shares, so it can increase EPS (earnings per share.) A good example of a blue chip company that shows a lot of treasure stock is the Coca Cola Company. The shareholders equity section of its balance sheet for year-end 2004 is shown below:

Coca Cola Shareholders Equity as of 12/31		
	2004	**2003**
SHAREHOLDERS EQUITY		
Common Stock	$ 875	$ 874
Capital Surplus	$ 4,928	$4,395
Reinvested earnings	$29,105	$26,687
Accumulated other income	$(1,348)	$(1,995)
	$33,560	$29,961
Less treasure stock at cost	$(17,625)	$(15,871)
TOTAL EQUITY	$15,935	$14,090

This tells us right away that the company is purchasing its stock on the open market.

CEO's can increase Earnings Per Share (EPS) by spreading the net after tax profit among fewer shares, thus increasing EPS. Companies who feel that their stock is undervalued often use this strategy. If your prospective company is increasing its treasury stock, you can be sure that they will want to talk about how undervalued their stock is.

Finally, treasure stock allows the company to provide stock options to its employees out of treasury stock. For our purposes, we would look at this section of the balance sheet in the following manner.

Coca Cola Shareholders Equity as of 12/31		
	2004	**2003**
Stock	$(13,170)	$(12,597)
Reinvested earnings	$29,105	$26,687
TOTAL EQUITY	$15,935	$14,090

Consolidated Financial Statements

If you want some information specific to a division of a diversified company, you can oftentimes find the P&L statements broken out in the second section of the company's 10-K report. Even if you can't find breakouts, you can glean information from the consolidated returns even if you are looking for a specific division's information. I was once working with a division of a major Fortune 500 company, and although this divisions' financial returns were not broken out in their 10-K documents, the consolidated statements clearly showed that their cash cycle was lengthening. In addition, there were several other measures that pointed to pressures on the cash flow, from a corporate perspective. I used this point during my meeting with the company executives, and in fact the executive team I was meeting with had felt this pressure and felt that I had the problems in their company "nailed."

The overall performance of the business often will dictate programs and policies throughout the divisions in much the same way that if a two income family has one spouse that receives a 10 percent raise, and the other loses their job, chances are the family will probably cut back on expenditures. I have dealt with divisions within companies that have had strong years, but the weakness of the overall company had impacted their ability to invest. The consolidated statements will often times allow you to draw these conclusions, which you can then use to your advantage in the sales cycle.

Quarterly vs. Annual Returns

You have to be careful to note if you are using quarterly or annual financial returns when you are analyzing the Profit Strategies of a company. Since an income statement is for a _period_ of time, while a balance sheet is a _snapshot_ in time, looking at a quarterly P&L together with a balance sheet snapshot will give us skewed numbers unless we take into account this smaller time frame. So, when looking at a P&L of something less than one year, we need to annualize the numbers.

The Issue: Financial statements are difficult to understand, and you have a deal to close!

The Work Involved: You only need to look at a few, key metric to draw most of your conclusions..

The Bottom Line: Read through this chapter to understand the terminology and the concepts. Moving forward, the major stumbling block you want to avoid is confusion about quarterly or annual numbers

Notes to the Financial Statements

During the Enron scandals, much of their financial tricks were hidden deep in the notes to the financial statements. The following was taken from Enron's 1999 10-K filings with the SEC.

> *In June 1999, Enron entered into a series of transactions involving a third party and LJM Cayman, L.P. (LJM). LJM is a private investment company which engages in acquiring or investing in primarily energy-related investments. A senior officer of Enron is the managing member of LJM's general partner. The effect of the transactions was (i) Enron and the third-party amended certain forward contracts to purchase shares of Enron common stock, resulting in Enron having forward contracts to purchase Enron common shares at the market price on that day, (ii) LJM received 6.8 million shares of Enron common stock subject to certain restrictions and (iii) Enron received a note receivable and certain financial instruments hedging an investment held by Enron. Enron recorded the assets received and equity issued at estimated fair value*

While I won't pretend to know what all of that means, it does send up a "red flag" when an Enron officer is involved in a related party transaction and it is buried so deep in the notes.

When I was in the consulting business dealing with closely held commercial construction firms, I learned a lesson very quickly: read the notes to the financial statements. I was calling on the CEO and owner of a large construction company trying to convince him that the consulting services our firm offered could impact his company profitability. Sitting across the desk from me, he reached over and handed me three years of audited financial statements.

"Tell me how my company is doing," he said.

I looked at the statements, quickly making some mathematical divisions, and then came to a quick conclusion that the increase in overhead the last year negatively impacted net profit.

"Gross profits were up, so you were able to expand on the negotiated portion of your work, but your overhead jumped considerably. This might be due to you structuring the organization to learn how to get into this market, and drive growth and profitability. This is where some consulting may be valuable. As an outside advisor..."
He cut me off and quickly told me the reason that his overhead increased so dramatically.

"I wrote myself a $3 million check at the end of the year as an executive bonus," he said.

I learned two things at that moment. Always read the notes to the financial statements - and I was in the wrong business.

Internal Financial Statements

You may find yourself in the position of looking at internally generated financial reports. These financial statements are often different in layout because they are used for management reports, rather than financial reporting.

For example, manufacturing plants often utilize full absorption costing, where all manufacturing costs, both variable as well as fixed, are charged to the product, whereas financial reports would hold costs in inventory until the product is sold, then expensed against revenue.

Factory ABC for month ended	June	July	August
Revenue	$100,000	$100,000	$100,000
Beginning inventory	$55,000	$55,000	$55,000
+ Purchases	$50,000	$50,000	$55,000
- Ending inventory	$(55,000)	$(55,000)	$(55,000)
COGS @ standard costs	$50,000	$50,000	$55,000
Gross Margin (before variances)	$50,000	$50,000	$45,000
Manufacturing Variances			
Direct material	$ -	$(5,000)	$ -
Direct Labor	$ -	$ -	$5,000
Variable MFG O/H	$ -	$ -	$ -
Fixed MFG O/H	$ -	$ -	$(3,000)
Total Variances	$ -	$(5,000)	$2,000
Gross Margin with variances	$50,000	$45,000	$47,000
Marketing & administrative costs	$20,000	$20,000	$20,000
Operating profit	$30,000	$25,000	$27,000

In the example of a factory P&L shown above, we see that the standard costs of the number of parts produced was $55,000. Over the three-month period the factory produced the same number of parts (because the sales revenue stayed the same) yet in July they paid $5,000 more for materials. In the following month, the factory incurred an additional cost for fixed manufacturing overhead (perhaps installing a new machine) that saved $5,000 of labor costs. The variance, then, shows us what additional costs the factory incurred to manufacture its parts. If the production will require the additional fixed manufacturing overhead costs demonstrated, and save on the labor as shown, then at some point they will revise their standard costs to reflect this change.

Keep an eye out for different stock classes. Consider the stock classes that Ben & Jerry's Homemade, Inc. had prior to their being acquired. Class A Common Stock was publicly traded and had one vote per share on all matters, and Class B Common Stock that was not publicly traded, and had ten votes per share on all matters. Ben & Jerry (along with another executive, Jeff who really got hosed when it came to naming the company) held shares representing 46 percent of all voting power, permitting them to control the company. The lesson here – read the notes to the financial statements. And be sure to be in the office the day they decide to name the company.

It is important to understand what drives the business at this lower level of financial returns, and how manipulation of the business can drive these financial returns. Many factories are cost centers. This means that due to the complexity of the distribution channel, the end product or part does not go into Finished Goods Inventory to get sold to a customer, but goes into the distribution channel for sale.

In examples like this, in order to gauge the effectiveness of the factory and factory manager, the plant manager gets sales credit for the number of units that they produce. A standard sales price is assigned to the units and the manufacturing costs are absorbed to get a measure of plant profitability. What I have seen happen quite a bit is that if no other incentives are used and plant profitability is the sole measure used, the plant's numbers can be manipulated to show great profitability, while implementing a strategy that can be detrimental to the company. For example, the factory manager can pay overtime to manufacture more units, and deliberately increase inventory levels.

This additional sales revenue credit from the per unit sales multiplier and the manipulating of the COGS formula by increasing inventory may show increased profitability. However, the company can run the risk of getting its supply and demand out of whack and increasing working capital requirements to fund this.

Okay, what all of that technical discussion means is that with numbers like we see below, the plant manager is cashing bigger bonuses for having a more productive plant, while the company must finance it through working capital.

In the next chapter, we will show you how to analyze a company's supply chain efficiency, manufacturing efficiency, and demand planning efficiency so as to draw some conclusions as to the effectiveness of their manufacturing operations.

Factory ABC for month ended	June	July
Revenue	$100,000	$110,000
Beginning inventory	$60,000	$55,000
+ Purchases	$50,000	$65,000
- Ending inventory	$(55,000)	$(60,000)
COGS @ standard costs	$55,000	$60,500
Gross Margin (before variances)	$45,000	$49,500
Manufacturing Variances		
Direct material	$(1,000)	$(1,000)
Direct Labor	$(500)	$(3,000)
Variable MFG O/H	$	
Fixed MFG O/H	$	
Total Variances	$(1,500)	$(4,000)
Gross Margin	$43,500	$45,500
Marketing & administrative costs	$20,000	$20,000
Operating profit	$23,500	$25,500
Each unit = $20 in sales credit		
Units produced	5,000	5,500

Consolidated Statements of Stockholders Equity

The Statement of Stockholders Equity generally shows a three-year detail of where the shareholder equity went, broken out by whatever buckets that company has its shareholders equity broken out in. This is an excellent tool to use if you require specific information about impacts to the shareholders equity section of the financial returns.

Foreign Financial Returns

Let's revisit the formula as we use it.

$$\textbf{HAVE } = \textbf{ OWE } + \textbf{ OWN}$$

or

$$\textbf{ASSETS} = \textbf{LIABILITES} + \textbf{EQUITY}$$

Let's revisit our house example and put some numbers to it, and say that we have a $100,000 house with an $80,000 mortgage. Our balance sheet would look like this.

$$\underline{\text{ASSETS= LIABILITES + EQUITY}}$$
$$\textbf{\$100,000= \$80,000 + \$20,000}$$

Looking at the world differently, Europeans will net this out so that you are focused on the net amount of assets, or the total equity that you have. The numbers don't change, but the emphasis does. The "new balance sheet math" according to the Europeans is:

$$\underline{\textbf{HAVE} \quad - \quad \textbf{OWE} \quad = \quad \textbf{OWN}}$$

$$\underline{\textbf{ASSETS - LIABILITES = EQUITY}}$$

So, if that house were in England, your balance sheet would look like the following:

$$\textbf{\$100,000 - \$80,000 = \$20,000}$$

In reality it is a bit more complex because whereas in the USA, the balance sheet always begins with the most liquid asset first, in Europe, it is just the opposite. The balance sheets of BP are shown below.

BP plc Balance Sheet English Style

BP plc as of 12/31	2004	2003
Assets		
Total Fixed Assets	$127,230	$123,011
Total Current Assets	$63,878	$47,651
Total Current Liabilities	$64,525	$50,584
Net Current Assets	$(647)	$(2,933)
Total Assets less Current Liabilities	$126,583	$120,078
Long Term Liabilities	$49,927	$49,482
Shareholders interests	$76,656	$70,596
Shareholders interests represented by		
Stock	$38,893	$37,143
P&L Account	$37,763	$33,453
Shareholders Interests	$76,656	$70,596

Chapter 8: Seeing Through the Fog

One of the things that we can see immediately with this return is that they have done us the favor of calculating net working capital in the traditional method of current assets less current liabilities. To calculate this in our manner, we would take this number and then subtract cash from it. You can see that English returns also net current liabilities from total assets.

The analysis that we use to uncover the company's Profit Strategies does not change based on the presentation of the financial statements. You just might find it more difficult to find the accounts that we are looking for to perform this analysis. Figures 1 and 2 will compare the presentation of financial returns side by side to give you a better feel for how they are presented.

Foreign returns show the P&L statement in just about the same way, except for a few differences in terminology. For example, they call sales "turnover," and COGS, or cost of goods sold, can also be called replacement cost of sales, as well as other terms.

Finally, the style in which they demonstrate a company's cash flow is not as in depth as we are used to seeing. Here, there is simply a summary note called cash inflow from operating activities. If we wanted to dig deeper to find out what made that cash flow (decrease in inventories, or perhaps an increase in accounts payable) we would have to do this by looking at the balance sheets ourselves. There is no summary for this in the financial statements as presented in the European manner.

BP plc year ended 12/31	2004	2003
Net cash inflow from operating activities	$28,554	$21,698
Dividends from joint ventures	$1,908	$131
Dividends from associated undertakings	$291	$417
Net cash outflow from servicing of finance	$(342)	$(711)
Taxes paid	$(6,378)	$(4,804)
Net cash outflow for capital expenditure	$(8,712)	$(6,124)
Net cash outflow for acquisitions/disposals	$(3,242)	$(3,548)
Equity dividends paid	$(6,041)	$(5,654)
Net cash inflow (outflow)	$6,038	$1,405
Financing	$6,777	$1,129
Management of liquid resources	$132	$(41)
Increase (decrease) in cash	$ 871	$317
	$ 6,038	$1,405

125

While accounting rules around the world are probably close to US rules, remember that they won't be equal. Figures 8-1 shows a balance sheet comparison between UK companies, and how those balance sheets would look the way we are analyzing them.

Figure 8-2 Balance Sheet Comparison			
Rolls Royce plc English Style		Rolls Royce plc USA Style	
as of 12/31	2004	as of 12/31	2004
Assets		Assets	
Total Fixed Assets	$2,793	Total Current Assets	$4,979
Total Current Assets	$4,979	Total Fixed Assets	$2,793
Total Current Liabilities	$2,774	TOTAL ASSETS	$7,772
Net Current Assets	$2,205		
		Liabilities	
Total Assets less Current Liabilities	$4,998	Total Current Liabilities	$2,774
Long Term Liabilities	**$2,691**	Total LT Liabilities	$2,691
Shareholders interests	**$2,303**	TOTAL LIABILITIES	$5,469
Shareholders interests represented by Stock	$516	Equity	
		Stock	$516
P&L Account	$1,787	Retained Earnings	$1,787
Shareholders Interests	**$2,303**	TOTAL EQUITY	$2,303

You will find deferred revenue in manufacturing companies that build large, complex products, and you will find under billings and over billings in the construction industry.

Deferred revenue and deferred profit are what we are going to refer to as an "over billing" because the company billed for this service, collected the money, but cannot recognize them yet due to some reason. It is a current liability because within the next twelve months from the date of the balance sheet, we must provide the service to the customer. However, this account will always contribute to cash flow, because this means in effect that the company is "into the customer" (we "over billed") for this amount. We can also have an "under billing" which would be a current asset, because the customer has provided the service and we haven't billed for it yet.

Credence Systems Balance Sheet as of	2005
Assets	
Current Assets	$476,672
Fixed Assets	$696,434
TOTAL ASSETS	$1,173,106
Liabilities	
Deferred revenue	$ 14,654
Deferred profit	$ 9,718
Total Current Liabilities	$179,995
LT Liabilities	$204,903
TOTAL LIABILITIES	$384,898
Equity	
Stock	$1,037,527
Accumulated Deficit	$(249,319)
TOTAL EQUITY	$788,208

The explanation in the Credence notes to the financial statement states that deferred revenue, which is included in accrued expenses and other liabilities on the balance sheet, includes deferred revenue related to maintenance contracts (and other undelivered services) and products that were sold with more than the standard one year warranty. Deferred profit is related to equipment that was shipped to certain customers, but the revenue and cost of goods sold were not recognized because either the customer-specified acceptance criteria has not been met as of the fiscal period end or the product is not classified as mature as of the fiscal period end and has not been accepted by the customer. An under billing has the direct opposite effect on cash flow as an over billing. An under billing means that the customer is "into us" for the amount. So while it is in the current asset category, we know that it will be turned into cash within a year, but until then, it is a cash drain.

> **The Issue:** Deferred revenues impact the Cash2Cash cycle and are important to businesses that have them.
>
> **The Work Involved:** You will probably have to re read this section several times the first time you try analyzing a prospective client with these on their balance sheet.
>
> **The Bottom Line:** You will not normally see over or under billings on balance sheets unless the company is in an industry that takes significant amounts of time to deliver the product. Some examples would include construction, long manufacturing such as some capital equipment manufacturers, or perhaps a software company that sells a product that has to be developed on site with the client.

That's Why They Call it an Annual Report

While I know what they were drinking, I have no idea what the executives at Robert Mondavi were thinking as their year ended on June 30, 2002. An annual report is called that not only because it summarizes the year, but it is also used for the next entire year by everyone to summarize the organization. Robert Mondavi is a Napa Valley winery that was a publicly traded stock until Constellation Brands acquired them in 2004 for $1.36 billion. Their balance sheet as of June 30, 2002, their year-end, showed a negative cash balance.

Now, although the cash account itself doesn't mean that much as a snapshot in time, looking at this balance sheet that shows $ 0 in cash and just under $3 million in an overdraft account does draw into question the treasury function of the organization and what in the world were they thinking the last week of June? Looking at some other measures, cash flow from operations increased from just over $5 million to over $33 million, the most cash flow the operations generated in three years, but the Cash2Cash Cycle increased 79 days, from 533 days in 2001 to over 612 days in 2002. (This industry has one of the longer Cash2Cash Cycles that you will find, but when you think about the industry you can understand why. Wine isn't manufactured like an automobile!) In any event, when looking at the results as we've shown here, you have to wonder if there is some issue in the area of financial control within the company.

In addition to thinking that a six percent tip shows appreciation for outstanding service, Europeans use what we can only be called "balance sheet new math."

Robert Mondavi As of 6/30

	2002	2001
Assets		
Cash	$ -	$7,189
Total Current Assets	$493,308	$480,900
Total Fixed Assets	$362,257	$383,458
TOTAL ASSETS	$855,565	$ 864,358
Liabilities		
Book overdraft	$2,734	$
Total Current Liabilities	$74,884	$93,570
Total LT Liabilities	$349,402	$368,319
TOTAL LIABILITIES	$ 424,286	$461,889
Equity		
Stock	$113,364	$110,070
Retained Earnings	$317,915	$292,399
TOTAL EQUITY	$431,279	$402,469

I once did some management consulting for a closely held company that found itself in similar financial shape as Robert Mondavi. They were short on cash, and had just weeks before their year-end.

We assumed that the company would have to go to their bank for capital during the coming year, and since their annual report was audited, and would probably be used to represent the company throughout the coming year, I recommended that they take out a short-term loan and put the money in their cash account. They paid it back the day after their year-end, so the overall financial cost to them was minimal. Yet their year end balance sheet – the one that they would be showing for the next year – would show a positive cash balance.

These are the issues that CEO's are thinking about, and they're the issues that anyone who sells to them must be aware of in order to figure out a company's Profit Strategies.

Wall Street Selling Implications - Lifting the Fog

While it is imperative to become fluent in the language of business by understanding the three key financial statements, you don't need to worry about every single category or items that you will find in them. Focus on the major points we discussed in this chapter, and remember to read through the notes.

One of the reasons that I began to focus my efforts on the points that were to become the Wall Street Selling Methodology™ is that I found that it was a way to tilt the playing field to my advantage. I came to this conclusion quickly the first time I had to walk through a manufacturing plant. I didn't understand anything about manufacturing, but after asking to see the company financial statements, and finding the manufacturing efficiency metric, I was pretty sure they had a problem. The company manufactured phone systems, which took, on average, sixteen weeks to manufacture. The company President didn't see manufacturing as his problem; rather, he viewed the problem as being that his company was losing market share. In his view, marketing was the main issue.

We discussed the strategic implications of speed to market in manufacturing with the ability to capture more market share, and after that conversation, we were both convinced. He was convinced, incorrectly, that I understood manufacturing, and I was convinced, correctly, that if I could understand the strategic implications of Profit Strategies I just might make a living in the manufacturing industry.

If you understand the methodology presented in this book, you will find yourself with at least as great of an understanding of the concepts than most executives you will meet. Tying these financial points into a discussion on strategy and market opportunity will allow you to show insight and gain the trust and respect of the executive you are calling on.

Another reason for executing the Wall Street Selling Methodology™ is because of the competitive environment you are operating in. The company that you so dearly call a prospect has numerous other sales people calling on them, just about every one of whom would probably set up his own mother with Robert Blake if it meant getting a deal. You must differentiate yourself against your competitors also, and the best way to do that is to follow the methodology and demonstrate to the executives you are dealing with that like them, you truly can think like a CEO.

"Know your strengths...so you know where to fight!"

Deep Dive for VALUE

A GRIZZLY BEAR CAN WEIGH up to 1,500 pounds, and can accelerate faster than your family minivan. A swipe of its paw can take a cow's head off.

An alligator's jaws can exert 300 pounds of pressure per inch, and it can hold its breath for over 45 minutes. It can swim faster than Mark Spitz, and run faster than Bob Hayes.

Who wins a fight between a grizzly bear and an alligator?

While they are both formidable foes, the answer is easier than it seems. *It depends on where they are fighting.*

Chances are, you aren't an expert in your prospect's business, so you had better find something that you can use to drive an advantage to you in the sales cycle. You already understand the value proposition your product will drive. To think like a CEO you need to expand this knowledge to the overall business environment. This chapter will help you to find the financial equivalent of the San Andres fault in just about any company, no matter how strong they might seem.

Become an expert in the concepts outlined in this book, and you will always be fighting opponents on your terms. Many people you face in your sales cycle don't have the vision or understanding of business that the C-Level executives have. After all, that's why they *are* C-Level. Your challenge is to then educate them so that they begin to have this understanding. This chapter will give you some additional tools to execute this strategy. While you may not use these metrics very often, there will be times where you will refer to this chapter to develop your sales strategy.

The first factory analysis that I ever did resulted in a sale. I closed the deal despite spending the entire morning on the factory floor with the plant manager learning the operations of "his" machines. He was demonstrating the manufacturing flow with machines that he called chuckers, brake presses, water jets, lathes and even one unique looking machine called a multi spindle screw machine. The noise was deafening, sparks were flying, grease was gathering on the floor, as he explained tolerances, dye changeovers and factory throughput. I was thinking to myself, "Let's see…righty loosie…no, righty tightie, lefty loosie? Yea, that's it."

After our tour we had an hour before our scheduled meeting with the Division President, so we sat down and he asked me,

"So, can I answer any questions that you have from the plant tour?"

I proceeded to tilt the playing field to my area of expertise as my line of questioning revolved around markets, margins, and productivity. I pulled their annual report out of my briefcase, went through several quick metrics, and started to tie these to his factory. This wasn't his strength, but I convinced him that his boss, the VP Operations would be focusing on these metrics, and the Division President certainly would.

During the meeting with the Division President, this factory manager began discussing how my solution could begin to drive stronger company metrics that would then be reflected on Wall Street.

The basic analysis that we have been working on thus far is what matters to C-Level executives. They manage to these numbers because they have to put up with everyone from bankers to Wall Street analysts focusing on them. Now we are going to give you the tools that you can use to analyze a company to uncover a point that you can use to craft a sales strategy. Now let's talk about dragging that gator into the mountains.

Deep Dive Liquidity

Our *Fast Five* metric of net working capital is where we will start in our Liquidity analysis. We will continue using working capital in our analysis by looking at the relationship between working capital and sales in two related metrics, working capital as a percentage of sales and working capital turnover. Both of these are different ways of representing the same thing: the amount of investment in each sales dollar that goes to "keeping the wheels of business greased."

> **Net working capital = (Current assets – cash) – current liabilities**

We now want to look at the relationship between working capital and sales. We can describe this as either a turnover or a percentage of sales.

> **Working capital TO = Sales / net working capital**

> **Net working capital as % of sales = (Net working capital / Sales revenue) * 100**

For example, let's take two similar companies in similar industries and look at their working capital turnovers. If company A has a working capital turnover of 10X, and company B has a working capital turnover of 20X, you would generally surmise that the second company is more profitable, being able to operate on less capital that is tied up in a low yielding asset. However, if Company B had working capital turns over the last three years of 10X, 15X, and now 20X, well, that's a big red flag that the company is bleeding working capital. If the turns have been consistent around 20X, with maybe some movement in them explained by management, then you might assume that it is a company that can operate on less working capital, and may be better managed than company A.

Whenever a company is seeing deteriorating working capital, your C-Level prospect will be focused like a laser beam to liquidity. These various liquidity metrics tell the same story, but will allow you to use different presentations to sell the message. Take a dollar, talk about working capital percentages and then tear that percentage off of the dollar. Laser beam focused.

Deep Dive Operations

The fixed asset % will provide some insights as to the operations of the company, and the barriers to entry that the companies in the industry might provide. The higher the fixed asset percentage, the more of a barrier to entry, financially speaking, the company has.

As an example, let's look at how difficult it is to get into the construction business. You need a license. You need workers that for the most part you can directly bill to the job, making them variable costs. If you need any machinery you can lease it on a short-term basis, or purchase it. You bill your customer monthly, based on how much work you have done. Now, compare the ease of starting a construction company with a manufacturing company.

A manufacturer will need equipment, and a factory to put that equipment in. You have to purchase raw materials, take the time to add value with your labor and equipment to make a product, and then sell that product. Financially, there is a much larger barrier to entry, to say nothing about the complexity of forecasting, matching demand and supply, etc.

We'll demonstrate how we can see the difference by looking at the fixed asset % for DR Horton, and Fluor, two publicly traded construction companies, and Lennox International, a company that manufactures air conditioners that go into the jobs that Fluor and DR Horton run.

Fixed asset % Fluor = 31%

Fixed asset % DR Horton = 23%

Fixed asset % Lennox International = 44%

Since this number in and of itself won't drive action, compare your prospect's fixed asset percentage with their competitors. You might also look at how this number has changed over the years. We will use a percentage to express this number, like 55%.

> **Fixed asset % = (Total fixed assets / total assets) * 100**

Another way that we can begin to understand what is happening in an organization is to look at the changes in what we classify as miscellaneous + / -. Changes that can drive this metric include restructuring charges, income or loss from discontinued operations, and other factors that are not part of the company's regular operations. If you see a lot of changes in miscellaneous, you will have a lot to analyze and perhaps, discuss. This number is expressed as an actual number, such as $250,000.

> **Change in Miscellaneous + / - = Masc. +/- expenses for year two –**
> **Misc. +/- expenses year one**

The changes in investing cash flow will give us some ideas as to a company's strategy. If this number drops substantially, this demonstrates that the company is cutting back on its investment, and signals either a strategic shift or conservation of cash.

Change in investing cash flow = Investing cash flow year two – investing cash flow yaer one.

Deep Dive Risk

Since there is risk associated with businesses we want to look at how we can quantify this risk, as well as gauge how the risk profile has changed. Consider two individuals and how they approach their personal risk profiles. We'll call the first person Mr. Big Spender and the second Mr. Conservative (thank you to Grandpa Kuta!) Mr. Big Spender maxes out his mortgage line, and lives in a large house, buys stocks on margin, and finances his Mercedes cars. His balance sheet looks like the following.

Mr. Big Spender Balance Sheet		
Have =	Owe +	Own
$2,500,000	$ 2,000,000	$ 500,000

Mr. Conservative, on the other hand, lives in a house much more within his means, pays cash for his cars, and never buys anything on his credit card without being able to pay it off immediately when the bill comes due. His personal balance sheet looks like this:

Mr. Conservative Balance Sheet		
Have =	Owe +	Own
$1,500,000	$1,000,000	$500,000

Note that they both have the same amount of Own (net worth,) but Big Spender is living a much more lavish lifestyle. We can't make a judgment as to which balance sheet is the better one, but we can look at the risk profile of the two. The wild card here is income. Assuming that they both have similar earnings potentials, the Mr. Big Spender balance sheet requires much more income to keep it going, and if something happens to that income, there is more risk to Mr. Big Spender keeping up that standard of living.

Just like Mr. Big Spender, the more debt financing the organization has the more risk it is taking on. So one of the standard measures that we will use is the percentage of long term debt compared to equity. This ratio will immediately demonstrate the risk the company is undertaking. The higher this number, the riskier the organization is. Different industries require different amounts of LT debt. For instance an industry that requires heavy investment in fixed assets to generate its sales (we looked at the fixed asset % ratio above) will likely have a greater LT debt to equity ratio, as well as higher interest expenses. The LT debt to equity ratio will be shown to one decimal point, ex. 6.5 to 1.

LT Debt to Equity = LT Debt / Total Equity

That interest that a company takes on must be repaid, no matter what they taught at WorldCom U. The times interest earned formula allows you to enter into a discussion on risk based on the financing strategy that your prospect is executing. The trend in this metric will be key to drawing conclusions on how much risk the company is taking on.

This is expressed as a decimal taken to the tenth place, such as 3.2.

Times Interest Earned = Operating profit / interest expense

The Issue: While the Wall Street Selling Methodology is built on speed, you may need to dig deeper in order to support your value proposition, or fine a pain you can focus on.

The Work Involved: You may need to revisit some of these metrics on occasion. Use this as a reference.

The Bottom Line: With these additional tooks you will be able to dissect your prospects business better than they can. Be sure to welcome that 'gator to the High Country.

Deep Dive Key Metrics

We will now add several other specific measures that you can look at in order to draw out needs in your prospect's organization.

Manufacturing Metrics

Manufacturing companies take raw material or purchased parts, provide some value added through labor and machinery, and then sell the product to their clients. They try to estimate the demand that they will have so that they can hopefully have their product where you want to buy it when you want to buy it. This requires them to provide their suppliers with estimates for raw materials or purchased parts; they then manufacture them, and then put them in a warehouse until they are sold. You can gauge how efficiently companies are doing this, and put some value to the opportunity to become more efficient in these tasks. We will start by using a metric you already understand, days outstanding of inventory, or Inventory DSO's.

Inventory DSO's = (Inventory/COGS) * Days in Period

In the notes to the company's financial returns, you can find how inventory is classified in a table that will look like the one below.

	20XX
	Company ABC
Raw Material Inventory	$250
WIP Inventory	$500
FGI Inventory	$150
TOTAL INVENTORY	**$900**

We want to use the percentage of each inventory category to further understand a company's efficiencies.

Raw Material Inventory	$250	$250/$900 =	28%
WIP Inventory	$500	$500/$900 =	55%
FGI Inventory	$150	$150/$900 =	17%
TOTAL INVENTORY	**$900**		**100%**

Raw Materials DSO's = Supply Chain Efficiency

Looking at the number of days of inventory a company has in raw material will tell us how efficient the company's supply chain is. If a company can't address the variability of lead times, they have to hold more raw material inventory. The more effective that a company can collaborate with its suppliers in matching the supply and demand functions, the fewer raw material inventory days they will have to stock. If your prospect is implementing programs with their suppliers, you should see their supply chain efficiency increase.

Supply Chain Efficiency = (Inventory Days * Raw Material Inventory %)

Work In Process (WIP) DSO's = Manufacturing Efficiency

After we get an idea of the supply chain efficiency, we want to look at manufacturing efficiency, which we can understand by calculating the number of days it takes a company to send products through its factories. Looking at the WIP DOS's will give us an excellent understanding of the efficiency of the company's manufacturing process. We want to consider both the trends in this number as well as the comparisons between different companies.

The closer a company can manufacture products in their work content time by taking out non-value added waste, the smaller the number of DSO's they will have. For example, let's say that a company can "expedite" an order for one of their products in one shift, or eight hours. They do this by moving the parts through the process without having them sit in queues, or wait in front of machines. If a company can do this on a regular basis, their WIP DSO's should be somewhere around one day, perhaps another day or two for WIP inventory throughout the process. If that same company has seven days of WIP DSO's, that is an indication that although they might be able to expedite products through the manufacturing process quicker, on average, it takes seven days to manufacture the product. If one can ascertain this difference between what the company can do and what they do on average, you can begin to see the value of focusing on manufacturing efficiencies.

Manufacturing Efficiency = (Inventory Days * WIP Inventory %)

Finished Goods Inventories (FGI) DSO's = Demand Planning Efficiency

Companies need to stock finished goods inventories to address either manufacturing capacity issues, or lead time issues. For example, in some industries the sales of their product is skewed towards certain events, or may be seasonal in nature. A company that manufactures lights for Christmas trees will sell the vast majority of their product in the thirty to sixty days before Christmas. They will stock FGI inventory to help balance the manufacturing capacity throughout the year. In other industries, if one's customers have a lead time less than the manufacturing company's lead time, they must stock FGI inventory to satisfy this demand or risk losing sales. If it takes four weeks to manufacture a widget, but customers will only wait two weeks to get this widget, the company must either learn to manufacture the widget within that two -week period, or carry finished goods. In this example, a company will generally hold about two weeks of finished goods inventory to meet that demand. The third reason that a company may have finished goods is that they did not do a good job predicting what products the market would want. In this way, the performance of FGI DSO's will give us some insight on the company's demand forecasting methods.

> **Demand Planning Efficiency = (Inventory Days * FGI Inventory %)**

Cash2Cash Cycle Analysis

To demonstrate these calculations, let's use the following information taken from our balance sheet and P&L statements.

P&L	
Sales	$100,000
COGS	$70,000
Balance Sheet	
Assets	
A/R	$25,000
Under billings	$500
Raw	$10,000
WIP	$10,000
FGI	$5,000
Total Inventory	$25,000
Liabilities	
A/P	$15,000
Over billings	$1,000

Working our metrics as shown above yield a Cash2Cash Cycle of 142 days. The chart below outlines the formula and the results.

DSO's	($25,000 / $100,000) * 365	1
Inventory Days	($25,000 / $70,000) * 365	130
Under billings	($500 / $100,000) * 365	2
A/P Days	($15,000 / $70,000) * 365	(78)
Over billings	($1,000 / $100,000) * 365	(4)
Cash2Cash Cycle		**142**
Cash per day		$192
Cash to be financed		$27,150

It takes our company four and a half months to turn their products into cash. If you want to quantify that number, divide the COGS by 365 days to give the average cost incurred per day. Dividing $70,000 by 365 means that on average, this company incurs $191 per day in costs. Since they are taking 142 days to turn their product into cash, that means they have to finance $27,150 ($192 * 142).

While most companies do not track this metric, one company that does is Dell. Dell has built their focus on cash conversion to capture significant market share from their competitors, and build a business model that is allowing them to move beyond personal computers and into other retail electronics, while still dominating their market. Looking at two years of Dell results compared to Compaq, who was at this time an independent company and a major competitor to Dell, will allow us to draw some conclusions regarding their Profit Strategies.

	2001	2000	2001	2000
	Dell	Dell	Compaq	Compaq
P&L Data				
Sales	$ 31,888	$25,265	$33,554	$42,222
COGS	$25,445	$20,047	$26,442	$32,417
Balance Sheet Data				
Raw Material Inventory	$95	$129	$298	$540
WIP Inventory	$305	$262	$172	$298
FGI Inventory			$932	$1,323
TOTAL INVENTORY	**$400**	**$391**	**$1,402**	**$2,161**

We can see from the chart above that by focusing on their manufacturing efficiencies, Dell only has to finance four days of inventory versus fifteen days in

Compaq's case. Adding in the supply chain efficiencies, Dell's materials and parts move through their warehouse, manufacturing, and distribution to the customer in just over one week, while their competitor takes almost a full two weeks longer. There is no effective way to compete with execution differences like this, and in fact the next year saw Compaq acquired by Hewlett-Packard.

	Dell 2001	Dell 2000	Compaq 2001	Compaq 2000
Raw Material Days	2	2	4	6
WIP Days	4	5	2	3
FGI Days	0	0	13	15
Total Inventory	6	7	19	24

Value Indicators

There are several ways to estimate the value of a company. Not one single method provides the most accurate metric, and in fact it is probably impossible to get an exact value for a company at any time other than an instant during trading on an exchange. In fact, advisors who make their living valuing companies generally use several of these methods to estimate the value, and it isn't an exact number either. Probably the only way to answer the question as to how much a company is worth is to see what someone will pay for it. This book precludes a deep analytical discussion on the positives and negatives of each of these methods, but after reading through the various methods, you should be able to draw some conclusions as to value based on several of these methods. For our examples, we will use the following balance sheet and P&L statement as examples.

Book Value

The first method we will look at when putting a value on a business is simply to value the company at book value, or equity. Based on valuing the company in this way, this company would have a value of $2.1 billion. This method in particular is a good, conservative way to value closely held companies.

Book value = Total shareholders equity

Big Valuable Company			
(Numbers in Millions)	2007		2007
Assets		Sales	$2,000
Total Current Assets	$1,000	COGS	$1,250
		Gross Profit	$750
Goodwill	$1,000		
Total Fixed Assets	$2,500	O/H	$450
TOTAL ASRSETS	$3,500	Operating Profit	$300
Liabilities		Interest Expense	$125
Current Liabilities	$500	Misc. +/-	$
LT Liabilities	$900	Pre Tax Net Profit	$175
TOTAL LIABILITIES	$1,400		
		Taxes(benefit)	50
Equity		Net Profit	$125
Stock	$600		
Retained Earnings	$1,500		
TOTAL EQUITY	$2,100		
Total shares outstanding of 100 million shares			

Adjusted Book Value

This method is like the book value method above, but you subtract out the goodwill to give you an "adjustment" to book value. Subtracting $1 billion from $2.1 billion yields $1.1 billion in adjusted book value for Big Valuable Company.

> **Adjusted book value = Book value (total shareholders equity) - goodwill**

Multiples

Professionals as well as investors can find just about anything to compare companies. The idea behind multiples is to look at a certain aspect that is important to the business, and value the company based on this. For example, during the late 1990's, also referred to as the "boom boom years," many companies were losing money, but still had sky-high valuations, both in the financial markets as well as the Mergers & Acquisitions marketplace as they were scooped up by others. One of the key factors that was quoted and used at the time was a multiple of sales. If we were to value Big Valuable Company at 2X sales, we would arrive at a value of $4 billion. I would caution you not to put much value in a sales multiple as a way to value a company.

While the Cash2Cash Cycle does not equal profit, it definitely impacts profitability. If a company can reduce the cash cycle they would not require as much short- term debt to finance working capital. This cash can also be turned into profits if a company uses it to offer better terms to their suppliers. Any savings generated this way will show up in gross profit, and then fall directly to the bottom line.

Multiple of Earnings

One of the most widely used means to value companies is the earnings multiple, also known as the P/E Ratio, or the price earnings ratio. This is generally shown as a trailing multiple, or the past four quarters of earnings, but is also shown as a forward P/E using estimated earnings. In our example, Big Valuable Company has 100 million shares outstanding, and booked $125 million in its last four quarters of earnings; it would have an earnings per share, or EPS, of $1.25. If the market is valuing their stock at a P/E multiple of twenty, this would value the company at a total value of $2.5 billion. Generally speaking, if two competitors have vastly different Price Earnings ratios, the market has greater expectations as to the future results of one of the companies.

> **Price to Earnings Ratio (PE Ratio) = Price of stock /
> last twelve months earnings**

Financial Market Performance

Another group of metrics that we want to look at if we are looking at a publicly traded company is the stock market performance of the company. Wall Street pro's are fond of saying, "The trend is your friend," so look at trends over the last several years and compare them to their competitors.

Market Capitalization

Market capitalization is the value of all shares outstanding times the current quoted price. This gives a good evaluation of the value of the company relative to others in the market. Sometimes this metric can tell you a lot, such as when you see that Southwest Airlines has more market capitalization than all the other airlines combined, and other times it is misleading, as when i2 Technologies had a market cap of over $30 billion, while GM had a market cap of less than $10 billion.

By now, you can look at a company's financial returns and understand how they are performing. Now we are going to learn how to use what we know to figure out where the CEO is placing his emphasis. We will look at different strategies, and see how they show themselves in the financial returns. Once you understand this, you simply integrate your value proposition into the CEO's and you will begin to see results!

Wall Street Selling Implications - Lifting the Fog

While you may not find yourself using all of the financial metrics that we outline in this chapter, you may want to focus in on some of these that are specific to the company – or industry – that you are calling on.

Having worked in the manufacturing industry, I knew there were numerous times when it was important to bring up in the sales cycle the metrics revolving around manufacturing efficiencies. Whether they were focused on planning, manufacturing execution or the supply chain, the ability to gauge my prospect's effectiveness relative to their strategic focus allowed me to build a compelling case for change. Simplifying the analysis allowed them to "name the problem" – as in, "that's the Dell Way" and generate interest in it.

Using the metrics described above, I could quantify the current manufacturing cycle time, and estimate the best-case scenario for change. Being able to quantify the problem in both days and dollars was a sure way to build a compelling case for change. While senor level executives certainly understood the problem, when I would draw some quantifiable numbers and goals around it, their response was usually, "Get it done."

Several of the metrics outlined here would be key for anyone involved in managing a project that wasn't a sales cycle. The concept of a Break Even Point (BEP) is critical to not just a Go/No Go decision, but the entire project management. We will go over this, as well as some other basic fundamentals useful for just about any internal project in the chapter on creating a value proposition.

Learn the methods outlined in this chapter for the specific "deep dive" needs of your product or solution, and you will be much closer to getting the sale, or driving value within your organization.

PART THREE

Profit Strategies

"Okay coach, what's your strategy for success?"

Profit Strategies

CONSULTANTS OFTEN GIVE SEMINARS as a way to educate companies on their philosophies of doing business. Of course, just as important, it's a way to drum up business. For several years after B-School I found myself on the "seminar circuit" with the consulting company I was working for. I would often begin a certain section by leading a discussion of brainstorming, having teams of four think up as many oxymorons as they could. Here are some from one of those sessions.

Jumbo Shrimp	Military Intelligence
Republican Party	Educated Guess
Strategic Management (ouch!)	Internal Revenue Service
American Culture	Truth in Advertising
Safe Bet	Firm Estimate
Bus Schedule	Bull Rider
Young Adult	Excessive Profits

That last one led to a discussion of profit, and if there was such as thing as excess profits. Should toy manufacturers be penalized for profits made during the Q4 Christmas season? What about candy manufacturers that earn the majority of their profits over Halloween? Who is to decide which profits are excessive? The result of our impromptu discussion was that the market is the only way to decide if profits are excessive. See, if a company is making profits far and above what others in the market are making, open markets will guarantee that competitors will enter looking for their share of those profits. The result will drive prices down for the consumer, and drive increased productivity – or death -- for the company. The description of this phenomenon was penned the "invisible hand" by Adam Smith. This chapter will outline the strategies that companies use to increase profits, and teach you to understand these business strategies on a company's financial returns. You will be able to see if a company is executing on its strategy, or whether it is being honest in how it is describing the strategies that it is undertaking.

The people developing strategy in businesses – the ones you are selling to - are an educated group. According to the 2005 Spencer Stuart annual CEO study of the S&P 500 companies, the percentage of CEO's who hold MBA degrees is approximately 38 percent. Another 29 percent hold an advanced degree other than an MBA degree, and 11 percent hold law degrees (I said educated, not ethical.) The importance of this issue scales when one realizes that there are over 55,000 businesses in the United States and Canada alone that are larger than $100 million dollars in revenue. While this means that there are at least 55,000 CEO's, there are probably hundreds of times that number of front line personnel who are the ones making or breaking the Profit Strategies of the company. Many CEO's have lamented that the staff below them down through the organization just doesn't understand how they impact the business, and – at times – doesn't share the sense of urgency that the senior managers have. If there was a way to educate everyone so that they consistently make the conscientious decisions that follow the organization's strategy and focus on profits, the impact to American business would be substantial.

While there are many different strategies for businesses to follow, this chapter will summarize them into three basic strategies that companies follow, and teach you how to uncover their impacts to the financial statements. From there, you will be able to understand the impacts of strategy and execution, and gain insight into the thrusts of the organization. We will not focus on the process by which strategy is developed, because in practice it can range from a strict process controlled by some high-priced consultants to the executive and his key advisor sketching out a flow chart of strategy on the back of a napkin. In fact, much strategy that presents itself in the form of acquisitions often happens apart from the company's formal strategic sessions. Effective strategies that allow companies to gain even a small competitive advantage over their competition can generate significant results and really open up tremendous profit opportunities. To demonstrate this, let's do a quick analysis using the "rule of 72."

The Issue: Taking financial information and turning it into a repeatable message that helps to sell your deal.

The Work Involved: Learn what it takes to recognize the different Profit Strategies; Growth Strategies, Operating Strategies, and Profit Strategies.

The Bottom Line: You will have the inside track to closing the deal if you can align your product or solution to your prospects Profit Strategies.

The Rule of 72

The rule of 72 is a good quick tool to demonstrate the impact of growth. Dividing a number into seventy-two will tell you how many years it will take to double. For assistance, if a company is growing earnings at 10 percent per year, it will take just over seven years to double earnings from their current levels. Seventy-two divided by ten is 7.2 years. So using our Rule of 72, if a company can consistently earn just 5 percent more on sales than its competitor, and assuming that their revenues are equal, in approximately fourteen years (72/5=14.4) they will have twice the retained earnings in the equity section of their balance sheet. If they are investing this wisely to capture more market share, well, before long you have an RC Cola trying to do battle against Coca Cola. This type of scenario might play out over years if the market is automobiles or over months if the market is a short lifecycle market like technology and its equipment. If one company is showing significantly better financial returns, this will generally be reflected in its stock price.

We will look at three basic strategies that companies use to garner these advantages; *Growth Strategies*, *Profit Strategies*, and *Operating Strategies*. Growth strategies are what companies use to increase revenues, market share, or both. An increase in revenues does not necessarily correlate to an increase in market share, if these revenues are growing at a slower pace than either the market itself, or the revenues of their competitors.

Profit strategies are strategies intended to increase the "bottom line" of the company, which in a publicly traded company means increased EPS. Finally, we'll look at operating strategies whose intent it is to manage the enterprise on an ongoing basis, with the intent of increasing the value of the business by focusing on market share, revenues, earnings, etc. The strategies are not always mutually exclusive, in that a strategy focused on growth does not inherently rule out an increase in the bottom line. The intent of this chapter is to show you the results key initiatives have on the financial statements, so that you can understand what strategies the company is executing on.

GROWTH STRATEGIES

Ramping up the current organization to increase revenues, called "organic growth," requires additional raw materials, labor, logistics, perhaps increasing the sales staff, employing more marketing, etc. Another way to grow the company is by acquiring other companies, and just like organic growth, this too requires cash. If your prospective company's strategy is growth, your value prop had better be pitching cash flow too.

As an example, the Novellus Systems Inc. financial returns of 2004 show what happens when the company grows. From 2003 to 2004, revenues increased 47 percent, and the Cash2Cash Cycle increased from 189 to 208 days, with each day representing just under $2 million. That is significant, because when it comes to cash, there are only three ways to get it. You can use the cash the business is generating, you can borrow it, or you can issue stock for it. Novellus used current cash in the bank, reducing cash & securities by almost $500 million, and taking on an additional $160 million in LT debt.

Whenever you hear the word "growth", you should immediately think "cash." Just like the teenager who begins to eat you out of house and home, in the business world, any type of growth strategy requires cash.

A business that generates enough cash to not need either bank financing or an infusion of cash via the stock market is a rare breed. Somewhere along the lifecycle of the business, they will need the ability to issue stock to expand its operations. Many companies with high stock prices use those prices as currency with which they can raise capital to expand operations and grow the business.

Growing a business can be risky in labor-intensive industries such as restaurants, construction companies, etc. Privately held companies that don't have access to the capital markets also run this risk. In many of these industries, companies go out of business "through the top," by expanding their business and growing too quickly, as often as they go out of business through lack of sales. We will revisit this concept of going out of business "through the top" when we look at the various players in the airline industry.

Buy the Business Strategy

While texts will tell you that executives acquire companies to increase market dominance, or customer touch points, among many other reasons, my experience has led me to believe that CEO's also buy companies for the same reason many consumers spend so much of their paychecks. First of all, it feels good. Just as you might not have really needed that extra set of tools, acquiring companies gives executives new divisions, markets, people, etc. They are addressing what sociologists have shown to be a powerful human need. The second reason that they acquire companies is that like people who find themselves with a windfall, the CEO might simply have some additional means with which they can acquire companies. These additional means might be a growing stockpile of cash, or an increased credit line, or maybe even a high -flying stock price.

The Buy the Business strategy is without a doubt the most prevalent growth strategy used by public companies. It is difficult to look through a public company's financial statements for even a few years without seeing acquisitions that they have made. However, when we are referring to this strategy, we are looking at businesses that focus on acquisitions in order to increase their top and bottom lines. As part of my research for writing this book, I looked through over 2,000 financial returns of companies in just about every industry, and I would say that between fifty and seventy-five percent of these companies had acquisitions in their financial returns. Because this strategy is so common, we will take a look at how you can recognize it, and provide some guidance as to whether you feel a company is doing smart buying, or acquiring just to demonstrate the results quickly.

Within the Buy the Business strategy are several visions that companies seem to focus on as they execute this strategy. Consider the example of Proxymed, Inc. and see if you can look at their balance sheet and immediately understand how they approach growing the business.

In this case, we don't even need to go to the P&L or cash flow statements to see that acquisitions are a major strategy for Proxymed. You can see the acquisition increasing goodwill, and being paid for partly out of LT debt and issuance of additional stock. The company bought just under $5 million in account(s) receivable, and showed a profit in 2002 of just under $2 million, as accumulated deficit decreased by this amount. The P&L statement shows a sales increase of about 16 percent as sales went from $43 million to just over $50 million, and that profit of just under $2 million. The past years also showed write offs of just under $3 million for impairment of assets. While this strategy is booking more profits, they are clearly increasing the risk of the shareholders, they are at least booking more profits.

	2002	2001
Assets		
A/R	$10,060	$5,589
Total Current Assets	$30,737	$21,961
Goodwill	$32,797	$7,961
Total Fixed Assets	$57,967	$3,921
TOTAL ASSETS	$88,704	$35,882
Liabilities		
Total Current Liabilities	$21,988	$12,567
Total LT Liabilities	$37,969	$13,009
TOTAL LIABILITIES	$37,969	$13,009
Equity		
Stock	$146,008	$120,094
Accumulated deficit	($95,273)	($97,221)
TOTAL EQUITY	$50,735	$22,873

How to Recognize the Buy the Business Strategy

1. Investment cash flow on the cash flow statement is increasing.

2. Increase in cash flow statement under acquisition of business.

3. Goodwill is increasing.

4. The company is raising cash through LT debt increasing, ST debt increasing, or additional issuing of stock.

Buy the Business: Size Matters Strategy

One of the big reasons given for acquisitions is the price concessions that companies believe that they can wring out of their suppliers. The March 1, 2005 issue of the Wall Street Journal noted that a major benefit of the Federated acquisition of May was the ability to force price concessions on their main suppliers, the apparel manufacturers. Other reasons behind this strategy are more options for the customer (Compaq-HP), or more market penetration through customers, locations, etc. (Computer Associates.)

A good example of the Size Matters Strategy is the acquisition binge that Oracle embarked on from 2002 to 2005, acquiring Peoplesoft for

Much like in a certain other room, many people in the boardroom believe that size matters. Many company mergers are done under the idea that bigger is better.

approximately $11.1 billion. Looking at four years of balance sheets you can see how these acquisitions affected Oracle.

Oracle Corp. As of 5/31	2005	2004	2003	2002
Assets				
Cash & ST Securities	$4,802	$8,587	$6,519	$5,841
Total Current Assets	$8,479	$11,336	$9,227	$8,728
Goodwill	$10,376	$80	$345	$446
Total Fixed Assets	$12,208	$1,427	$1,837	$2,072
TOTAL ASSETS	**$20,687**	**$12,763**	**$11,064**	**$10,800**
Liabilities				
ST Debt	$2,693	$9	$153	$ -
Deferred revenue	$2,289	$1,497	$1,409	$1,241
Total Current Liabilities	$8,063	$4,272	$4,158	$3,960
Total LT Liabilities	$1,787	$496	$586	$723
TOTAL LIABILITIES	**$9,850**	**$4,768**	**$ 4,744**	**$4,683**
Equity				
Stock	$6,794	$5,612	$5,228	$4,907
Retained Earnings	$4,043	$2,383	$1,092	$1,210
TOTAL EQUITY	**$10,837**	**$7,995**	**$6,320**	**$6,117**

You can see that the acquisition binge drove total equity to increase 77 percent from just over $6 billion to just under $11 billion. However, when you subtract the goodwill from this total equity to get an idea of adjusted book value, equity actually dropped to $461 million. While the cash flow statement will show us exactly where the money came from to pay for this acquisition, the balance sheet shows us the results. The company is much more leveraged, as debt grew by just under $4 billion (short term debt increased by over $2.6 billion, and long-term debt increased approximately $1.3 billion) stock increased over $1.1 billion, and cash decreased by just under $4 billion. Oracle has always operated with negative working capital, but this working capital dropped almost $3 billion after the deal, from -$1.523 billion in 2004 to -$4.386 billion in 2005.

Oracle Corp. Cash Flow for years ended 5/31		
	2005	**2004**
Operating Cash Flow		
Increase in deferred revenue	$394	$91
TOTAL OPERATING CASH FLOW	**$3,552**	**$3,195**
Investing Cash Flow		
Purchases of investments	$(7,101)	$(10,310)
Proceeds from sales in investments	$12,194	$8,009
Acquisitions, net of cash	$(10,656)	$(21)
Capital expenditures	$(190)	$(226)
TOTAL INVESTING CASH FLOW	**$(5,753)**	**$(2,548)**
Financing Cash Flow		
Payments to repurchase stock	$(1,343)	$(1,499)
Proceeds for issuance of stock	$596	$354
Proceeds of borrowings	$12,505	$6
Payments of debt	$(9,830)	$(150)
Distribution of minority interests	$(44)	$(31)
TOTAL FINANCING CASH FLOW	**$1,884**	**$(1,320)**

The deal did buy some deferred revenue, which since it is a liability account acts like an "over billing." This is a net cash positive impact of $792 million, and when added to the $1.4 billion in cash that Peoplesoft had on their balance sheet (once Oracle purchased them, this cash became theirs) we get the $11.1 billion that the acquisition cost. The cash flow statement makes this easy to see.

The bet that Oracle is making by embarking on the Size Matters Strategy is that they will reap significant cash rewards when companies looking for enterprise software can only look at SAP and Oracle. Running the numbers on the IRR of the additional cash flows that will be generated by the Peoplesoft organization just don't seem to exceed Oracle's opportunity cost as outlined by their cost of capital. It will be interesting to see how this bet on the market shakes out for all Oracle shareholders.

How to Recognize the Size Matters Business Strategy

1. Investment cash flow on the cash flow statement is increasing.

2. Increase in cash flow statement under acquisition of business.

3. Goodwill is increasing.

4. The company is raising cash through LT debt increasing, ST debt increasing, or additional issuing of stock.

5. The company is acquiring its competitors.

Buy the Business: The Horizontal Bop Strategy

Another way company's can expand their customer base is via acquisition in a related market. Keeping with the theme that business can indeed be fun, we call this the Horizontal Bop Strategy. I got a first hand look at this vision when i2 Technologies found themselves the provider of eMarketplaces, and utilizing the content services of Aspect Development. Aspect Development saw i2 as a good delivery system for their content services, and worked to integrate the two software packages. Their executive team in the meantime worked to strike deals with i2's competitors, including Arriba and SAP. Whether prodded by Aspect's management or not, i2 decided that if they could dominate this horizontal market they could in effect lock out the competition. The result was a $9 billion dollar takeover of a company whose best year produced just under $100 million in sales and approximately $10 million dollars of pre tax income. Take out the taxes, and i2 paid almost 1,200 times Aspect's earnings. While i2 was looking for a significant increase in sales by expanding its customer base with Aspect's customers, their judgment was skewed by the irrational exuberance the market was showing for their stock.

How to Recognize the Horizontal Bop Strategy

1. Investment cash flow on the cash flow statement is increasing.

2. Increase in cash flow statement under acquisition of business.

3. Goodwill is increasing.

4. The company is raising cash through LT debt increasing, ST debt increasing, or additional issuing of stock.

5. The company is acquiring companies on the periphery of their main markets.

Buy the Business: The Shopping Center Strategy

This vision is often one that the executive as when looking at a business that he just can't do without. There is often very little overlap among marketing or distribution channels, or even customers or suppliers. Having said this, one can't assume that a lack of synergy in the business units lead to bad acquisitions. If a company can lend executive talent, provide access to capital, or provide marketing expertise, they can actually run the newly acquired business with better financial results. If a company can't provide this expertise, they will still earn the revenues and profits that will contribute to the consolidated results.

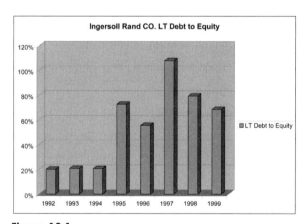

Figure 10.1

The reason that many feel this can be a risky strategy is because by investing in various companies, an investor can get the same diversification as if they invest in a diversified company.

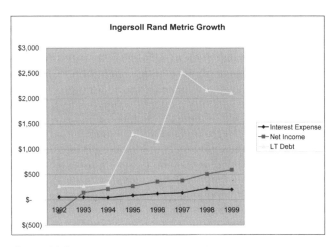

Figure 10.2

Ingersoll-Rand under CEO Jim Parella undertook this strategy, growing revenue from approximately $4.5 billion to over $7.5 billion in the years from 1994 to 1999. Ingersoll-Rand found themselves selling everything from compressors to door openers to door locks. Figures 10-1 and 10-2 show the results of this Shopping Center Strategy for Ingersoll-Rand, on net income, debt and interest expense. While this strategy certainly drove earnings and stock price, it left the company in a riskier position due to its leverage.

How to recognize the Shopping Center Strategy

1. Investment cash flow on the cash flow statement is increasing.

2. Increase in cash flow statement under acquisition of business.

3. Goodwill is increasing.

4. The company is raising cash through LT debt increasing, ST debt increasing, or additional issuing of stock.

5. Many different profit centers or organizational P&L's.

Grow the Business - The Organic Strategy

Another way to achieve growth in the business is to grow the business internally, also referred to as "organic growth." Companies that grow this way don't use their capital to acquire other companies, but rather invest in their current situation and business infrastructure. Although companies are constantly trying to increase sales and profits, few companies that are not storefront-based utilize this strategy exclusively to grow their business. First of all, it is very difficult to execute. If the business is currently a well-managed business, there is only so much that can be done to increase both the top and bottom lines. This strategy of organic growth often takes longer than acquiring a company, and one thing CEO's are not is patient. However, I've found that companies that can consistently grow their business significantly through organic growth are some of the best-run businesses and organizations around.

Increasing the distribution channel is another way companies grow organically. This could mean setting up additional distribution centers for increased customer response, new branches of service organizations, or even investing in property plant & equipment for new manufacturing capacity.

How to recognize the Organic Strategy

1. Revenues are rising, while the goodwill account is staying the same.

2. If gross margins remain the same or grow, the growth is due to market growth and or business execution.

3. If gross margins shrink, the company is buying the business or the market is tightening.

4. Increase in additional markets, such as overseas, additional industries, etc.

Grow the Business – The Storefront Strategy

Companies that have businesses run from "storefronts" are the most effective organically grown businesses. Some examples of this would be construction companies that set up offices in different locations, and financial institutions that grow organically by opening branches and retail outlets that open up new stores to grow. Companies that grow in this manner run the risk of cannibalizing their current storefronts, and it is not uncommon for companies to have issues with their distribution channel as they grow locations.

The famous quote from McDonalds that they were not in the hamburger business, but rather the real estate business, demonstrates how important it was for them to increase their touch with storefronts. What McDonalds does is to acquire the real estate and rent it out to franchisees. In fact, based on the 2004 McDonald's 10-K, rents and service fees made up over 25 percent of the corporations $19 billion in sales, and McDonald's has over $21 billion in contractual cash inflows stretching out beyond 2009.

Let's look at two of the most dominant "category killers" out there, Wal-Mart and Home Depot. Both of these companies have driven sales by putting new stores up, as you can see from Figures 10-3 and 10-4.

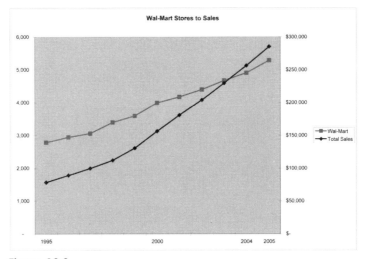

Figure 10.3

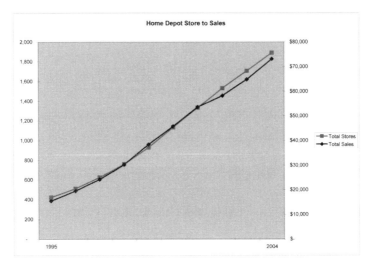

Figure 10.4

This strategy requires tremendous investment, and looking at the financial returns can tell us how aggressive the company is in expanding. Comparing the LT debt that both retailers took on to grow demonstrates that Wal-Mart's long-term debt grew from approximately $7.8 billion in 1995 to over $20 billion in 2005. However, equity grew even higher, dropping the LT debt to equity ratio from sixty-two percent in 1995 to forty-one percent in 2005. Home Depot's debt grew from $720 million to approximately $2.1 billion from 1995 to 2004, and their LT debt to equity ratio also shrunk, but from 14.4 percent to 8.9 percent. So we can see that both companies have experienced a positive effect from the concentration of capital as more stores generated more cash. We can also see that Home Depot is much more conservative in using debt capital to grow their business.

The risk companies that are storefront-based run is that sooner or later, they run out of locations to put more stores, and then they had better be ready to really grow internally, through increases in same store sales.

You may be asking yourself at this point why companies have to continue to grow. Could, say, Wal-Mart not simply reach the saturation point, and rather than increase same-store sales, simply maintain, continually turning a profit and holding onto whatever market share is theirs? Yes they could, but their stock would take a beating, and many of their top management staff would probably end up leaving. If you have ever worked for a company that was satisfied with the status quo and did not try to increase profits, you understand. If you were the owner of such a company, my bet is you struggled with turnover problems.

How to recognize the Storefront Strategy

1. Revenues are rising, as are the "storefronts."

2. The cash flow statement shows increased investment in the business.

3. Increase in number of distribution outlets.

4. The company is raising cash through LT debt increasing, ST debt increasing, or additional issuing of stock.

Grow the Business - Execute the Sales Team Strategy

The first mantra a CEO usually spews to Wall Street when he discusses organic growth is "sales execution." The issue for them is generally executing on sales, with nary a thought of questioning the marketplace strategy, or customer needs, etc. The primary way companies execute on the sales team to achieve growth is to simply increase the number of sales representatives in the market. This will generally call for increased marketing, sales expenses, and even maybe advertising dollars. Getting sales people on board is expensive, and putting them in front of customers is more expensive yet. This is an opportunistic strategy to capture market share while the market is growing, and in my experience tends to work better in industries that are not "zero sum games." An industry in a "zero sum game" is one that must resell new deals to hit the yearly sales revenue. An excellent example is the software business. A software company that sells $100 million dollars of software would probably only have 20 percent or so guaranteed the following year, assuming that the support revenues are 20 percent of software revenues. So in this example, in year two, they would have $20 million coming in on support contracts, but have to go sell another $80 million in new contracts to have another $100 million dollar year. Throw in a significant growth target that software companies over the last several years have been striving for, and this type of math catches up to companies quickly.

A more traditional industrial company that sells, say, fasteners, might have long-term contracts with customers, or have a customer base that has its yearly revenue much more consistently forecasted. Let's say, for example, that this traditional fastener company sells their product to a wide range of industrial manufacturers of everything from pumps, to automotive parts, to machinery manufacturers. Their customers will continue to sell those pumps, cars, etc. even during economic slowdowns. So, if they sell $100 million of fasteners, they might have both a limited downside and upside of, say, 20 percent or so. So if contracts are cancelled, business for their customers stalls, etc. they might only sell $80 million or so. Likewise, their upside may be more limited also. Hit it out of the park, and they might sell $120 million or so.

With that understanding, investing in the sales & marketing of a company to spur internal growth can be an effective strategy, but smart companies are effective about this. Ideally, companies should only resort to this when there is a significant change in the market requiring more coverage, when current sales staff is stretched too thin, additional sales staff is needed due to new product introductions, etc. Otherwise, it can be an expensive and risky strategy. To see the risk in this strategy, let's revisit the software industry. Most managers in the software industry feel that the key to increasing sales is to hire proportionately more salespeople. That is to

Cut back on the sales staff. Put new uncertainty in front of the sales team as they see the blood flying, and moral can drop like a brick. Sales generally follow the same path.

say, if the company is selling $1 billion with 500 salespeople, the way to take the company to $2 billion is to double the sales staff. The company now hires an additional 500 salespeople pushing the same message, resulting in huge overhead expense. If the market hasn't expanded, what you get is 1,000 salespeople covering the same number of accounts. While this does provide more coverage to some customers, unless the sales staff is hitting it out of the park, as described above, the company will increase its sales expense much more than the resulting increase in revenues. What management now must decide is how long they want to play this corporate game of "chicken." If there is a hiccup in the market, or the company management gets tired of paying out the overhead associated with salaries and labor burden, the quickest way to protect profits is to get out of the situation.

i2 Technologies played this corporate game of "chicken", and ended up seeing the market change the same way someone driving the wrong way on the Ventura Freeway might-- as a hood ornament for a Kenworth. They increased their salespeople from 730 as of December 1999 to 1,700 by February of 2001. As the market softened, sales dropped over 12 percent. Judgment day had come for the sales staff, as on their next 10-K, i2 reported 300 salespeople, firing a breathtaking 1,400 from their sales staff. If you see the SG&A percentage rising or even steady at a higher rate than others in the industry, this is a strategy that the company is embarking on.

How to recognize the Execute the Sales Team Strategy

1. Revenues are rising.
2. The company has significant increases in its sales and marketing personnel (outlined in their 10-K.)
3. SG&A expenses are growing.

Grow the Business – The Service Strategy

An internal growth strategy that can pay huge dividends is the Service Strategy. Companies may develop a service business by offering service contracts on their products, aftermarket parts and installation, or even consulting services. This is one strategy that can be effective in driving revenues and perhaps margins of product sales, if the company is in an industry where better customer service results in increased customer loyalty.

There are several classic business case examples of companies that have driven growth in revenues, as well as profits through a focus on the service business. General Electric is one example, and IBM is another. IBM in the early 1990's found itself in an industry that was becoming increasingly commoditized. Hardware, which made up over 57 percent of total revenue in 1991, was slowing down, margins were being squeezed, and another industry based on software code was developing. In the three years between 1990 and 1993, gross profit margin dropped from over 50 percent to approximately 38.5 percent. Big Blue was in trouble.

In order to drive growth and profitability, Big Blue decided to focus on the services business. They have grown the services business to approximately 48 percent of total 2004 revenues, just over $46 billion. Remarkably, IBM's services revenue gross margin is just over 25 percent, near the 29-30 percent margins that they earn from hardware. Without this shift into services, Big Blue might very well have been Big Black & Blue now. Figure 10-5 shows IBM executing on the Service Strategy.

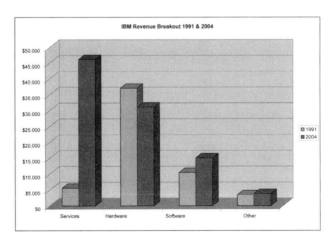

Figure 10.5

These changes are reflected in the abbreviated P&L statement shown below.

IBM P&L for years ended 12/31				
	1991	**1991 Margins**	**2004**	**2004 Margins**
Revenue				
Services	$5,582		$46,213	
Hardware	$37,093		$31,154	
Software	$10,498		$15,091	
Other	$11,593		$3,835	
Total Revenue	$64,766		$96,293	
COGS				
Services	$4,531	18.8%	$34,637	25.0%
Hardware	$18,571	49.9%	$21,929	29.6%
Software	$3,865	63.2%	$1,919	87.3%
Other	$5,106	56.0%	$1,776	53.7%
Total COGS	$32,073		$60,261	
Gross Profit	$32,693	50.5%	$36,032	37.4%

As management utilized a Services Strategy to grow their total revenues 48 percent, they also addressed the shrinking industry margins by restructuring their business. The result was so successful that at the same time gross profit dollars increased less than $4 billion, EBIT increased thirteen-fold to over $12 billion. The cuts in R&D and SG&A are shown below.

		% of Revenue		**% of Revenue**
R&D	$6,644	10.3%	$5,673	5.9%
SG&A	$21,375	33.0%	$19,348	20.1%
EBIT	$939	1.4%	$12,028	12.5%

Because he drove these changes in strategy so successfully, Lou Gestner will go down in the CEO Hall of Fame.

How to recognize the Service Strategy

1. Growth in service revenues.

2. Check gross margins to find the differences between the markets.

3. Check goodwill to see if the company is growing the Service Strategy via acquisition.

Grow the Business – The Innovator Strategy

In addition to growing the top line revenue, innovation can help companies to defend their pricing policies in rapidly changing markets. One company that is focusing on innovation to drive growth and profitability is Ultratech, Inc., a manufacturer of capital equipment for the integrated circuit industry. Since it is very expensive and difficult to install and integrate this equipment into the manufacturing lines, Ultratech is defending its market share by embarking on a strategy of innovation. Their innovation has resulted in a commercial product utilizing new Laser Processing technology that the company expects to be useful for many product generations.

Looking at the last several years of financial returns provides some insight as to the impacts of this strategy. First of all, the company realized a significant increase of 60 percent in sales revenue throughout a difficult industry cycle. Equally impressive is the growth in gross margins, which increased over 1.5 percent as they grew these sales. When we look at how they achieved this you can see that the company focused on R&D spending, and ramped up the sales process by increasing overhead significantly. Because of this double whammy, operating profits dropped. Without the payback in the revenue and gross margin side, this might be cause for greater concern.

These financial statements demonstrate that growth requires cash flow, and you can see that the company financed this growth strategy primarily through cashing in some of their marketable securities (short term investments) and taking out a larger line of short term credit, as their notes payable increased over $5.5 million.

Ultratech P&L for years ending 12/31			
	2004	**2003**	**2002**
Products	$93,392	$85,799	$52,400
Services	$16,500	$14,322	$16,106
Total Sales	$109,892	$100,121	$68,506
Products	$48,466	$46,999	$45,770
Services	$8,733	$6,511	$7,886
Total COGS	$57,199	$53,510	$53,656
Gross Profit	$52,693	$46,611	$14,850
R&D	$25,936	$21,309	$23,522
SG&A	$29,186	$23,058	$23,744
Total O/H	$55,122	$44,367	$47,266
Operating Profit	$(2,429)	$2,244	$(32,416)
Interest Expense (Benefit)	$(3,498)	$(4,024)	$(6,258)
Misc. +/-	$ -	$728	$(4,090)
Pre Tax Net Profit	$1,069	$6,996	$(30,248)
Taxes(benefit)	$445	$(570)	$(4,866)
Net Profit	$624	$7,566	$(25,382)

Using the short-term credit strategy tells me that they are expecting the tremendous returns from this strategy to happen quickly. As the cash flow statement points out, they also sold some additional stock to raise some capital.

Ultratech Balance Sheet as of 12/31	2004	2003
Assets		
Cash	$151,627	$165,902
Inventory	$27,842	$19,037
Total Current Assets	$201,539	$196,785
Total Fixed Assets	$29,007	$23,963
TOTAL ASSETS	$230,546	$220,748
Liabilities		
Notes Payable	$7,900	$2,564
Accounts Payable	$13,587	$7,729
Total Current Liabilities	$31,918	$26,284
Total LT Liabilities	$5,338	$3,725
TOTAL LIABILITIES	$37,256	$30,009
Equity		
Stock	$206,457	$204,528
Accumulated deficit	$(13,167)	$(13,789)
TOTAL EQUITY	$193,290	$190,739

Ultratech cash flow for period ending 12/31	2004	2003
TOTAL OPERATING CASH FLOW	$(10,459)	$11,677
Investing cash flow		
Capital Expenditures	$(9,868)	$(6,073)
Investments in securities	$(102,513)	$(165,056)
Proceeds from sales of investments	$137,195	$161,938
TOTAL INVESTING CASH FLOW	$24,814	$(9,191)
Financing Cash Flow		
Proceeds from ST debt	$37,900	$15,315
Repayment of ST debt	$(32,564)	$(22,584)
Proceeds from issuance of stock	$3,120	$12,055
TOTAL FINANCING CASH FLOW	$8,456	$4,786
TOTAL CHANGE IN CASH FLOW	$22,811	$7,272

How to recognize the Innovator Strategy

1. Growth in R&D and overhead accounts.

2. The cash flow statement shows increased investment in the business.

3. The company is raising cash through LT debt increasing, ST debt increasing, or additional issuing of stock.

4. Check the gross margins. A penetration strategy will put pressure on gross margins, but entering into new markets with a value strategy should defend or increase gross margins.

PROFIT STRATEGIES

Profit strategies are the specific actions that the company is undertaking to drive earnings growth. While the growth and operating strategies that we have discussed above are of course driven to drive profits, these tend to be focused on profit on an even shorter term.

Profit Strategies - The Right Sizing Strategy

Jack Welsh was once called "Neutron John" in his early days as CEO of GE. The Neutron Bomb was a weapon that the USA developed for tactical warfare that would explode and emit radiation, killing everyone around, but leaving the buildings intact. He earned this nickname because his continuous focus on productivity resulted in him firing thousands of workers, but keeping the factories around. If a company can continue to generate revenue with fewer employees, they become more productive, as measured by sales per employee.

One strategy for growing the business organically is to innovate. If the company does not develop the right products, or the adoption curve is slower than anticipated, the Innovator Strategy can quickly become the Pioneer Strategy. (There is a saying in business that the definition of a pioneer is a person laying face down in a puddle with an arrow in his back.)

Many companies that utilize the Right Sizing Strategy will take a charge against earnings for the costs associated with this strategy. Eastman Chemical reduced its total employees from 15,000 in 2003 to 12,000 in 2004, resulting in a charge against earnings as demonstrated in their financial statements below. These restructuring charges are outlined in the P&L statement as shown below.

Eastman Chemical		
For years ended 12/31		
	2004	**2003**
Sales	$6,580	$ 5,800
COGS	$5,602	$ 4,990
Gross Profit	$ 978	$ 810
Selling G&A & Overhead	$ 597	$ 588
Impairments and restructuring	$ 206	$ 489
Operating earnings (loss)	$ 175	$ (267)
Net Income	$ 175	$ (270)

You will always find the amount added back into the cash flow statement, because this is a non-cash charge.

Eastman Chemical		
For years ended 12/31		
Cash Flow from Operations	**2004**	**2003**
Net Earnings (loss)	$ 170	$(270)
Impairments and restructuring	$ 206	$ 489

While this restructuring resulted in big gains in productivity - sales per employee jumped from approximately $386K to over $548K - this strategy could also generate huge bottom line savings. For example, if you assume each employee had a fully burdened cost of $100K (this would include Social Security, state unemployment taxes, etc.) then this could result in an annual savings of $300 million per year. Now you are thinking like a CEO. While everyone realizes that losing this many employees may impact service to the customer and many other key results, these downsizings are generally done in concert with various organizational and process changes.

If you see restructuring charges several times over the recent past in a company's financial statements, this is a large, waving red flag. You can safely assume that there has either been significant management turnover, a complete failure in strategy, or a possible example of a company "managing earnings." When a company accrues for a charge such as restructuring, and then does not use all of it, the remainder falls back into earnings. This accounting fact, teamed with management's general philosophy that they should lump the bad news into one quarter, often results in companies overestimating what restructuring will truly cost. So when you see many recent restructurings, assume earnings management.

How to recognize the Right Sizing Strategy

1. The number of employees drops significantly from one year to the next.

2. The company reduces the number of factories, branches, or "storefronts."

3. The company shows a restructuring charge.

Profit Strategies - Kill The Dogs

Just as a laser beam is more powerful than a flashlight, companies often find that focusing on their key competencies – what they do best – is often the ticket to increasing profits. In any event, this strategy finds an executive who decides to sell the underperforming business units, or those that he has decided (sometimes differently than his or her decision just a few years prior) to divest. IBM provides a good example of a kill the dogs strategy over the past years as they have attempted to focus on selling the enterprise marketplace and letting others fight it out in the challenging consumer marketplace. Consistent with this strategy, on December 31, 2002, IBM sold its hard disk drive (HDD) business to Hitachi, Ltd. (Hitachi.) This business unit had sales that were dropping dramatically over the prior two years, and IBM was racking up losses of over $400 million. While this may have been viewed as an excellent buy from Hitachi's standpoint, for IBM it was clearly time to kill the dog.

While the purchase price was approximately $2 billion, like any contract the terms were negotiated so that IBM received $1.4 billion at closing, with the remainder to be received one and three years after closing. The net cash flow to IBM was just over $240 million in 2002, and $97 million cash inflow in 2003. While IBM received this cash on the deal, the P&L statement showed a loss from discontinued operations of $1,755 million in 2002, net of tax. Included in these losses was a loss on sale of $382 million.

While you can see these impacts to the financial returns in both the cash flow statement (cash from divestures) and the P&L (loss from discontinued operations), if you use the current financial return to look at past results, you could miss the business impacts of this unit, because GAAP requires the company to take these results out and "reformat" the past results. For example, looking just at the revenue line in the P&L for the 10-K reports for year ended 2001 and 2002, we see the following:

IBM for years ended 12/31 in millions	As reported in 2002 10-K Annual Report for Year End 2001	Reclassified 2001 to confirm with 2003 10-K Annual Report for Year End 2002
REVENUE		
Global Services	$34,956	$34,956
Hardware	$33,392	30,593
Software	$12,939	12,939
Global Financing	$3,426	3,426
Enterprise Investments/Other	$1,153	1,153
TOTAL REVENUE	$85,866	$83,067

When one looks at the notes to the financial statement, we find that the HDD business had revenues of $2,799 in 2001, the difference that we see between the initial 2001 return presented, and the reformatted presentation. Impacts from this divestiture flow all the way through the financial statements so that reformatted numbers can give us differences in everything from revenues, to operating profits, to equity. The net profit line will stay the same, but there will be a line for discontinued operations that will have either the profits or losses of these operations summarized there.

How to recognize the Profit Strategies – Kill the Dogs Strategy

1. Executives that divest are usually more than happy to tell shareholders about it in the letter to the shareholders, because after all, it does set a new agenda, can result in minimizing losses, and should generate to the lifeblood of the business, cash flow.

2. Look at the investing cash flow section of the cash flow analysis. Unless the company either gave the business away, or got taken to the cleaners in the negotiations, you will see some positive cash flow impacts from the divestiture.

3. Look at the miscellaneous +/- for discontinued operations. If discontinued operations shows a positive number, the company is making a strategic shift

out of the business, and they should have a strategy to replace these profits. While not all dog business units are money losers, if the discontinued operations number is negative, you can be sure that the business unit was a drain on their earnings and the company did the right thing by getting it off their books.

4. Companies that divest businesses often take restructuring charges. Keep in mind that this restructuring charge is spent over time, and as such the amount shown for restructuring will generally be put back into the cash flow statement.

5. The company can use the divested business funds in various ways, and as discussed earlier, this is the function of finance. If they use the proceeds of this sale to reduce their debt, look for the interest expense to be reduced on the P&L, which is almost always a good thing no matter what strategy was employed.

6. Depending on how many acquisitions the company also does, you may see a reduction in total assets. If there are not offsetting acquisitions, total assets will almost always be reduced. This makes sense, because if you are divesting of a business, you usually sell the assets of that business. This drop in assets could be reflected in a drop in goodwill or maybe fixed assets like property, plant & equipment.

Profit Strategies – Sell the Value Strategy

The Value Strategy is a brand driven strategy that focuses on a real or perceived value in its product versus the competition. In order to execute this strategy, the company must have some differentials over their competitors. Morton's Salt is an example of a company that has focused on the Value Strategy, as they have sold their table salt on value for a number of years. Morton was one of the early innovators in the salt industry, coming up with such innovations as a salt that would not stick together in wet weather, additives for cattle block salt, and salt substitutes. This innovator strategy contributed to growing sales, so Morton's decided to price their table salt at a premium. Supported by both marketing dollars and brilliance (fill in the blank, "When it rains, it _____") they remain the premium priced product for table salt.

Like Morton's salt, there are many brands that utilize a Sell the Value Strategy that you recognize. Nike shoes, Ralph Lauren clothes, Exxon Mobil gasoline,

GMC trucks and just about anything from Nordstrom. The value strategy requires significant marketing expenses, so you can expect companies to protect the value in their brand by having higher (or more effective) marketing expenses. Companies executing the Sell the Value Strategy will protect their margins at the cost of increased sales, which explains why you will never see Nike product in the bargain bin.

While the Sell the Value Strategy is easy to explain, its execution is loaded with land mines. As an example, let's look at professional football in the sixties. The American Football League was created in 1960 to fill America's insatiable appetite for professional football. Focusing mostly on cities where the NFL didn't have a franchise, the AFL was struggling for survival while the National Football League closed a major television contract to broadcast games on CBS. Prior to this deal, each NFL franchise had its own contract with smaller, regional broadcasters that were often undercapitalized. The NFL convinced CBS to focus on regional telecasts for the early game, and then follow them up with a nationally televised game. The power of a national network teamed with local exposure in each market resulted in professional football replacing Major League Baseball as not only the national pastime, but the national passion.

In order to appease the franchise owners who made most of their revenues by selling tickets, in the early 60's the NFL blacked out the local team's home games, and didn't put another game on to replace it. The AFL strategically aligned with NBC, and began filling this dead time with their games, taking advantage of a ready-made market already developed by the NFL. They captured so much market share so fast that within six years they forced a merger between the leagues. The NFL tried to differentiate itself by limiting its exposure and focusing on value, and the AFL took advantage of it and captured tremendous market share quickly.

How to Recognize the Sell the Value Strategy

1. Chances are, a company executing on this strategy will have stronger gross profit margins than their competitors.

2. If you read the word "brand" all over their 10-K's or annual report, you know they are trying to drive to this strategy.

Profit Strategies - Low Bid Buyer Strategy

One example of a company that has built an excellent business model on the

Like New Coke or whoever decided to invite Ozzie Osborne to sing *Take Me Out to the Ballgame* at Wrigley Field, the NFL made a key mistake trying to protect its image as the value added product. And this was a big one.

Low Bid Buyer Strategy is Cott Corporation, one of the finest companies that you have never heard of. If you have ever picked up a Safeway soda rather than a Coca Cola product, you are one of the people that do this hundreds of millions of times per year. They own approximately 68 percent of all private label carbonated drinks sold in the USA, 97 percent in Canada, and 38 percent in the UK. The gross profit margin tells the story as Coke sells value, and achieves gross profit margins of over 65 percent. Cott sells the low bid and sees gross margins below 20 percent. Since Cott isn't buying commercials during the Super Bowl, the Stanley Cup, or anytime, and really doesn't worry about driving a consumer to its private label brand, its SG&A expense is much lower than Coke's. While their EBIT pushed 26 percent, Cott's remains consistent at between eight and ten percent. Figure 10-6 shows a financial comparison between a Value Strategy and a Low Bid Buyer Strategy. They have carved out a niche on top of the Coca Cola Company, and they are profitable and in all likelihood, happy. Their shareholders certainly are, as since Cott went public in 2000 their shares have outperformed Coke's.

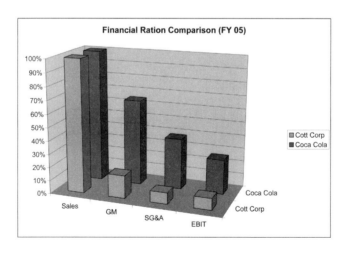

Figure 10.6

How to recognize the Low Bid Buyer Strategy

1. The company will generally have lower gross profit margins.

2. The company may embark on a follower or "me too" strategy.

3. Companies that follow this strategy often try to re brand their "me too" product in the hopes of protecting some additional gross profit.

4. Low Bid Buyers won't have the R&D expenses of market innovators.

Profit Strategies - Wallet Share Strategy

The Wallet Share Strategy allows companies to sell more to their current market channel by offering additional value added services. This strategy can range from the "no brainer" of cable companies beginning to offer high-speed internet connections to their customers to other strategies that sometimes are more difficult to see. FedEx had the Wallet Share Strategy in mind when they acquired Kinko's, the copying and document management retail outlet.

FedEx already had a partnership with Kinko's, which provided access to the full range of FedEx day-definite ground shipping and time-definite global express shipping services. Rather than continue this partnership, FedEx felt that complete control would allow them to increase their touch point into small businesses. Based on the 2004 10-k, Kinko's contributed $521 million in sales and $39 million in profits for a margin of 7.5 percent. Since this revenue and profit was not for the whole year, when you make that adjustment the sales figures round to between $2 to $2.5 billion, with profits, based on that 7.5 percent margin of just over $170 million. Based on an acquisition price of over $2.4 billion, FedEx paid just over fourteen times earnings. Kinko's had 1,220 outlets, each averaging just over $1.8 million in sales and just under $140,000 in profits per outlet. FedEx paid almost $2 million per outlet of Kinko's to execute their Wallet Share Strategy.

The main changes you will see in the financial returns are minimal impact to revenues and profits, but an increase of just over $1.5 billion in goodwill, $1.1 billion in long-term debt. FedEx is financing a significant amount of this acquisition through their short-term cash flow that they are generating by better current liabilities management.

How to recognize the Wallet Share Strategy

1. When a company is expanding into similar markets through acquisition of innovation, they are executing the Wallet Share Strategy.

2. This strategy will require financing of some kind. Look for additional equity sales or debt used to finance the growth into this strategy.

3. Note that if a company utilizes this strategy through a partial ownership of shares, if they own less than 20% of the company, they will not show any of the financial results on their financials. The 10-K will outline which other business relationships the company has.

OPERATING STRATEGIES

Companies have different strategies on how to operate what can be a vast network of factories, storefronts, divisions, clients, and assets.

Operating Strategies Expand the Brand Strategy

We showed how Wal-Mart executed a Grow the Business Storefront Strategy and drove sales by putting up more stores. However, they also executed an Expand the Brand Strategy, as the Wal-Mart name began to show up on different types of stores, increasing their sales per store by over ninety percent over the ten-year period 1995 to 2005. Looking at the Figure 10-7 you can see where Wal-Mart's growth really began to accelerate. Clearly, this was a company that was executing on their strategies.

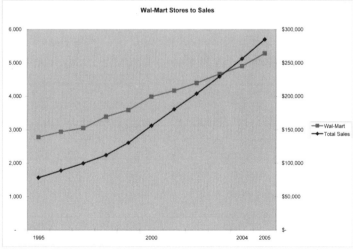

Figure 10.7

Today, Wal-Mart has a significantly different mix of brands than they did ten years earlier. Figure 10-8 shows the growth in Wal-Mart brands.

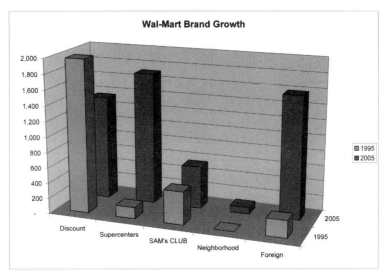

Figure 10.8

Another example of the Expand the Brand strategy was the 2003 acquisition of Airborne by DHL. DHL is a worldwide express mail and logistics company that just happens to also be the Deutche Post, or the German Post Office. While having significant world market share, they had very little market share in the largest single market in the world, the USA. DHL acquired the ground operations of Airborne and spun off the air express operations into ABX Air. Airborne's ground operations had sales of just over $1.25 billion, and with the acquisition DHL immediately became the third largest player in the US market. Their revenues for the Americas jumped over 50 percent., a gain of almost $1.5 billion. Due to double coverage and excess capacity across the North American market, they subsequently shut down many of their DHL offices, and integrated the Airborne operations into their brand. The 2,700 layoffs that they admitted to publicly will bring somewhere around $200 million annually to their bottom line. That in and of itself is a nice value proposition for the merger, unless, of course, you're one of the 2,700 who were laid off.

How to recognize the Expand the Brand Strategy

1. Most companies with a strong brand identity should probably try to embark on this strategy. This will be outlined in the 10-K under the "strategy" section.

2. If you are seeing the brand used in many different ways, you are witnessing the Expand the Brand Strategy. Think of Coca Cola Classic, Coke, Diet Coke, Caffeine Free Coke, Vanilla Coke, well, I'm sure you get the picture.

3. If the company is experiencing strong growth without the added investment of fixed assets this may be an indicator of this strategy.

Operating Strategies - The Fort Knox Strategy

Balance sheet decisions play a key role in operating strategies also. Companies that have efficient capital structures are able to raise debt capital at better rates than their competitors. If a company can borrow funds more efficiently, the obvious benefit is that they will end up repaying less interest. Just as important is their ability to go raise these funds quickly, offering much more flexibility to their business. Different industries tend to have different norms for capital. For instance, in the software industry, companies often have large amounts of liquid assets, either in cash or in marketable securities. In 2005 Standard & Poor's lowered their debt ratings on GM and Ford stock to junk status. As the stock market factors in expectations of future cash flows, that same day that this was announced GM's stock fell almost 6 percent, and Ford's was down over 4 percent. Standard & Poor's credit score for Toyota Motors during this same time was AAA.

An example of a company that utilizes the Fort Knox Strategy is General Electric. Taking a look at GE and some of the competitors that they face in their businesses demonstrates that yes, they in fact have more financial flexibility, and pay less in interest than their competitors.

General Electric Co.	AAA/Stable/A-1+	AAA/Stable/A-1+
Siemens AG	AA-/Stable/A-1+	AA-/Stable/A-1+
Emerson Electric Co.	A/Positive/A-1	A/Positive/A-1
United Technologies Corp.	A/Stable/A-1	A/Stable/A-1
Honeywell International Inc.	A/Stable/A-1	A/Stable/A-1

A complete discussion of how Standard and Poor's categorizes these classifications is in the chapter on financial markets.

How to recognize the Fort Knox Strategy

1. First of all, any company executing on this strategy will have an outstanding balance sheet.

2. Moody's or Standard and Poor's will have the company rated at their highest levels.

3. The interest rates that the company is paying on their debt and commercial paper will be less than their competitors, who are not able to execute to this strategy.

Operating Strategies - Fundamental Football Strategy

Some companies' strategy is to focus on what they do best, minimize risk, and grow as the market grows. Often, these companies will have similar year over year financial statements, and with the exception of economic slowdowns or dramatic industry changes they may continue in their niche. The best run of these companies can use the natural market growth to accelerate their growth beyond their competitors in the market.

Hurco Companies, Inc. is an example of a company executing this Fundamental Football Strategy to outdistance its competitors. Hurco manufacturers interactive computer controls, machine systems, and software and has been focusing like a laser beam on what they do best. While the market has driven some growth, let's take a look at what they delivered in 2004.

Finally, there is the strategy that far too many companies take. I call this the Buffalo Springfield Strategy, after their hit song that started off, "There's something happening here. What it is ain't exactly clear..."

Revenue grew twenty-six percent, and the accompanying gross margins increased jumped from 30.4 percent to 33.9 percent. This drove operating margins up from 8.9 percent to 13.1 percent, and worked like a lever on RONA, moving it from just over 12 percent to 17.5 percent. During this growth, they were able to become more productive, as sales per employee jumped 11 percent. This funded this internally generated growth by compressing their Cash2Cash Cycle from 133 days to 113 days.

This resulted in free cash flow increasing from $4.8 million to just under $9 million.

Hurco Fast Five Balance Sheet	2005	2004
Fixed asset %	22%	23%
Net working capital	$25,498	$17,821
Change in LT Debt	$(457)	$4,866
Change in goodwill	$329	$5,818
Leverage factor	1.6	1.9
Fast Five P&L		
Revenue Growth Rate	26%	32%
Gross Margin	33.9%	30.4%
Operating Margin	13.1%	8.9%
Change in Interest expense	$(113)	$(190)
Net profit margin	13.1%	6.3%
Fast Five Cash Flow		
Change in operating cash flow	$5,169	$6,808
Free cash flow	$8,937	$4,756
Sales & acquisitions of business	$	$
Debt capital financing	$(147)	$(4,052)
Equity capital financing	$797	$2,128
Fast Five Key Metrics		
Asset TO	1.3	1.4
Pre Tax RONA	17.5%	12.1%
After Tax RONA	17.5%	8.5%
ROE	27.9%	16.3%
Cash2Cash Cycle	113	133
Revenue per employee	$ 441,933	$ 398,288

The industry as a whole was up, but if you look at some other players in the industry, you will see that Hurco outperformed them, too, as demonstrated by the comparison chart below.

	Hurco	Hardinge, Inc.
Sales Growth	26%	32%
Gross Margin Increase	3.5%	0%
Increase in Rev/Employee	11.0%	9.7%
Cash2Cash Cycle in Days	113	259

In the next chapter, we will look at a company that is so focused on the fundamentals that you would think Vince Lombardi himself was the CEO. The company is Southwest Airlines and dominates the airline business like the Packers of the late 1960's.

How to recognize the Fundamental Football Strategy

1. A company executing this strategy will probably have financial statements that are similar in layout year after year.

2. If you see a company generating consistently better metrics, you know that they are focusing on doing what they do best.

3. Companies executing a Fundamental Football strategy won't have a lot of divestitures on their financials.

4. A Fundamental Football strategy will minimize, and perhaps even eliminate restructuring charges. While a company may certainly take these charges, you definitely won't see a Fundamental Football company taking them every year or two.

The Buffalo Springfield Strategy

There are CEO's who for whatever reason cannot focus their company's energies and investments on specific Profit Strategies. Without the ability to differentiate themselves, capture market share, or increase profits, they explore numerous different directions, and usually end up asking, "What happened?" The Buffalo Springfield Strategy.

Wall Street Selling Implications – Profit Strategies

This is one of the most critical sections in the Wall Street Selling Methodology™. By now you understand how to look at a company's financial returns and understand completely what they represent. If you can quantify this into the strategies that management is utilizing so we can begin to align and integrate our value proposition to these strategies.

Likewise, if the company is not executing on the strategies, you can begin to formulate your value proposition around helping them to change their strategic initiatives. If your product can help them to adapt to market changes and deliver greater results to "Wall Street," you will develop a compelling message.

It is only by understanding Profit Strategies that you can answer the inevitable WIFFM question that your sales team will encounter as they move up to the highest levels of the organization. (WIFFM is an acronym for "What's In It For Me.") Show the executives that you understand what they are struggling with and you will get their interest – and be another step closer to gaining their sponsorship.

The famous mathematician Archimedes was focused on a problem that he drew in the sand when his Roman captor ordered him to get moving. "Wait until I have finished my problem," were the last words he spoke, as the soldier killed him. Listen to whoever has the power.

The Business Lifecycle

The Wonder Years	*The Blunder Years*	*The Thunder Years*	*The Plunder Years*

How to Learn Any Industry in 30 Minutes or Less

IT HAD BEEN A TOUGH NINETY DAYS. In typical US big business fashion, the software company for whom I was working had tried to wring every last opportunity out of the pipeline to satisfy Wall Street. It ended up being a great quarter – for me, anyway. Although my team closed four deals selling supply chain software to the aerospace and defense industry (A&D industry,) it seemed like the companies in this unique industry needed our solutions about as much as the Pope needs a double bed. The software helped companies minimize its inventory, and increase its efficiencies in everything from design engineering to operations. To most companies, the idea of producing the same amount of sales with less working capital is a huge positive. If you can get that product manufactured in half the time while saving that investment in working capital, you can transform not just your company but the entire industry (see Dell Computers.) The accounts that my team were calling on were in the A&D market, where the rules were different.

Think of a Destroyer, for example. The US Navy orders a Destroyer in January of 2005 and expects delivery in, say, September of 2008. Just staffing the ship is a huge logistical investment, so they outline in the contract when they want it. And they don't want it early. Therefore, there is no value proposition for software to help them deliver it early.

As if that weren't enough, the accounting standards of A&D did not lend themselves to our value proposition. That destroyer is built cost plus, which means that whatever costs the company incurs they mark it up by an agreed upon percentage, and then bill the government. And since they billed what is called the percentage complete method, the bill for that Destroyer is sent out as the costs are incurred. These methods don't encourage productivity, and allow companies to influence both sales and profits by getting that inventory delivered on site early, not Just-In-Time. This was the environment that our team was operating under.

Some initial industry analysis allowed us to understand these nuances so that we could speak to the senior managers of these businesses understanding their operating environment, and seeking their input as to ways to impact their metrics and profits. Coming at the problem like this - after substantial pre call planning – we were able to integrate our value proposition into just a manufacturer of Navy ships. It seemed that the Navy, much like a typical customer, would change its mind about the features they wanted in its ships. If these changes came in later in the manufacturing, this caused our client to have to jump through hoops to deliver that ship on time, or to lose the incremental revenue by not accepting these change orders. We restructured our value proposition integrating our value with our customer's problems. The only way you will be able to do this is to understand the industry that you are selling to by understanding the nuances of the industry, and the strategies and financial returns of its players.

This chapter will outline a methodology that you can follow to understand the industry dynamics that your prospect – and their competitors – are in.

Looking at statements of publicly traded securities in the same industry will allow you to draw enough conclusions to help you understand the nuances of the industry. One thing working in your favor in this example is simple economics. In a free market, capital will move to the areas that are producing the highest returns. As this happens, businesses are created to handle the demand, increasing the supply. This in turn drives the price down and creates other opportunities in other markets. What this means in real life is that most companies in the same industry will have similar profitability numbers. Not exactly the same, but if there is a large difference, this will generally be reflected in the stock price.

The Product Lifecycle

The way in which this is played out can be summarized by something called the Product Lifecycle, and is shown in Figure 11-1. Interestingly enough, the concepts behind the product lifecycle can also be applied to companies in general. When you look at products – or companies – they are born, grow, and then either grow some more or die. The Product Lifecycle represents this lifecycle approach in four stages, the Wonder Years, the Blunder Years, the Thunder Years, and the Plunder Years.

Figure 11.1

As the name implies, when the product first comes out, management may be unsure of where it fits, how to price it, etc. They make a lot of mistakes, and are really **wondering** what is going on. From there, they begin to make changes to the strategies, maybe make some strategic mistakes, but despite of or because of these **blunders**, they begin to understand the market, the competition, and how to take advantage of their strategic differentials. This leads to the third stage, where they begin to "catch their stride" and really become profitable, and hopefully, dominant. They are truly **thundering** in the marketplace. After some time, the laws of economics take over, and other market entrants might begin to take market share. If the company cannot bring out new products, the product lifecycle begins to decline, with the product continuing sales, but at a decreasing level. The product, and company, begin to **plunder**. This product lifecycle curve can also be applied to companies. If a company cannot grow, introduce new products, perhaps gain entry into new markets, it will slowly – or sometimes not so slowly – die off.

The objective that companies have is to introduce new products at that point in the lifecycle where sales are beginning to diminish. This is a very difficult task, because introducing new products too soon could result in sales of the new product cannibalizing the older product. Product introductions need to be managed because they require investment in parts and inventory throughout the supply and logistics chain. Because of these and many other complexities, the ability to introduce new products in an efficient manner can be a strategic advantage for companies. (See Figure 11-2.)

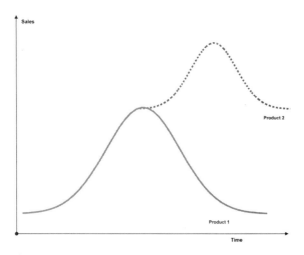

Figure 11.2

There are a number of items that we are going to check for in the financial returns of companies competing in the same or similar industries. Looking at these metrics over several industry players will allow us to draw conclusions about the industry as a whole. Like the analysis that we are doing on individual companies, it's important to keep in mind that these metrics will not provide all the information that we need all of the time. To cover this fact, we'll look at several categories of metrics, and compare these with their trends over several years to try to deepen the analysis. The categories that we will look at are:

- Competitive Structure
- Asset Structure
- Operating Environment
- Key Benchmarks

It is important to have a good understanding of the industry fundamentals, as the industry wields a tremendous influence over the profits and business financing requirements. The metrics we discuss in this book will allow you to make judgments as to the effectiveness of management in organizations.

Competitive Structure

The first thing that we will look at is the overall competitive structure of the industry. The more competitors the industry has, the more competitive pressure a company will see on its prices for its goods or services. Additionally, the concentration of these competitors will impact profitability, depending on where the company lies. In the Enterprise Requirements Planning (ERP) software industry in the late 1990's and early 200's, SAP was the dominant player with approximately 56 percent world-wide market share, and 38 percent market share in the US. The rest of the market share falls

No matter how well one may determine the company is managed, I like to keep in mind the quote by Warren Buffett that puts this all in perspective. "When a manager with a reputation for excellence meets a business with a reputation for difficult economics, it's usually only the business that leaves with its reputation intact.

to Oracle, PeopleSoft, JD Edwards, and then a bevy of smaller players. This concentration of market share in SAP forced consolidation in the industry, with Oracle, PeopleSoft and JD Edwards soon becoming the same company. Finally, in order to quantify this phenomenon, we'll look for the amount of goodwill on the company's balance sheets. As we'll learn in the next chapter, acquiring companies generally overpay for their acquisitions, and as such will carry a good amount of goodwill on their books (occasionally writing this off and generating a huge loss to net profits.) Some of the specific accounts we'll look at are:

- The number of competitors
- The concentration of competition
- The amount of consolidation demonstrated by the goodwill account

Asset Structure

After we look at the competitiveness of the industry, we will look at the asset structure the companies require to compete in this industry. This will help us to begin to understand what concentration and type of financing the companies must consider. These assets in turn generate sales. Different industries generate different sales from their asset bases, and require different amounts of "grease" in the form of working capital to keep the wheels turning.

We also want to understand the differences between fixed and variable costs associated with the various industry players. Looking at the gross profit margins and fixed assets on the balance sheets will help us to draw some conclusions in this regard. If a company has gross margins of greater than less than 50 percent, meaning a COGS of greater than 50 percent, they are more cost-sensitive than sales-sensitive. The same percentage increase in sales or a decrease in costs will result in a greater increase in profits if the company focuses its resources on decreasing costs.

	Original financial structure # 1	10% Decrease in Costs	10% Increase in Sales	Original financial structure # 2	10% Decrease in Costs	10% Increase in Sales
Sales	$100.0	$100.0	$110.0	$100.0	$100.0	$110.0
COGS	$51.0	$45.9	$56.1	$75.0	$67.5	$82.5
GP	$49.0	$54.1	$53.9	$25.0	$32.5	$27.5
O/H	$39.0	$39.0	$39.0	$15.0	$15.0	$15.0
EBIT	$10.0	$15.1	$14.9	$10.0	$17.5	$12.5
Increase in EBIT		51%	49%		75%	25%

If the company has gross margins of more than 50%, they are more sales-sensitive than cost-sensitive, as demonstrated by the same spreadsheet showing companies with gross margins over 50 percent.

	Original financial structure # 1	10% Decrease in Costs	10% Increase in Sales	Original financial structure # 2	10% Decrease in Costs	10% Increase in Sales
Sales	$100.0	$100.0	$110.0	$100.0	$100.0	$110.0
COGS	$49.0	$44.1	$53.9	$25.0	$22.5	$27.5
GP	$51.0	$55.9	$56.1	$75.0	$77.5	$82.5
O/H	$41.0	$41.0	$41.0	$65.0	$65.0	$65.0
EBIT	$10.0	$14.9	$15.1	$10.0	$12.5	$17.5
Increase in EBIT		49%	51%		25%	75%

Note that in each of these scenarios, we assume that an increase in sales drives the same percentage increase in direct costs, or COGS. There is also the idea of fixed costs that we want to address. Fixed costs do not increase as do variable or direct costs, until a certain sales increase drives capacity at that fixed level requiring an investment in additional fixed resources. As demonstrated in Figure 11-3, the most profitable place for a company to be is the maximum sales achievable without an increase in fixed costs. This is represented graphically by the red arrows.

The competitive market also influences industry profitability. For example,

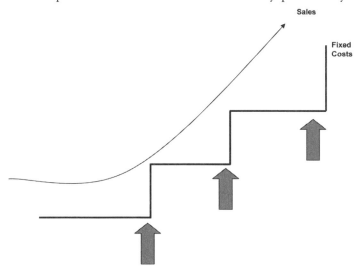

Figure 11.3

in the fall of 2005 the United States saw gas prices jump to unprecedented levels as the gulf coast was decimated by hurricanes. The result of the rapid price rise was an outpouring of sentiment among those buying gas that the oil companies were taking advantage of consumers. Since the people that buy gas also buy newspapers, watch news shows, and write emails to their congressmen, Congress acted and called the executives of five oil companies to Washington to grill them on their excessive profits. I pulled up the financial returns of the five companies involved, looking at quarterly statements for Q3 2005, Q3 2004, and complete year 2002 returns. Figure 11-4 shows that except for Shell, Exxon Mobil and all of the companies called to testify were marking up their cost of oil less as the price of oil was rising.

So how can you explain all of those large year over profit increases? Although the gross margins decreased, the absolute dollars increased, and since more expensive oil does not require additional investment in fixed costs the results of the additional dollars drop to the bottom line. There was no increase in fixed costs for the oil companies, because they were not increasing their profits due to additional capacity, or shipping additional barrels of oil; that oil just cost more. See Figure 11-5.

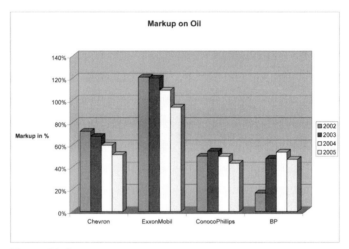

Figure 11.4

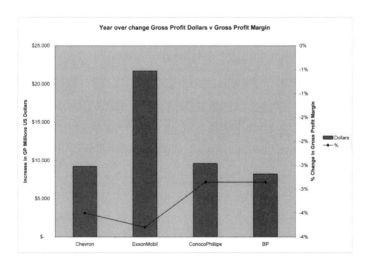

Figure 11.5

As we try to get our hands around the asset structure piece of the puzzle, we'll look at the following specifics in our financial returns:

- Asset Turnover – This will give us a good first look at the productivity of the company and industry. Some industries require significant assets to generate sales (an electrical utility may have to operate a coal plant, for example.)

- Debt/Equity – The higher the debt to equity ratio, the more risk the company is taking on, and the higher the interest payments will be. Since long-term debt generally finances fixed assets, we need to ensure that this additional debt is going to investments that bring in more than their capital cost.

- Net Working Capital % Sales – This ratio will give us an idea as to how the company is utilizing its short term operating assets.

- Leverage Ratio – This is a different take on the debt to equity ratio that will allow us to immediately quantify how changes in Return on Assets will drive equity value.

- Fixed Asset Ratio – Different industries have different asset structures. We want to understand what types of fixed asset requirements the industry is placing on the companies competing in this space.

The Issue: How various industries impact a company's operating environment, and how you can use this in your sales cycles.

The Work Involved: earn what it takes to recognize the different Profit Strategies; Growth Strategies, Operating Strategies, and Profit Strategies.

The Bottom Line: You will have the inside track to closing the deal if you can align your product or solution to your prospects Profit Strategies.

Operating Environment

We want to look at how the individual competitors get their sales, and the margins associated with these sales. This will require an analysis of the revenue buckets, cost structure, and associated margins. Sometimes, competitors in the same field have significantly different business strategies. In order to draw conclusions in this area of analysis, we'll try to get the following metrics:

- Product Line Revenue
- Product line profitability
- Cost Structure
- Gross Margin
- Operating Profit Margin

Key Benchmarks

Finally, we want to compare three key measures that will quickly tell us how efficient the company is at managing its balance sheet, its cash, and its individual productivity. The metrics that we will look at to help us judge the competitors as well as the industry are:

- Revenue per employee

A company's revenue per employee is an excellent means to uncover its core productivity. The higher the sales per employee, the more productive – in general – the company is.

- Cash2Cash Cycle

Figure 11-6 demonstrates the Cash2Cash Cycle.

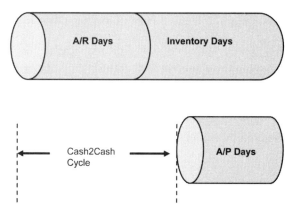

Figure 11.6

Several years ago, I was selling to both Honeywell Aerospace and General Electric, when GE tried to acquire Honeywell. I had intimate knowledge of both companies, and my idea that if the merger went through there would be a bloodbath at Honeywell was confirmed by a conversation I had with a GE executive. "Honeywell has huge inefficiencies that we can take advantage of. Their sales per employee are in the $200,000 range, while ours is up over $350,000. We'll have to decimate their organization to get the productivity up where in needs to be."

To bring our understanding to a defined metric that will tell us how the company has been doing in collecting its cash, we will look at both the balance sheet and the income statement, and turn the key metric into time. We'll look at the time it takes to turn the parts into products - emphasizing the manufacturing efficiencies - sell the product and then collect the cash from sales. We'll subtract from this the time the company is aging its suppliers, and the difference is the time that the company must finance its operations.

- Cash Flow Statement
- Break Even Point (BEP)

We are going to look at an industry in three specific ways. Although we might not get definitive numbers in each of the categories that we are looking at, a solid understanding will be gained by looking at them in aggregate.

Now that we have the framework we'll use to analyze an industry, let's take a look at several industries to see if we can glean some understanding of how they operate. As you do this in your sales cycles, you will be able to match your value proposition to the nuances of the industry and the specifics of your prospect's Profit Strategies.

Car Dealerships

Have you ever wondered just how much money your car dealer is making? After a quick search on the internet, I found five automotive distributors, who are technically classified as "specialty retailers." Taking a look at the three balance sheets for our automotive retailers, we see that the two largest companies have invested in more fixed assets than their three smaller competitors, whose current assets take up the lion's share of total assets, with a range of between 58 to 60 percent. As you would expect, a large investment in fixed assets is not required to generate sales in this industry, as anyone who has purchased a car in a dealer's metal building will attest to.

All of the industry players are heavily leveraged. Net working capital is as small as you will find it, with the totals ranging from an unbelievable sixth tenths of one percent (60 basis points for the banking industry readers) for the dominant player, Autonation, a high of just over 5 percent of sales for Asbury Automotive. These companies do not require the "grease that keeps the wheels of business going" because the automotive OEM's are supplying this for them. They are then using the long-term debt that they are raising to grow their business through acquisition, as demonstrated by the high amount of goodwill as compared to equity.

As of 12/31/04	Autonation	United Auto	Sonic	Group 1	Asbury
Assets					
Cash	$107,000	$11,061	$82,082	$37,750	$28,093
A/R	$773,000	$382,098	$306,498	$76,678	$148,196
Contracts in transit				$172,402	$105,350
Inventory	$2,640,000	$1,326,553	$1,046,909	$877,575	$761,557
Total Current Assets	$3,677,000	$1,764,136	$1,554,197	$1,205,215	$1,143,506
Goodwill	$2,976,000	$1,064,126	$909,091	$366,673	$461,650
Total Fixed Assets	$5,021,000	$1,768,665	$1,132,032	$742,005	$754,453
TOTAL ASSETS	**$8,698,000**	**$3,532,801**	**$2,686,229**	**$1,947,220**	**$1,897,959**
Liabilities					
Accounts Payable	$2,697,000	$1,487,862	$1,059,947	$957,180	$704,026
Total Current Liabilities	$3,411,000	$1,691,708	$1,196,929	$1,049,762	$847,510
Total LT Liabilities	$1,024,000	$766,058	$790,967	$330,284	$570,426
TOTAL LIABILITIES	**$4,435,000**	**$2,457,766**	**$1,987,896**	**$1,380,046**	**$1,417,936**
Equity					
Stock	$2,087,000	$769,154	$295,534	$248,243	$392,118
Retained Earnings	$2,176,000	$305,881	$ 402,799	$318,931	$87,905
TOTAL EQUITY	**$4,263,000**	**$1,075,035**	**$698,333**	**$567,174**	**$480,023**

Taking a quick look at the P&L statement, we can see that gross margins are similar, ranging from 14.7 to 15.7 percent, and operating profit, or EBIT, is within a range of 1.8 to 3.9 percent. We can see the importance of an access to capital, as the impact of interest expense allows the larger player, Autonation, to utilize its own capital to lessen the negative impact of the cost of interest to its Pre Tax Net Operating Profit. As a result, interest expense only consumes approximately 60 basis points as Autonation books a 3.3 percent pre tax NOP margin from a 3.9 percent EBIT.

Year end 12/31/04	Autonation	United Auto	Sonic	Group 1	Asbury
Sales	$19,424,000	$9,886,000	$6,422,000	$5,435,000	$5,301,000
COGS	$16,412,000	$8,436,000	$5,415,000	$4,603,000	$4,487,000
Gross Profit	$3,012,000	$1,450,000	$1,007,000	$832,000	$814,000
O/H	$2,246,000	$1,187,000	$772,000	$733,000	$671,000
EBIT	$766,000	$263,000	$235,000	$99,000	$143,000
Interest Expense	$157,000	$92,696	$62,329	$44,648	$60,504
Misc. +/-	$34,000	$9,263	$1,123	$(6,400)	$(1,059)
Pre Tax Net Profit	$643,000	$179,567	$173,794	$47,952	$81,437
Taxes(benefit)	$210,000	$67,880	$67,230	$20,171	$31,364
Net Profit	$433,000	$111,687	$106,564	$27,781	$50,073

It is difficult for these auto retailers to control the price of the OEM's cars they sell, so the avenue they have available to increase gross profit is to get more money for the cars by focusing on more effective negotiating. As this is becoming harder with the free flow of information that many purchasers have available, the best route for these companies to increase their gross profit is to focus on service sales, and the sales of used cars. Looking at the numbers confirms this, and the auto retailers are putting investment into this part of the business in order to increase overall returns. (See Figure 11-7.)

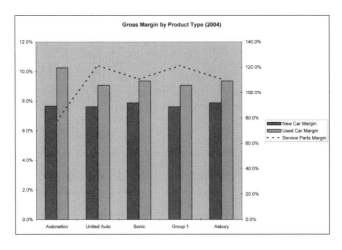

Figure 11.7

Insurance Industry

Insurance companies build a business on the idea of OPM – *Other Peoples Money.* Looking at the balance sheets of three publicly traded insurance companies, Metlife, Inc., Lincoln National Corporation, and Prudential Financial, Inc. shows us how OPM generates cash.

Each company's balance sheet shows that of total assets, Prudential has 83 percent of their assets in investments, while Metlife has 90 percent of its assets in investments. A deeper dive into the balance sheets gives us some insights as to the individual strategies these companies are undertaking. An insurance company holds two different kinds of investments on its books. Those investments it makes on its own behalf are under the investment category, while investments the company manages for other are tracked under an account called separate account assets. The assets in the separate account assets do not bear investment risk - to the insurance company, that is, and are not available for creditors should the company go bankrupt. The owners, of course, bear this investment risk. Lincoln National places more emphasis on managing others' money as they have almost half of their assets in this account. All three companies have the vast majority of their investments in fixed maturity assets.

Balance Sheet						
As of 12/31/04	Metlife		Lincoln		Prudential	
	Millions		Millions		Millions	
ASSETS						
Investments						
Fixed maturities	$176,763		$34,700		$153,715	
Equities	$2,188		$3,398		$4,283	
Mortgages	$32,406		$3,856		$	
Real estate	$3,981		$191		$	
Policy loans	$8,899		$1,870		$8,373	
Other investments	$10,748		$492		$50,253	
Total Investments	$234,985	66%	$44,507	38%	$216,624	54%
Separate account assets	$86,769	24%	$55,204	47%	$115,568	29%
Goodwill	$633		$1,195		$564	
Total Assets	$356,808		$116,219		$401,058	
LIABILITIES						
Contract liabilities	$190,713		$102,607		$177,530	
Other liabilities	$134,414		$6,174		$189,513	
ST debt	$1,445		$214		$4,044	
LT debt	$7,412		$1,048		$7,627	
Total liabilities	$333,984		$110,043		$378,714	
NET WORTH						
Stock	$16,216		$2,586		$19,493	
Retained earnings	$6,608		$3,589		$2,851	
Total Net Worth	$22,824		$6,175		$22,344	
TOTAL LIAB&NW	$356,808	15.6%	$116,218	18.8	$401,058	17.9

The liability side of the balance sheet consists of all the money that they are liable to give back, if asked. Insurance benefits consist of the interest credited to the accounts, and the –(according to these companies) *mortality experience*. The rest of the liabilities are primarily made up of the money that the insurers are borrowing.

With all that OPM coming in, the way that insurance companies make money is to earn both a stable and high spread between investment income and interest that must be credited to their policies. Correctly managing this asset liability strategy, (ALM strategy) directly impacts their profits, and has risks as interest rates both rise and fall. Since insurance companies generally guarantee a minimum return, if rates stay low, they run the risk of losing market share if they lower their minimum return. If they don't lower this minimum return, their interest margins are squeezed, resulting in lower returns to the shareholders.

So, these companies generally do better in a rising rate environment. If you find this hard to believe, look at what Lincoln National spells out in their 10-K.

The continuation of historically low interest rates creates a challenge for our products that generate investment margin profits, such as fixed annuities and universal life insurance.

P&L Statement						
Year ended 12/31/04	**Metlife**		Lincoln		Prudential	
	Millions		Millions		Millions	
Revenues						
Premiums	$22,316	57%	$298	6%	$12,580	44%
Policy fees	$2,900	7%	$1,586	30%	$2,317	8%
Investment income	$12,600	32%	$2,704	50%	$9,079	32%
Other income	$1,198	3%	$783	15%	$4,372	15%
Total	$39,014		$5,371		$28,348	
Policy benefits	$22,662	58%	$2,303	43%	$12,896	45%
Interest to policyholders	$2,998	8%	$100	2%	$4,819	17%
Dividends	$1,814	5%		0%		0%
Total COGS	$27,474	70%	$2,403	45%	$17,715	**62%**
Gross margin		30%		55%		38%
O/H	$7,761	20%	$1,931	36%	$7,346	26%
Pre tax profit	$3,779	10%	$1,037	19%	$3,287	12%

However, if rates rise too high too quickly, they could lose business as their clients will "cash out," crimping the flow of funds into the business. Insurers have assumed rates in their pricing model, and variation to these rates can also impact profits. Lincoln National refers to this as a lapse rate, and their laps rates were falling to only 8.9 percent in 2004 from 10.5 percent in 2002. Since these rates were less than assumed in the financial models, the impacts to profits were greater.

Lincoln is the most profitable of the three, with a pre tax net profit of 19 percent. Pre tax ROA is a metric that is used as a standard in the banking industry. Lincoln's ROA is .9 percent (90 basis points), .8 percent for Prudential, and 1.1 percent for Metlife. You won't find many companies with more sales per employee, with Metlife and Prudential just under $725,000 per employee, while Lincoln National's 5,441 employees generate just under $1 million in sales revenue per employee. Given these favorable metrics, as you can imagine, insurers generate tremendous cash flow, as shown by the chart below. Very few companies you look at will have operating cash flow three times their net after tax income, as Metlife and Prudential have. (See Figure 11-8.)

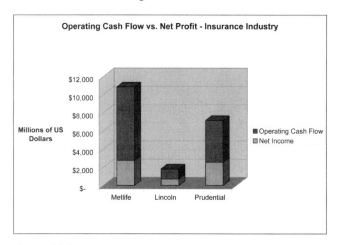

Figure 11.8

Each of these companies is in excellent financial shape, but I wouldn't be surprised to see Lincoln National as a possible acquisition target sometime in the future, as its market capitalization is just over $9 billion, less than a third of the others.

Banking Industry

We are going to look at several of the largest banks in the USA. JP Morgan Chase and Citigroup are large banking groups focused on many different markets, including corporate banking and investment banking. Washington Mutual (WAMU) is a consumer-focused bank.

When looking at a bank's numbers, net interest margin is roughly equivalent to gross profit margin, and Citigroup has the highest of the three banks here, which would lead us to assume that they are either more efficient, or get a better price for their products. This bears out as Citigroup has a quarter of its loans in foreign countries, where there is high demand for capital, and competes less in the ultra competitive retail market. Citigroup takes advantage of this strategy by receiving a much higher percentage of their income from fees than either JP Morgan or Wamu. JP Morgan has fewer than 10 percent of their loans in foreign countries and Wamu is focused on the domestic real estate market, where fully 98 percent of their loans are. With this strategy, Citigroup has a much larger provision for credit losses, as you would expect. Figure 11-9 shows these loan portfolios in a graphical format.

P&L Statement			
Year ended 12/31/04			
	JP Morgan Chase	**Citigroup**	**Wamu**
Interest Income	$30,595	$66,709	$11,350
Fee Income	$2,672	$16,772	$1,999
Total Non Interest Income	$21,790	$23,133	$2,310
TOTAL INCOME	$55,057	$107,445	$15,659
Interest Expense	$13,834	$22,086	$4,234
Net Interest Margin	$41,223	$85,359	$11,425
Net Interest Margin %	74.9%	79.4%	73%
Provision for credit losses	$2,544	$10,034	$209
O/H –	$34,359	$52,201	$7,535
Gain/loss on sale of investments	$1,874	$831	$303
Net income before taxes	$6,194	$23,955	$3,984
Income tax expense	$1,728	$6,909	$1,505
Net income	$4,466	$17,046	$2,479

Balance Sheet as of 12/31/04	JP Morgan Chase	Citigroup	Wamu
Assets			
Cash & equivalents	$56,848	$47,445	$4,537
Investments	$531,998	$694,149	$24,807
Loans (net of loan loss)	$394,794	$537,560	$205,770
Goodwill	$43,201	$31,992	$6,196
All other assets	$130,407	$172,955	$66,608
TOTAL ASSETS	**$1,157,248**	**$1,484,101**	**$307,918**
Liabilities			
Deposits	$521,456	$562,081	$173,658
Other Liabilities	$434,717	$604,819	$94,536
LT Debt	$95,422	$207,910	$18,498
TOTAL LIABILITIES	**$1,051,595**	**$1,374,810**	**$286,692**
Stockholders Equity			
Stock	$75,444	$7,137	$3,274
Retained Earnings	$30,209	$102,154	$17,952
TOTAL EQUITY	**$105,653**	**$109,291**	**$21,226**

A key indicator as to the strategy that a bank takes can be found by looking at the degree they are loaned out. Wamu has 118 percent of their deposits loaned out, whereas the business-focused banks have much less.

The notes to the financials spell out the types of loans that the banks are granting, and demonstrate their different strategies. Wamu has fully 98 percent of its loans secured by real estate. Real estate loans generally generate less risk, and in fact their provision for credit losses is only .1 percent, or 10 basis points.

Financial institutions often deal with numbers in the tenths of a percent, and in order to keep these numbers from getting too confusing, they refer to these as basis points. One percent is one hundred basis points. One half of one percent is fifty basis points. In the world of banking, fifty basis points can be a huge difference.

Some of the key metrics that banks use are shown in the chart below. The Capital Adequacy Ratio is important to C-Level banking executives, as it serves as the safety net of the bank, and is regulated. Anything below 5 percent is cause for

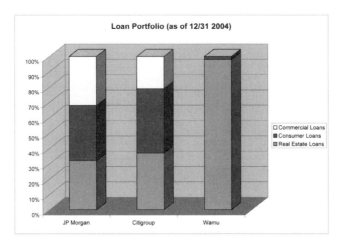

Figure 11.9

concern with banks, with that number raising to 7.5 percent for credit unions.

The provision for loan losses show how risky the bank's loans are. This number can be impacted by poor underwriting – taking on risky loans – or poor processes in the collections end. The loan product is also a huge contributor here, as the discussion regarding Citigroup's foreign loans show.

One of the challenges banks face is how to manage their loans and deposits, called Asset Liability Management in banking terms. While at first glance it seems that the answer is easy – get deposits and loan that money out at a higher rate – in practice it is much more complex due to constantly shifting rates, and different maturity dates on both the loans and the deposits. The measures below will help you to see how the C-Level executives are managing their business, and you can see that Wamu has a very aggressive loan strategy, as they have loaned out almost twice as much as a percentage of their assets as the other banks.

Finally, the yardstick for profitability in banking is Return on Assets, or ROA. C-Level bankers are constantly measuring themselves on this number, and as we can see below, the 34 basis points higher in ROA that Citigroup earns versus Wamu and the 76 basis point difference between Citigroup and JP Morgan Chase is the banking equivalent of the Harlem Globetrotter versus the NJ Generals.

Pull the bank's quarterly numbers from the sites we spoke about in Chapter Six, and be sure you are speaking in terms of these metrics when you sell to the banking industry.

Year End 12/31/04	JP Morgan Chase	Citigroup	Wamu
Capital Adequacy Ratio			
Net Worth / Total Assets	9.1%	7.4%	6.9%
Asset Quality Ratio			
Provision for credit losses / Loans	0.6%	1.9%	0.1%
ALM Ratio			
Loan / deposits	76%	96%	118%
Loans / total assets	34%	36%	67%
Earnings Ratio			
ROA	0.39%	1.15%	0.81%
Operating expenses / Assets	3.0%	3.5%	2.4%

Automotive Manufacturing

You don't have to look any farther than the stock market to see that US automotive manufacturers are in trouble. For the year ended 2004, Ford, GM, and Daimler Chrysler had combined sales of over $546 billion, and as of mid January 2006, a combined market capitalization of approximately $84 billion, or just over 15 percent of sales. Toyota had sales of approximately $171 billion, and a market cap of approximately $172 billion. Why the discrepancy? Let's look at our manufacturing efficiency metric to shed some light on this.

When looking at the financial returns of the US auto companies over the past ten to fifteen years, one can immediately see the focus that they put into manufacturing. One way to measure the operating effectiveness of a company is to look at the time it takes them to turn raw materials into sales. The inventory days metric gives us this insight. To take it to the next level, we can look at how long it takes them to manufacture their products through their factories. Since this is the main focus of a manufacturing company, this leads to much investment, and much lost opportunity if the manufacturing is not *World Class.*

To take a specific look at the manufacturing effectiveness, we can look at work in process days, which is the time, on average, that it takes the company to manufacture the product. Figure 11-10 shows how GM has focused on compressing the cycle time that they require to move product through their factory.

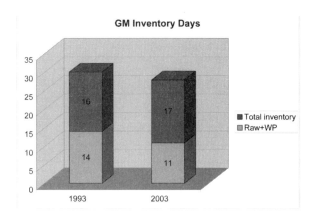

Figure 11.10

While this chart is certainly good news for GM and their investors, they still trail Toyota in manufacturing efficiency. The numbers above lump both raw material and work in process time together, because that is how Ford and GM display it in the notes to their financial statements. Toyota breaks out the WIP inventory, so we can tell that it takes, on average, four days to move products through their factories. In addition to the investment this requires in fixed assets, every day of inventory costs GM over $400 million, so those four extra days free up over $1.2 billion for Toyota. That cash can be used for, among other things, paying their suppliers quicker in order to gain price concessions. Toyota pays its suppliers in about 104 days on average. GM and Ford each stretch their suppliers, on average, 250 days. When you add in the costs for expensive union direct labor, you find that Toyota's gross margin is over 18 percent, while the US carmakers remain under 8 percent. (See Figure 11-11.)

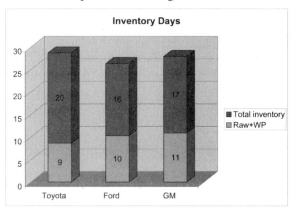

Figure 11.11

While Ford and GM have made giant strides to match the manufacturing effectiveness of Toyota, they still considerably trail in just about any measure of productivity. The chart below shows the effectiveness of the organization in generating revenue from employees, as well as assets. Figure 11-12 shows this productivity comparison.

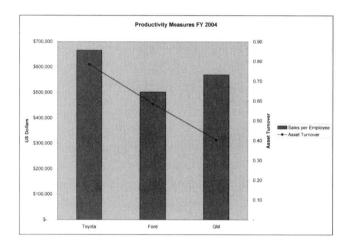

Figure 11.12

As you can see, Toyota is significantly more productive than either GM or Ford. When you also consider the huge amounts of cash flow that must go to fund pension liabilities and the difficulty in raising cash in the debt and equity markets, you realize how difficult it will be for American automotive manufacturers to compete and win against Toyota.

Airline Industry

The market capitalization for Southwest Airlines in early March of 2005 was over $11 billion. The market capitalization of United Airlines, American Airlines, Delta Airlines and Northwest Airlines was less than $3 billion – combined. How did these carriers get into such a mess? Let's see if their financial returns provide any insight. The chart below summarizes some key financial metrics of the five different airlines. Let's see if we can take a closer look at how these companies are competing in this industry.

Airline	Market Cap	Employees	Sales	Assets	Rev / Emp	Asset TO
NW Airlines	$595	39,342	$11.30	$14.0	$286,691	0.80
Delta	$645	69,250	$15.0	$21.8	$216,635	0.69
United	$118	58,900	$13.70	$20.7	$233,005	0.66
American	$1,460	92,100	$18.60	$28.8	$202,443	0.65
SW Air	$11,250	31,011	$6.50	$11.3	$210,570	0.57

Surprisingly, you see that the most efficient airline of the bunch, based on revenue per employee and asset turnover, two measures of productivity, is NW Airlines. SW Airlines is the most inefficient, based on these measures. However, when we look at their balance sheets, we begin to see a big difference. Every airline except Southwest holds a tremendous amount of long-term debt, and is in fact insolvent. Remember, when your liabilities exceed your assets, your assets in jail. Right Mr. Skilling?

Looking at a vertical analysis allows us to begin to see some problems that the traditional carriers have. Interestingly enough, this also shows us that Southwest Airlines does not have the lowest labor cost. What they do have is a focus on what they do best. They didn't try to expand into additional markets too quickly, and don't fly into unprofitable markets. The major airlines do, and oftentimes lose money doing it. You can see this in the P&L below, because Southwest does not pay anything to regional carriers.

In order to capture the feeder traffic, the major airlines pay regional carriers to use their name and services. Not only do they pay these regional carriers, but they lose money on the deal, too.

While the increase in fuel has hit the industry hard, Southwest Airlines saw their fuel prices rise only about 30 percent over the last three years, while most of the other airlines have seen increases of over 50 percent. Although Southwest uses the same fuel as the others, they purchase this fuel on advanced contracts, which allows them to lower their prices.

Balance Sheet	Delta	American	Northwest	United	Southwest
PERIOD ENDING 12/31	**2004**	**2004**	**2004**	**2004**	**2004**
Assets					
Current Assets					
Cash & Equivalents	$1,811	$598	$707	$2,100	$1,305
Short Term Investments	$336	$2,809	$1,904	$78	-
Net Receivables	$731	$836	$460	$1,047	$248
Inventory	$203	$488	$217	$234	$565
Total Current Assets	$3,606	$4,971	$3,578	$3,914	$2,172
Property Plant and Equipment	$16,556	$19,137	$8,270	$14,174	$8,723
Goodwill	$227	-	-	-	-
TOTAL ASSETS	21,801	$28,773	$14,042	$20,705	$11,337
Liabilities					
Current Liabilities					
Accounts Payable	$3,481	$6,212	$2,145	$5,558	$1,996
Total Current Liabilities	$5,941	$7,018	$4,497	$6,461	$2,142
Long Term Debt	$21,656	$13,524	$8,023	$301	$1,700
TOTAL LIABILITIES	$27,597	$29,354	$16,866	$28,385	$5,813
Net Worth					
Common Stock	($1,423)	$182	$1	$1	$790
Retained Earnings	($4,373)	$1,294)	($1,999)	(7,946,000)	4,089,000
TOTAL NET WORTH	(\$5,796)	(\$581)	(\$3,087)	(7,680,000)	5,524,000

P&L Statement	Year Ended 12/31/04		
Operating Revenues	United	Northwest	Southwest
Passenger	76%	75%	96%
Regional Carriers	12%	10%	0%
Cargo	4%	7%	2%
Other operating revenues	8%	8%	2%
TOTAL REVENUES	100%	100%	100%
Operating expenses			
Salaries and related costs	31%	34%	37%
Aircraft fuel	18%	20%	15%
Regional affiliates	15%	11%	0%
Purchased services	9%	0%	0%
Landing fees and other rent	6%	5%	6%
Depreciation and amortization	5%	6%	7%
Aircraft maintenance	5%	4%	7%
Cost of sales	4%	0%	0%
Aircraft rent	3%	4%	3%
Commissions	2%	0%	0%
Other operating expenses	8%	21%	16%
TOTAL COSTS	105%	104%	92%
EBIT	-5%	-12%	8%
Interest expense	-3%	-5%	-1%

After surviving the competitive environment and incurring additional fuel costs, the carriers then get hit with the cost of all that debt we looked at above in the form of interest expense. Based on the industry returns we are seeing (except for Southwest and a few other niche players) pigs might have a better chance of flying – and surviving - than these companies. Cash in those frequent flyer miles and buckle up. It's going to be a bumpy ride and an even rougher landing.

Movie Theaters

The movie theater business used to be highly fragmented, but in today's competitive environment it is dominated by four companies: AMC, Cinemark, Regal Entertainment Group, and Carmike Cinemas, Inc. The first thing we see is something that anyone who has ever attended a movie suspected: the theater makes more margin from the popcorn than from the movie itself. While only making up from 26 to 33 percent of sales, concessions provide from 36 to 49 percent of gross profit, as the gross margins for concessions run from 85 to 90 percent. Admissions still make up approximately two thirds of revenues, with a still strong gross margin of 47 percent. The majority of the gross profits are eaten up by overhead in both Regal and Carmike, who see 47 percent of revenues going towards overhead. This overhead will probably require a lot of fixed assets, and in fact the balance sheet shows that Regal has 76 percent of their assets tied up in land, property, and equipment, while Carmike has 73 percent of their assets tied up in the same.

P&L	Regal		Carmike		Regal	Carmike
Year ended	12/30/2004	1/1/2004	12/31/04	12/31/03	Regal	Carmike
Revenues						
Admissions	$1,657	$1,690	$331	$332	67%	67%
Concessions	$636	$646	$162	$161	26%	33%
Other Revenue	$173	$153	$	$	7%	6%
Total Revenue	$2,466	$2,489	$493	$ 493	100%	106%
COGS						
Film rental	$878	$908	$174	$180		
Cost of concessions	$94	$92	$16	$17		
Total COGS	$972	$1,000	$190	$197	39%	39%
Gross Profit	$1,494	$1,489	$303	$296	61%	61%
O/H	$1,173	$1,110	$232	$225	48%	47%
EBIT	$321	$379	$71	$71	13%	15%
Interest expense	$95	$72	$26	$42	4%	5%
Misc. +-	$(84)	$(1)	$3	$3		
Pre Tax Net Profit	$142	$306	$48	$32	6%	10%
Taxes(benefit)	$59	$121	$18	$(74)		
Net Profit	$83	$185	$30	$106		

The investment in fixed assets requires both of these companies to raise debt capital. More debt leads to more interest expense, as well as operating risk. Regal's times interest earned dropped from 4.5 to 3.4 times, while Carmike increased their times interest earned from 1.7 to 2.7 times.

In Millions	Regal 2004	Regal 2003	Carmike 2004	Carmike 2003
EBIT	$321	$321	$71	$71
Interest Expense	$95	$72	$26	$42
Times Interest Earned	$321/$95 3.378947	$321/$72 4.458333	$71/$26 2.730769	$71/$21 1.690476

You will also note on the Regal balance sheet that the company's net worth dropped by over $700 million, while LT debt increased by over $500 million. While the consolidated statement of stockholders equity will outline what happened in this account, the cash flow statement below will also provide some insight as to what happened.

	Regal	
Balance sheet as of	12/30/2004	1/1/2004
Assets		
Cash	$243	$288
A/R	$49	34
Inventories	$7	$6
Total Current Assets	$321	$354
Property Land	$1,934	$1,817
Goodwill	$213	$197
Total Fixed Assets	$2,221	$2,095
TOTAL ASSETS	$2,542	$2,449
Liabilities		
A/P	$182	$194
Current portion LTDebt	$260	$31
Total Current Liabilities	$644	$390
Total LT Liabilities	$1,829	$1,265
TOTAL LIABILITIES	$2,473	$1,655
Equity		
Stock	$46	$730
Retained Earnings	$23	$64
TOTAL EQUITY	$69	$794

Looking at the cash flow statement will allow you to immediately see that the company paid $842 million in dividends in 2004, following dividends payments of $799 million in 2003. The cash flow statement also demonstrates that the company is doing an outstanding job of acquiring other assets, as they invested $223 million in cash and only increased the goodwill account by $16 million.

Regal Entertainment Group Cash Flow Statement		
For year ended	12/30/2004	1/1/2004
Operating Cash Flow		
TOTAL OPERATING CASH FLOW	**$387**	**$476**
Investing Cash Flow		
Cash for acquisitions	$(223)	$(97)
TOTAL INVESTING CASH FLOW	$(306)	**$(181)**
Financing Cash Flow		
Cash used to pay dividends	$(842)	$(799)
Payments on LT Debt	$(926)	$31
Proceeds from LT Debt	$1,650	$315
TOTAL FINANCING CASH FLOW	**$(126)**	**$(281)**

Casinos

Everyone knows that those casinos in Las Vegas and elsewhere aren't built by the winners. Looking at some financial statements of various casinos, let us see what is really going on. Harrah's and Las Vegas Sands are primarily in the Las Vegas market, while Trump Hotels is in the Atlantic City Market, and Ameristar has hotels in the smaller markets of Kansas City, St. Louis, Mississippi, etc.

Harrah's is the only one of the group that gets the greatest gross margin from gaming. Now, that being said, the largest gross margin dollars are brought in by the gaming operations for all of the companies, although for the Las Vegas properties, gaming operations only bring just over 50 percent of all gross profits. While gaming certainly drives the business, it looks like the Las Vegas players really have diversified into other profitable areas.

P&L	2004	2004	2004	2004
Revenues	Harrah's Entertainment	Trump Hotels	Las Vegas Sands	Ameristar Casinos
Casino	$3,214,888	$1,210,065	$708,564	$856,901
Food & Beverage	$665,515	$130,498	$121,566	$114,010
Rooms	$390,077	$79,200	$312,003	$26,082
Other	$217,195	$44,570	$116,437	$23,166
TOTAL REVENUES	$4,487,675	$1,464,333	$1,258,570	$1,020,159
COGS				
Casino	$2,061,642	$570,892	$340,241	$379,909
Food & Beverage	$278,107	$46,605	$64,176	$63,758
Rooms	$66,965	$29,063	$77,249	$6,565
Other			$60,055	$13,687
TOTAL COSTS	$2,406,714	$646,560	$541,721	$463,919
GROSS MARGINS				
Casino	64%	47%	48%	44%
Food & Beverage	42%	36%	53%	56%
Rooms	17%	37%	25%	25%
Other	0%	0%	52%	59%
O/H as % sales	23%	19%	14%	15%
Depreciation as % sales	7.3%	7.0%	5.5%	7.2%

Finally, the depreciation as a percentage of sales shows that these casinos, despite popular belief, aren't built for cash. In fact, LT Debt to equity is greater than 1X for all the companies, a metric that would certainly seem high in most industries. (See Figure 11-13.) The Trump Hotel's long term Debt to equity is not shown in the chart due to scaling reasons. It is over 300X. This industry is about as close as one can get to truly printing money. As the gambling public drives these companies to invest in additional capital improvements and more glitz and glitter, they can finance the investment because if you build it, people will come.

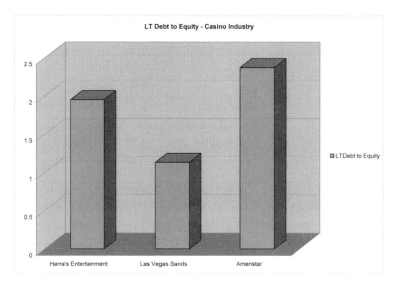

Figure 11.13

Professional Sports

Most professional sports franchises in the U.S. are closely held businesses, but one team that was listed and traded on the NYSE was the Boston Celtics Limited Partnership. The stock underwent reorganization after the Taxpayer Relief Act of 1997 and no longer trades publicly, but the June 30 year-end statements in 1998 give us a good insight as to the industry of professional basketball in the mid to late 90's.

You can begin to see the league economics changing as the Celtics COGS increased by 42 percent. This shift is even more dramatic when you look at the makeup of the COGS over a five-year period from 1994 to 1998. The cost of the team increased from $22.5 million to almost $40.5 million, while the direct costs on a game basis stayed the same. There was something happening in the industry-- even though you can see that the team had a pre tax net margin of over 18 percent.

Boston Celtics Limited Partnership			
P&L For years ended June 30	1998	1997	1996
Sales	$75,679	$62,997	$64,780
COGS	$43,221	$43,327	$30,497
Gross Profit	$32,458	$19,670	$34,283
O/H	$18,658	$18,948	$18,333
Operating Profit (EBIT)	$13,800	$722	$15,950
Interest Expense (Benefit)	$385	$737	$1,787
Misc. +/-	$(18)	$361	$(101)
Pre Tax Net Profit	$14,167	$1,820	$17,636
Taxes(benefit)	$1,900	$1,400	$1,850
Net Profit	$12,267	$420	$15,786

Since much of a professional basketball team's income from single games comes from season ticket holders, they are getting a good deal of cash up front. As you can expect, the treasury function that manages this cash flow is extremely important. You can see that much of the investing cash flow is the buying and selling of securities.

Boston Celtics Limited Partnership		
For the year ended June 30	1998	1997
Operating Cash Flow		
TOTAL OPERATING CASH FLOW	$16,301	$2,461
Investing Cash Flow		
Capital Expenditures	$(384)	$(136)
Purchase of Securities	$(789,121)	$(637,882)
Sales of Securities	$757,682	$665425
TOTAL INVESTING CASH FLOW	$(31,939)	$26,965
Financing Cash Flow		
Increase in LT Debt	$80,000	
TOTAL FINANCING CASH FLOW	$17,401	$(28,910)
NET INCREASE (DECREASE) IN CASH	$1,763	$ 516

Looking at these financial returns may give us an insight as to how the industry operates, but like you could see from the COGS section of the P&L, the business has changed. The best summary of this "salary inflation" is a quote by Joe DiMaggio.

"If I were sitting down with George Steinbrenner (to discuss a salary) and based on what Dave Winfield got for his statistics, I'd have to say, 'George, you and I are about to become partners.'"

The chart below outlines the changes that modern sports economics has brought to the business of sports.

	1985-86 Season		2004-5 Season	
League Minimum	$70,000		$385,000	
Average Salary	$370,104		$ 4,900,000	
		(millions)		(millions)
Top Team Payrolls	1. Lakers	$ 8.6	1. Knicks	$101.0
	2. Nets	$ 6.8	2. Mavericks	$90.2
	3. 76ers	$6.8	3. Trail Blazers	$84.5
	4. Knicks	$ 6.7	4. 76ers	$71.8
	5. Celtics	$6.6	5. Timberwolves	$70.2
		millions)		millions)
Top Player Salaries	1. Magic Johnson	$4.5	1. Shaquille O'Neal	$27.6
	2. Moses Malone	$2.1	2. Allan Houston	$17.5
	3. K. Abdul-Jabbar	$2.0	3. Chris Webber	$17.5
	4. Larry Bird	$1.8	4. Kevin Garnett	$16.0
	Jack Sikma	$1.6	5. Jason Kidd	$14.8
			5. Jermain O'Neal	$14.8

Additionally, many sports owners now own their own stadiums, and generate significant amounts of revenues from that income stream. Rather than lease the stadium and show a net outflow for the lease, they now have an earning asset and show a cash outflow to cover the debt that they took out to build the stadium. Of course, in many instances a fair amount of the financing was picked up by the taxpayers. So in some small way, you're helping to underwrite A-Rod's lavish lifestyle.

"Free Labor" – Prison Industries

The Utah prison system has a business that utilizes the captive labor of prisoners as labor. While we all know of the cliché of prisoners making license plates, which they do at the Utah Correctional Institute (UCI) organization, they also have a diversified reach into many different enterprises, as varied as furniture manufacturing to computer repair, to data entry, and even roofing operations. While the prison system maintains the main objective of this enterprise is to teach inmates functional skills that will be valuable once they are released, the organization did do over $12 million in their fiscal year ending June of 2002. As you would expect, revenue per employee is about as low as you will find it, at just under $20,000 per employee.

Utah Correctional Institute (000's)				
As of 12/31	**2002**	Year Ended 12/31	**2002**
Assets			
Total Current Assets	$3,774	Sales	$12,880
Total Fixed Assets	$2,013	COGS	$9,402
TOTAL ASSETS	$5,787	Gross Profit	$3,478
Liabilities		O/H	$2,660
Total Current Liabilities	$852	Operating Profit	$818
Total LT Liabilities	$1,190		
TOTAL LIABILITIES	$2,042	Interest Expense	$
		Misc. +/-	$(130)
equity		Pre Tax Net Profit	$688
Stock	$3,041		
Retained Earnings	$704	Taxes(benefit)	$
TOTAL EQUITY	$3,745	Net Profit	$688

While the system has a number of different companies, you can see that they are keeping the selling price down, as shown by their gross margins of about 27 percent. The ROE of over 18 percent is one that the taxpayers of Utah are probably pleased with.

The Vatican

In April of 2005, there were many stories about the finances of the Vatican, and I decided to see if I could develop a balance sheet and income statement from the information that was being distributed. The Vatican does not publish its financial statements, but gives instead a news conference once a year to discuss the situation of the Vatican[1]. Since the Vatican has three distinct and different entities; I tried to take the bits and pieces of information in the news, and apply some logic and experience to it and consolidate the Holy See (the Pope and his works and Vatican dignitaries), and Vatican City (the buildings and operation of the Vatican City.) The only information available on the Vatican Bank was the 1996 book ``Inside the Vatican" by Thomas Reese, a U.S. Jesuit priest, who said that the bank had at that time approximately $4 billion in investments. Depending on how the bank is run, this could be placed in investment accounts, or loaned out and multiplied many times over, and since it is difficult to assume which I left it out of the analysis.

While most of the income accounts I got from various news sources and the official Vatican press conference on the financial results, I backed into the investment number. Since 2003 saw the dollar lose 17 percent against the Euro, and we know the loss from this exchange rate risk was 32.8 million Euros, assuming this loss was realized and from the cash account, that gives us a cash balance of 193 million Euros, or $237 million dollars. Assuming a 50 basis point return on the Vatican's cash account (.5 of 1 percent) gave us an investment income from their "sweep accounts" of 970,000 Euros. In order to get the almost 33

The movie theatre industry has one of the lowest revenues per employee ratios you will see, with Regal generating just over $97,000 per employee, and Carmike generating just over $63,000 per employee. This ratio works for these companies because many of their employees – 47 percent in Carmike's case – work for minimum wage. Now that's a scary ending.

---

1 Since these are not published, I found the information I used for these statements from articles written by Gregory Viscusi on April 6th for Bloomberg, and AP article by Victor L. Simpson, as well as an article covering the Vatican finances at Znit.org

million Euros left that their investments showed, I assumed a 5 percent return on these investments, arriving at the amount of just under 657 million Euros. These organizations employ a total of approximately 4,000 employees, and have seen employee headcount increase since the Vatican Secretariat of State began holding formal diplomatic relations with over 170 countries.

Consolidated Vatican Income Statement for period ending July 31, 2003	Millions of Euro's	Millions of Dollars
Revenue	2003	2003
From churches	$79.60	$97.84
Real Estate Income	$49.50	$60.84
Media Income	$40.70	$50.03
Investment income	$33.80	$41.55
Total Revenue Holy See	$203.60	$250.26
Total Revenue Peters Pence	$45.40	$55.80
Total Revenue Vatican City	$145.90	$179.34
TOTAL CONSOLIDATED REVENUE	**$394.90**	**$485.40**
Expenses		
Exchange Rate Loss	$32.80	$ 40.32
Financial Loss	$11.60	$14.26
Media Expenses	$ 41.90	$51.50
O/H Expenses Holy See	$99.40	$122.18
O/H Expenses Vatican City	$154.70	$190.15
Peter's Pence assistance	$ 45.40	$55.80
Real Estate Expenses	$27.10	$33.31
Total Expenses	$412.90	$507.52
Operating Profit (Deficit)	($18.00)	($22.12)

Each Catholic church is "owned" by its parish as an independent stand alone not for profit organization. As such, these individual churches are not part of the Vatican's assets. The Vatican does "own" its own parish, as well as a significant amount of the most valuable art in existence. Since it is impossible to put a price on many of the Vatican's art treasures, they are listed on the Vatican balance sheet at 1 Euro each. While at first this seems like it significantly understates the obvious, upon further review it is probably as good a measure as any. The Vatican art can't be used as collateral for debt equity, and Italy won't allow any of these treasures to leave, but they do produce a significant amount of cash flow that could be valued on the asset section of the balance sheet. The problem is that the net cash flow produced by these treasure was negative, something that could be addressed by more market-based pricing.

Consolidated Vatican Balance Sheet	Millions of Euro's	Millions of Dollars
Assets		
Cash	$193.00	$237.23
Investments	$656.70	$807.19
Real Estate	$908.00	$1,116.08
TOTAL ASSETS	$1,757.70	$2,160.51
Liabilities		
Deposits	$	$
TOTAL LIABILITIES	$	$
Net Worth	$1,757.70	$2,160.51
TOTAL NET WORTH	$1,757.70	$2,160.51

What the Vatican is facing is no different than a company that embarks on a growth strategy. The number of Catholics more than doubled in the last thirty-five years, and this growth requires cash, making the last three years of running deficits even more difficult for the Vatican. While the Holy See is obviously not a corporation, they can address these issues with some fundamental football strategies that address the controllable aspects of their business.

The Vatican should optimize its pricing model for its art, and the Vatican City attractions. It should reorganize the Vatican media business to become more productive within the organization, and raise equity capital to offset further growth costs. Equity capital for the Vatican would mean to press for more donations from the far-flung Catholic dioceses, especially those in the United States who donate over a third of the income from churches. Of course, the tradeoffs to what seems like a logical fix to the Vatican's financial situation is that they are in the business of running the largest religion in the world, being a beacon of light and hope to mankind (at least the Catholics), and not just focused on bottom line profits.

The industry summary below will summarize some of the key metrics that you will want to understand when analyzing an industry. While an individual metric may not yield the insight that we are looking for, when taken in whole and in comparison with others in the industry, the information below is the minimum that you should investigate to get the answer.

INDUSTRY SUMMARY
Competitive Structure
Number of Competitors
Concentration of Competition
Goodwill
Asset Structure
Asset Turnover
Debt/Equity
Net Working Capital % Sales
Leverage
Fixed Asset Ratio
Operating Environment
Product Line Revenue & Margin
Cost Structure
Gross Margin
Operating Profit Margin
Key Benchmarks
Revenue per employee
Cash2Cash Cycle
Cash Flow Statement
Break Even Point (BEP)

Wall Street Selling Implications – Industry Analysis

"We're unique."

Those are the two words that no salesperson wants to hear, because if a prospective client says this, he believes it, and your sales challenge just got a lot bigger. The way to overcome this issue is to address it early by showing that you understand their situation, their company, and their industry.

This knowledge will allow you to more effectively craft your message around not just the company and its Profit Strategies, but within the context of the competitive environment that it finds itself. You may uncover some areas of weakness in some industry players that your prospect is attempting to capitalize on, or you may identify some constraints to strategy.

You can also use the knowledge that you gain in your analysis to develop some assumptions about your prospective company. Knowing the key industry metrics that we discussed above will allow you to more effectively craft your questions as you drive your sales cycle. It will also allow you to more fully understand the implications of the company's Profit Strategies.

Anytime you are dealing with closely held companies, you can develop a good understanding of the basics that the company is operating under by looking at some publicly traded companies in the same industry. With the US economy as competitive as it is, you are almost guaranteed to find some public companies in the market space you are selling into. While these may not be your targets, they will provide you with a good understanding of the industry, and you will have enough information to develop a set of assumptions that will be more accurate than not.

Let's Look at "Blue Chips"

THE US SECRET SERVICE is tasked to protect probably the two most important things to the United States: the President, and the currency. The US dollar is as good as gold, but much easier to forge. Bad guys have been trying for years, and despite advancements in everything from printing presses to computer scanners and printers, confidence and strength in the US currency is a strong today as it was 100 years ago. For that, we can all thank the US Secret Service. They teach a foolproof method to their agents that allows them to recognize counterfeit money, and this method is as simple as it is foolproof. They teach their agents to recognize *genuine* US currency. We'll do the same thing to learn about financial statements. We'll look at the financial equivalent of US currency, taking a look at some companies to see if we can uncover their profits strategies, and why they are tops in their field. Different industries will have different returns due to the challenges their business presents. Still, after looking at several blue chip companies, you will have some additional tools in your bag to be able to quickly analyze Profit Strategies, as well as their impacts on the company scorecards we call financial returns.

Wal-Mart

Let's take a look at the P&L statement of Wal-Mart, and its major competitor, Target, and see if we can see any differences in their Profit Strategies. Two years worth of P&L statements are shown below.

	Wal-mart		Target	
	2004	**2003**	**2004**	**2003**
Revenue	100%	100%	100%	100%
Gross Margin	23.2%	22.2%	34.0%	33.4%
Overhead	17.4%	16.6%	23.9%	23.2%
Operating income	5.8%	5.5%	7.3%	7.4%
Interest expense	0.4%	0.4%	1.2%	1.2%
Net Profit	3.5%	3.3%	3.8%	3.8%

Most people would begin by looking at the bottom line, or net profit, which shows us that they are both achieving about the same results. Let's see if we can understand more about their Profit Strategies by doing a more complete analysis, and drawing some conclusions to what we are seeing.

The first point that we look at is the gross profit margin, where we see Wal-Mart has almost 50 percent less margin, as a percentage of sales. This means that they are either less productive or sell their products for less. If you have ever been in a Wal-Mart you know that their prices are in fact very low, so we can see that their lower prices are reflected in the gross profit margin. Validating that they do run an efficient shop, the overhead line shows that they operate a company approximately four times as large with much less investment, as a percentage of sales, in overhead expenses. Yet the smaller gross margin that Wal-Mart has leads to a significantly smaller operating profit margin. Do you think that Wal-Mart's investors are willing to take less of a return on sales to accomplish their business model? Probably not, and we can see that they don't as we take a look at the amount of interest that both companies pay. The stronger financial position allows Wal-Mart to pay a third less, as a percentage of sales to interest as Target, thereby providing their investors with a return similar to Target. At this point we probably don't even need to look at the balance sheet, but a quick look shows that the debt/equity ratio is about 40 percent for Wal-Mart, and 92 percent for Target. Given similar returns on the net profit line, investors are taking a bigger risk with the higher leveraged Target, whose debt load will probably not allow them to match Wal-Mart's prices unless they can do so while taking less return, or significantly reducing the overhead factor. Both of these strategies are of the "says easy does hard" variety, and would probably take significant restructuring to accomplish.

Just about the time I got around to putting an 8-Track system in my car, cassettes began to get popular. Sony then came out with something that you may remember called a "Walkman." You could find this portable cassette player on just about everyone who was running, working out, riding their bikes, grocery shopping, and even swimming. In fact, the product was such a pop phenomenon that it became a generic term for any portable cassette player, in much the same way Xerox was often referred to as a copy. Then someone figured out how to make electronic ones and zeros carry music, and rather than move into the digital age, Sony got crushed by Apple. Today your typical teenager thinks that the term "Walkman" refers to those bars with tennis balls on the bottom that their grandparents use. The moral of the story: while the companies you see outlined here are on top now, I am using these examples so you can see what "Blue Chips" look like. Staying on top in the business game is tougher than winning back to back Super Bowls.

Dell

The PC industry is one of the most competitive industries in today's market. One company fundamentally changed the way that this business was done when a University of Texas student began to build and sell computers out of his dorm room. He utilized this direct sales model to compete in and later dominate the market for PC's.

Let's take a comparative look at Dell and their closest competitor, Compaq. Since Compaq was acquired by HP, it is difficult to hold a head to head comparison, so we will use the financial returns from each company for the years 2001 and 2000, the last two years of Compaq's existence as an entity. Dell's fiscal year-end for the purposes of these statements is the last day of January, or the first day of February, while Compaq's year-end is a calendar year, so the exact months will not match up, but the statements will give us a good comparison on a twelve-month year nonetheless.

	Dell		Compaq	
Assets	2001	2000	2001	2000
Cash	$4,910	$3,809	$3,874	$2,569
Accounts Receivable	$2,895	$2,608	$4,623	$6,715
Inventory	$ 400	$391	$1,402	$2,161
Total Current Assets	$9,491	$7,681	$13,278	$15,111
Other assets			$7,212	$6,314
Investments	$2,418	$2,721	$	$ -
Total Fixed Assets	$1,526	$1,069	$10,411	$9,745
TOTAL ASSETS	**$13,435**	**$11,471**	**$23,689**	**$24,856**
Liabilities				
ST Debt	$ -	$ -	$1,692	$711
Accounts Payable	$4,286	$3,538	$3,881	$4,233
Total Current Liabilities	$ 6,543	$5,192	$11,133	$11,549
Total LT Liabilities	$1,270	$971	$1,439	$1,227
TOTAL LIABILITIES	**$7,813**	**$6,163**	**$12,572**	**$12,776**
Equity				
Stock	$ 4,783	$4,048	$6,724	$6,733
Retained Earnings	$839	$1,260	$4,393	$5,347
TOTAL EQUITY	**$5,622**	**$5,308**	**$11,117**	**$12,080**

Looking at the asset structure of the two companies on the balance sheet, we see that Dell has been running on negative net working capital both years. In 2000 they operated on approximately $1.3 billion in negative net working capital, and this increased to a negative $1.9 billion in 2001, freeing up about $600 million. By using manufacturing as a strategic weapon, they are able to have their customers finance their business. Compaq, on the other hand, is not structured to operate like this, and 2001 saw working capital drop over $2.7 billion, a sure sign of a company in trouble.

	Dell		Compaq	
	2001	2000	2001	2000
Sales	$31,888	25,265	$33,554	$42,222
COGS	$25,445	$20,047	$26,442	$32,417
Gross Profit	$6,443	$5,218	$7,112	$9,805
O/H	$3,780	$2,955	$6,633	$7,513
Operating Profit	$2,663	$2,263	$479	$2,292
Interest Expense	$ -		$113	$112
Misc. +/-	$472	$188		
Pre Tax Net Profit	$3,135	$2,451	$(575)	
Taxes	$958	$785	$(210)	$280
Net Profit	**$2,177**	**$1,666**	**$(785)**	**$569**

We also see that both companies have an account called other "assets" under their fixed asset account. Dell's other fixed assets are securities held as investments. (Since these investments are in fixed assets, the company has no intention of selling them anytime soon, within the twelve-month window of the balance sheet.) Compaq also has other fixed assets, and the notes show us that these are loans that Compaq is holding on the purchases of their computers. Whenever you see this type of account – and it is prevalent in the auto industry – this shows that the OEM has to offer financing of their product to sell it.

Combining the P&L into our analysis, we see that Dell holds about six days of inventory, compared to Compaq's nineteen days. The difference is just over $1 billion in additional inventory that Compaq has to finance. Since liquidity is proving to be a main differentiator, the Cash2Cash Cycles proves this out as Compaq's Cash2Cash Cycle is thirty-nine days longer than Dell's, at sixteen days versus a negative twenty-three days for Dell. This tells us that Dell has the use of its customers' cash for twenty-three days before it has to pay its suppliers, while Compaq must finance over $1.1 billion to do its business.

Our liquidity analysis carries over to the cash flow statement, where one sees that Dell generated significantly more cash flow – almost 3X the amount of Compaq. While Compaq did generate positive operating cash flows, this was not sufficient to cover future operations as well as the investments that they needed to make, so they made this up by increasing debt, both short term and long term. Dell generates so much cash they are using this to repurchase their stock, increasing EPS even more as the net profit is spread over fewer shares. Looking at this analysis one really has to wonder what compelled Carly Fiorina, as HP's CEO, to seek to acquire Compaq, other than buying more time in the corner office.

	Dell		Compaq	
	2001	2000	2001	2000
Operating Cash Flow	$4,195	$3,926	$1,482	$565
Investing Cash Flow	$(757)	$(1,183)	$(955)	$(1,231)
ST Debt			$706	$258
LT Debt			$300	$575
Purchase of common stock	$(2,700)	$(1,061)		
Financing Cash Flow	$(2,305)	$(695)	$964	$298

COMPARATIVE ANALYSIS	Dell		Compaq
Step 1 – High Level Asset Structure		2.37	1.42
❑ Asset Turnover		2.37	1.42
❑ Debt/Equity		0.23	0.13
❑ Net Working Capital		$2,948	$2,145
❑ Leverage		2.39	2.13
Step 2 – High Level Operating Environment			
❑ Cost structure			
❑ Net Working capital as % Sales		9.24%	6.39%
❑ Net operating profit margin		8.35%	1.43%
❑ Net Profit Margin		6.83%	-2.34%

Step 3 - Key Benchmarks			
❏ Revenue per employee		$ 797,000	$528,000
❏ Product line profitability			
❏ Cash2Cash Cycle		(22.61)	16.07
A/R Days		33.14	50.29
Inventory Days		5.74	19.35
A/P Days		61.48	53.57
❏ Operating Cash Flow		$4,195	$1,482
❏ Operating Cash Flow		$(2,305)	$964
❏ Goodwill			
❏ Fixed asset ratio		11.36%	43.95%

Microsoft

One of the strongest financial returns you will ever see belongs to Microsoft Corporation. Looking at their balance sheet, you can see that cash and short-term investments add up to approximately half of all assets. Beyond the percentage, the numbers that we are talking about are huge. Note the drop in both cash and ST investments from 2004 to 2005. Looking at the cash flow statement, we see that they paid out $36 billion in dividends, and continued a strong stock repurchase program. In addition to ST investments, Microsoft has a number of long-term investments that show up in the fixed asset section of their balance sheets. Microsoft also has an over billing, showing in the balance sheet as both short term and long term unearned revenue. Unearned revenue represents customer billings for multi-year licensing that are either paid upfront or annually at the beginning of each billing cycle. It also represents undelivered elements or payments for other subscriptions where Microsoft has committed to delivering something in the future. They get the cash up front, however, so like all over billings, it is a liability but Microsoft gets the usage of the cash.

Microsoft Corp, as of June 30		
	2004	2005
Assets		
Cash	$14,304	$4,851
ST investments	$46,288	$32,900
Total Current Assets	$70,566	$48,737
Property Plant & Equip	$2,326	$2,346
Investments	$12,210	$11,004
Total Fixed Assets	$23,802	$22,078
TOTAL ASSETS	$94,368	$70,815
Liabilities		
ST unearned revenue	$6,514	$7,502
Total Current Liabilities	$14,969	$16,877
LT unearned revenue	$1,663	$1,665
Total LT Liabilities	$4,574	$5,823
TOTAL LIABILITIES	$19,543	$22,700
Equity		
Stock	$56,396	$60,413
Retained Earnings	$18,429	$(12,298)
TOTAL EQUITY	$74,825	$48,115

Microsoft Corp. year ended June 30	2003	2004	2005
Net Income	$7,531	$8,168	$12,254
Recognition of unearned revenue	$(11,292)	$(12,527)	$(12,919)
TOTAL OPERATING CASH FLOW	$15,797	$14,626	$16,605
Purchases of investments	$(91,869)	$(95,005)	$(68,045)

Maturities of investments	$9,205	$5,561	$29,153
Sales of investments	$77,123	$87,215	$54,938
TOTAL INVESTING CASH FLOW	$(7,495)	**$(3,342)**	**$15,027**
Common stock issued	$2,120	$2,748	$3,109
Common stock repurchased	$(6,486)	$(3,383)	$(8,057)
Common stock dividends	$(857)	$(1,729)	$(36,112)
TOTAL FINANCING CASH FLOW	$(5,223)	**$(2,364)**	**$(41,078)**

Microsoft's stock has been flat over the time period that we are looking at here due to weak growth. However, when you look at the absolute numbers, you have to wonder what Wall Street was thinking. They earn more in interest income than many companies earn on their business. We have already seen how Microsoft earns tremendous cash. Their earnings are 63 percent over the three-year period we are looking at here. Clearly, this is a company that has found the ingredients to the secret sauce.

Microsoft Corp year ended June 30			
	2003	**2004**	**2005**
Sales	$32,187	$36,853	$39,788
COGS	$6,059	$6,716	$6,200
Gross Profit	$26,128	$30,137	$33,588
O/H	$16,583	$21,103	$19,027
EBIT	$9,545	$9,034	$14,561
Interest Expense	$ -	$ -	
Misc. +/- (interest income)	$1,509	$3,162	$2,067
Pre Tax Net Profit	$11,054	$12,196	$16,628
Taxes(benefit)	$3,523	$4,028	$4,374
Net Profit	$7,531	$8,168	$12,254

Keep On Trucking

While Detroit is getting their market-share clock cleaned, one would make a mistake thinking the same thing about one American truck manufacturer. PACCAR, Inc. PACCAR manufactures Kenworth and Peterbilt trucks, and has been steadily increasing returns to the business, and those people lucky enough to have purchased their stock. Long known for manufacturing the highest quality trucks on the road, a look at their financial returns show how they are able to turn this brand equity into additional returns.

Like some of the automotive companies, PACCAR has a finance group that provides loans to their customers. This group earned an incredible 2.71 percent on assets, contributing an additional $200 million to PACCAR's bottom line. The trucking industry has been strong over the last several years, and PACCAR took full advantage of the Fundamental Football Strategy to solidify their position as the premier manufacturer of trucks. The company has invested heavily in R&D over the previous three years, and this investment paid off as truck gross profits actually grew by 30 basis points to 14.7 percent, even as revenue grew 23 percent. Managing for the bottom line, operating margins and net profit margins increased to 11.5 percent, and 5.9 percent, respectively. Net profit dollars increased a whopping 45 percent. Focusing on the future, the company rewarded their shareholders by increasing their dividend $199 million dollars, or 73 percent over the year prior. PACCAR has increased their dividend by an impressive – especially if you are one of those shareholders – 173 percent.

Companies growing sales organically as fast as PACCAR almost always require cash to finance that growth. PACCAR's short-term debt went down, and their long-term debt decreased by over 150 million. They generated 686 million in free cash flow, which was actually an increase of over $25 million from the year prior. The key metrics outlined below show that PACCAR is delivering on their investments in productivity, and based on the dividend increased outlined above, they are also delivering to their shareholders.

PACCAR 12/31	2005	2004
Inventory days	16	20
Asset TO	2.5	2.1
Pre Tax RONA	28.5%	22.4%
After Tax RONA	14.7%	10.4%
ROE	32.9%	25.1%
Cash2Cash Cycle	(27)	(33)
Revenue per employee	$607K	$528K

Business and Society

We've just seen a number of strategies that companies use to increase profits. In the next section, we will look at strategies that proved disastrous to the companies that executed them. Before we leave, let's take a look at why, despite what Michael Moore and just about everyone at the Sundance Film Festival would have you believe, it's in everyone's best interests that companies do well.

Simply put, a growing and profitable business provides more value to society than a business that is not growing. Labor goes toward higher paying jobs – or at least paying jobs -- direct costs goes to other organizations and businesses, and profit goes towards paying taxes, state, local, and federal.

Even not for profit companies pay a significant amount of taxes, when you add in the personal taxes that most business employee's pay: Medicare, Social Security, etc. Business is the basis of the tax -base.

The Odebrecht Group's Annual Report does an excellent job of summarizing this. The Odebrecht Group is a Brazilian engineering & construction group, and they term their annual report a "Social Report." It discusses not just the year's progress on the business front, but the social commitments the company stands for also. The 2002 report shows the following table that summarizes both its results – and its philosophies.

I'm sure that there are many high priced tax attorneys whose job it is to minimize the taxes that corporations pay, but I've looked through enough financial returns to know that companies pay a good deal of their net profits in corporate income taxes.

Odebrecht Group Year ended 12/31/02	
Economic & Financial Indicators (in millions or BRL)	
Gross Revenue	$13,241
Shareholder's Equity	$3,133
EBITDA	$2,461
Operating Profit	$1,720
Net Profit	$1,274
Investments	$1,055
Total Assets	$19,237
Economic Wealth Generated (in millions of BRL)	
Payment of Third Parties (Suppliers of goods & Services)	$8,763
Compensation for Work (Odebrecht members)	$1,103
Government Revenue (Taxes, tariffs and contributions)	$2,101
Return on Capital (Majority Shareholder)	$1,274

As you work with prospects during your sales cycles, and you compare their strategies and results with their competitors, you will begin to see and understand the trends and financial metrics that define that industry. As you expand your sales cycles, you will find similarities and differences between industries, and may even begin to see the interrelationships between industries. When you are at this point, the executives you deal with will see you not as a salesperson, but as a "trusted advisor."

Wall Street Selling Implications – "The Blue Chips"

Just like the US Secret Service who we started this chapter with, you will want to understand – immediately – how to recognize a "Blue Chip" company. As you go through financial returns in your sales cycles, you will begin to quantify these "Blue Chippers" and use this information to your advantage. This chapter was meant to give you some immediate experience in this endeavor.

Never forget that when you call on a senior level executive, you cannot be seen as a salesperson. A solid understanding of his company, his industry, and what it takes to be a "Blue Chipper" within it will gain you immediate credibility.

Finally, just like everything else in life, it is difficult to remain on top. Excellence in management is one differentiator that I have seen in my experience. Industries, competitors, and economies cannot just change, but be *rocked* by change. A company needs top executive talent that can recognize these changes, and quickly react or develop Profit Strategies to ensure their excellence.

The business landscape is littered with companies that were unable to adapt to changing markets. Pan Am helped define air travel for the world, but their refusal to invest and grow their domestic US business forced a crash landing. Pan Am's business model focused on overseas flights that were fed by passengers who would fly other airlines into the major international airports and then switch to Pan Am. Once the industry deregulated, those "feeder passengers" just stayed on those feeders and one of America's premier brands found themselves insolvent.

Depending on when you read this book, you may find some of the companies that we discuss in here in a completely different shape. For that reason, the examples in this book are not meant to demonstrate individual companies that are better than others, but rather are shown so that you can understand the concepts in the book and apply them to your sales cycles.

13

Profits in the Rear View Mirror

IN THE LAST CHAPTER we looked at the financial equivalent of US currency. Likewise, I have learned what the financial returns of companies going down the proverbial tubes looks like by, quite simply, looking at them. Whenever I hear about a company failing, having problems, or having its stock dropping, I note the name, and then pull up the financial returns on the internet, or get an annual report sent out to me. There are many varied ways for organizations to get into trouble, and after looking at enough of these statements, you begin to get an idea of what to look for, because the financial results are reported. Much has been made of the world-class scandals that plagued numerous large, public companies in the early 2000's. To a great degree, when analyzing financial returns, one is dependent upon management and the auditors to provide a fair and accurate representation of the financial situation of the company. Out and out fraud is going to be difficult to discover utilizing what we know about financial returns. Still, there are some warning signs for companies that, if used in conjunction with other means, might provide some "red flags" for you to consider.

K Mart

Let's take a look at the K Mart financial returns and see what we can uncover about the financial situation that should have raised a red flag among the investors and managers. We'll look at the four-year period from 1998 to 2001, to provide us even more information. We see that both operating profit and net profit dropped steadily, with a breathtaking drop of over $1.3 billion between 1999 and 2000.

K Mart				
Year ended	2001	2000	1999	1998
Sales	$36,151	$37,028	$35,925	$33,674
COGS	$29,936	$29,658	$28,111	$26,319
Gross Profit	$6,215	$7,370	$7,814	$7,355
O/H	$7,588	$7,415	$6,514	$6,245
Operating Profit	$(1,373)	$(45)	$1,300	$1,110
Interest Expense	$344	$287	$280	$293
Misc. +/-	$(1,504)	$ (46)	$(280)	$(69)
Pre Tax Net Profit	$(2,533)	$(378)	$740	$748
Taxes(benefit)	$(115)	$(134)	$337	$230
Net Profit	$(2,418)	$(244)	$403	$518

Looking at various key measures throughout the four year period show that with the exception of 1999, revenue growth was anemic, either negative or a slight 3 percent, while gross profit margin over this same time shrunk from 21.8 to 17.2 percent. Shrinking gross profit margins mean one of two things: either increasing costs to produce the sales, or price pressures on the products that result in lower sales volume. At the same time Kmart was experiencing price or productivity pressures, overhead growth steamed on. From 1998 to 2001, overhead grew by a total of $1.34 billion, until it was 21 percent of revenue versus only 18.5 percent in 1998. Let's play the part of manager here. If we assume a 20 percent gross profit, increasing overhead by $1.34 billion means we have to generate incremental sales of $6.715 billion to pay for that. ($1.34/.2 = $6.715.) At a time when sales are stalling, increasing them by another $6 or 7 billion is probably impossible. Thus, the profit comes out of net profits, and we see this as an almost $3 billion drop in net income as it goes from over $500 million in 1998 to a loss of over $2 billion in 2001.

K Mart	2001	2000	1999	1998
Revenue Growth	-2%	3%	7%	
Gross Margin	17.2%	19.9%	21.8%	21.8%
O/H as % Revenue	21.0%	20.0%	18.1%	18.5%
O/H Growth in $	$ 173	$ 901	$ 269	

We also see a growth in miscellaneous +/- items, which when you look at the audited P&L statement demonstrate significant fees for restructuring, discontinued operations, etc.

Kmart P&L takeaways:

1. Continued drops in gross margin signify a deteriorating operating environment.

2. Continued investment in overhead as gross profit drops signifies that management is either not addressing this change in operating environment, or is fully executing on the Buffalo Springfield Strategy.

3. Many charges in the +/- line for things such as restructuring is a huge red flag.

K Mart Balance Sheet	2001	2000	1999	1998
Assets				
Cash	$1,245	$401	$344	$710
Current Assets	$7,884	$7,752	$8,160	$7,830
Fixed Assets	$ 6,414	$7,080	$6,944	$6,336
TOTAL ASSETS	**$14,298**	**$14,832**	**$15,104**	**$14,166**
Liabilities				
Current Liabilities	$624	$4,001	$4,076	$3,691
LT Liabilities	$9,326	$3,861	$3,738	$3,512
TOTAL LIABILITIES	**$9,950**	**$7,862**	**$7,814**	**$7,203**
Equity				
Stock	$3,087	$2,952	$2,662	$3,144
Retained Earnings	$1,261	$4,018	$4,628	$3,819
TOTAL EQUITY	**$4,348**	**$6,970**	**$7,290**	**$6,963**
TOTAL LIAB & EQUITY	**$14,298**	**$14,832**	**$15,104**	**$14,166**

Taking a look at the balance sheets for the same time period several things jump right out at us. First of all, Kmart's net working capital (current assets less cash, less current liabilities) drops by $390 million. It increases dramatically in

2001, because the company paid off a lot of current liabilities as they took on an additional $5 billion + in debt. In fact, in every year, debt increases at least $100 million. Debt growth in and of itself is not necessarily bad, if the other key metrics, such as equity, are growing. Looking at Kmart's debt as a percentage of equity demonstrates that this debt growth is not necessarily good, as it increases from about a 50-50 split to over 2X equity.

Finally, look at how retained earnings have dropped. Remember, that is the "bottom line," so if it drops, that is bad.

Kmart balance sheet takeaways:

1. Continued drops in net working capital demonstrate trouble.

2. When debt increases much faster than equity, this is trouble.

3. Shrinking net worth is bad.

4. Increasing amounts of preferred stock are bad.

K Mart	2001	2000	1999	1998
Net Working capital	$6,015	$3,350	$3,740	$3,429
LT Debt	$ 9,326	$3,861	$3,738	$3,512
LT Debt growth %	142%	3%	6%	
LT Debt to Equity	214%	55%	51%	50%

American Standard

In most American cities it seems as if all the crime, disasters and new world developments occur between 9:00 pm and 10:00 pm – just in time for the evening news lead in. If you regularly watch the news at this time, you might be surprised that anyone is crazy enough to wander out in the city, seemingly open to be impacted by all this mayhem that surrounds them. Of course, that reporter live at the crime scene conveniently fails to mention that the police tape they are standing in front of was put up some ten hours earlier.

Just like the talking heads, sometime companies that have issues and challenges latch onto a concept and try to drive acceptance within the investor community. They accentuate the positive, while posting less than stellar financial returns. For example, American Standard in the mid 1990's could be accused of this strategy. After a leveraged buyout, the company went public and due to the huge debt load, was immediately undercapitalized. Their PR machine went into high gear talking about how *positive* it was that American Standard was operting on "negative working capital."

American Standard as of 12/31				
		1994	**1995**	**2004**
Assets				
Total Current Assets		$1,064	$1,294	$2,889
Total Fixed Assets		$2,092	$2,225	$3,952
	TOTAL ASSETS	$3,156	$3,519	$6,841
Liabilities				
Total Current Liabilities		$1,078	$1,306	$2,346
Total LT Liabilities		$2,875	$2,603	$3,565
	TOTAL LIABILITIES	$3,953	$3,909	$5,911
Equity				
Stock		$39	$334	$(216)
Accumulated Deficit		$(836)	$(724)	$1,146
	TOTAL EQUITY	$(797)	$(390)	$930
Net Working Capital		$(14)	$(12)	$543

It is interesting that once the company began having positive net working capital because they were finally financially strong, they stopped speaking about the methodologies focused to "negative working capital." Now that they are operating with more capitalization, they are pitching the Six Sigma trend that Jack Welch helped to popularize.

Morrison Knudson

Morrison Knudson (MK) was one of the top commercial contractors in the USA when Bill Agee took over as Chair, President, & CEO. Most of their business was in civil engineering and construction. In 1991 they made a decision that in hindsight turned out to be disastrous. They decided to go into the railroad business and acquired three companies over the next several years. These acquisitions allowed them to build new and rebuild mass-transit rail cars, as well as building new and rebuilding locomotives.

Like most bid centric construction businesses, MK was very much a cost sensitive business, with a gross profit of less than 3 percent, and interest income (shown below as Misc +/-) at a significant piece of overall earnings, almost equaling EBIT.

Morrison Knudson P&L				
Year ended 12/31	1992		1993	
Sales	$2,284	100.00%	$2,722	100.00%
COGS	$2,233	97.77%	$2,646	97.21%
Gross Profit	$51	2.23%	$76	2.79%
O/H	$38	1.66%	$41	1.51%
EBIT	$13	0.57%	$35	1.29%
Interest Expense	$12	0.53%	$3	0.11%
Misc. +/-	$23	1.01%	$25	0.92%
Pre Tax Net Profit	$24	1.05%	$57	2.09%

For most contractors, cash is the name of the business, and MK's Cash2Cash cycle in 1993 was negative two days. LT debt to equity was approximately 30 percent at the end of 1993, and consistent with contractors, the vast majority of assets were in current assets. With the large cash basis, MK's net working capital was only $13 million in 1993, although this increased over $1billion from the negative $1.1 billion in 1992.

While the return on sales looks anemic, it was really about average for the heavy construction industry. Contractors – like car dealers - make a small margin without a large investment in fixed assets. While the profit margin is small, multiplying the 2.09 percent by asset turnover of 2.22 yields a more respectable 4.6 percent RONA. When this profit margin is multiplied by the leverage factor of 3, the result is a Return on Equity, or ROE of a respectable 14 percent. It takes a carefully managed business to make sure that all the metrics add up to such a respectable return on equity. What Mr. Agee decided to do was to focus on the rail business. This was outlined in the cheery 1994 Proxy Statement:

When Mr. Agee became CEO of the Company, [he] targeted the rail transportation industry as one in which the Company could not only effectively compete but also become a national and world leader. Accordingly, although his plan clearly envisioned an expansion of the Company's locomotive and transit car remanufacturing operations, more importantly, it also envisioned future new designs for locomotives and transit cars, engineering departments staffed by competent professionals who would create such designs, manufacturing facilities strategically placed within and without the U.S. wherein such locomotives and transit cars with their new designs would be built, key alliances and acquisitions of other rail transportation companies where such alliances or acquisitions were in the Company's best interests, expanded services such as track maintenance and renovation of electrical lines powering commuter locomotives, major high-speed rail projects in key areas within the U.S. and the world in which the Company would help design, build, operate and maintain such projects. In summary, Mr. Agee's strategic plan was to take the steps necessary to position the Company at the front of a rail transportation renaissance. During the year, Mr. Agee continued to carry out the foregoing strategic plan with remarkable success.

Well, maybe not *remarkable* success. A manufacturing business is in many ways opposite of a construction business, in that it requires an investment in fixed assets to build product, and does not have its cash flow financed by clients. This strategy proved catastrophic for the company's main line of business as in an effort to fund the cash required by the rail business, the construction business changed its mix from 60 percent cost plus to 60 percent hard bid. By March of 1995 Morrison Knudson had had enough, and took a hit of almost $175 million dollars to divest itself of MK Rail, but by that time it was too late. One of the preeminent construction companies in the USA was mortally wounded.

Mr. Agee resigned in February of 1995 after destroying one of the country's largest construction companies. Happy Valentine's Day, shareholders.

Balance Sheet As of 12/31	1992	1993	1994	1995
Assets				
Cash & ST Investments	$1,177	$91	$66	$63
A/R	$160	$231	$177	$166
Inventory	$78	$133	$268	
Assets discontinued ops				$72
Under billings	$127	$185	$123	$87
Total Current Assets	$681	$793	$637	$484
LT Investments	$198	$183	$152	$87
Goodwill	$27	$36	$15	$4
Property & Equipment	$194	$213	$113	$56
Total Fixed Assets	$419	$432	$265	$144
TOTAL ASSETS	**$1,100**	**$1,225**	**$902**	**$628**
Liabilities				
ST debt	$1,005	$37	$192	$251
Accounts Payable	$209	$293	$194	$130
Overbillilngs	$58	$104	$104	$63
Total Current Liabilities	$608	$689	$639	$717
Total LT Liabilities	$114	$120	$201	$104
TOTAL LIABILITIES	**$725**	**$819**	**$845**	**$821**
Equity				
Stock	$259	$279	$305	$317
Retained Earnings	$116	$127	$(248)	$(510)
TOTAL EQUITY	**$375**	**$406**	**$57**	**$(193)**

Morrison Knudson

Year ended 12/31

	1992		1993		1994		1995	
Sales	$2,284	100.00%	$2,722	100.00%	$2,021	100.00%	$1,708	100.00%
COGS	$2,233	97.77%	$2,646	97.21%	$2,121	104.95%	$1,689	98.89%
Gross Profit	$51	2.23%	$76	2.79%	($100)	-4.95%	$19	1.11%
O/H	$38	1.66%	$41	1.51%	$52	2.57%	$129	7.55%
EBIT	$13	0.57%	$35	1.29%	($152)	-7.52%	($110)	-6.44%
Interest Expense	$12	0.53%	$3	0.11%	($4)	-0.20%	$23	1.35%
Misc. +/-	$23	1.01%	$25	0.92%	($193)	-9.55%	($174)	-10.19%
Pre Tax Net Profit	$24	1.05%	$57	2.09%	($349)		($261)	

Enron

While complete and utter business fraud is virtually impossible to uncover, there are some measures that one can take to see if a company passes the "smell test." A good example of this is one of the all time great financial frauds, Enron. I am not even going to place Enron's financial returns here because management did such a good job of falsifying them they are virtually useless. However, there are a few other red flags in their 10-K filings that may have given an indication that things just weren't quite what they seemed.

Looking at the four-year period of Enron's financial statements from 1997 through 2000 yields the following unbelievable results:

Enron	2000	1999	1998	1997
Revenue (Billions)	$100,789	$40,112	$31,260	$20,273
Employees	20,600	17,900	17,810	15,500
Revenue/Employee (millions)	$4.9	$2.2	$1.8	$1.3

Either Enron was the most productive company in the world, or something was wrong. From 1998 to 1999 they added ninety employees, and almost $9 billion in sales. That's $100 million in incremental revenue per employee.

The key to uncovering how this measure is causing red flags to wave everywhere lies in one of Enron's industry competitors, Exxon. (Exxon is now known as Exxon Mobil, having acquired Mobil in late 1999.) Each Exxon employee generated sales of approximately $1.5 million, the trend of which was steady over the same time period. This is just one example of why you must be familiar with sales per employee for companies in similar industries.

In addition to the unbelievable revenue per employee, the notes to the financial statements give us additional cause for concern. A comparison of Enron and Exxon subsidiary companies from their 10-K's shows Exxon with approximately 350 subsidiaries, the vast majority of which Exxon owns 100 percent of, with several where Exxon is only a 70 – 85 percent shareholder. I can tell you that I look through a lot of financial statements, and this is a lot of subsidiaries. By the same token, Exxon Mobil is a complex corporation. Enron's Exhibit of Subsidiaries by contrast shows over 2,500 subsidiaries, many of whom Enron owns small percentages of, in some cases as low as 1 percent. Because of what happened with Enron, if you find the parent company with thousands of subsidiaries, many of whom with no controlling interests, let's just agree to wave that red flag high. (By the way, General Electric, in their 2000 10-K showed about 25 subsidiaries, of which all but two were 100 percent owned by GE, and none were less than 55 percent owned.)

> Recognizing a loser can save valuable sales cycles. I once had a salesperson, Bill, who described an opportunity as, "...hotter than a twenty something Starbucks barista." This sounded promising until we pulled up the financials of the company. It turned out that their returns made them look more like a mid sixties diner waitress named Flo.

Enron also showed some of the most complex financial statements that have ever appeared in SEC documents. Once again, think back to the Warren Buffet quote regarding understanding financial statements and in the future, if you find a company that makes it this difficult to read about their financial conditions, assume the worst.

Sunbeam

One of the biggest disasters in modern business history was the leadership of "Chainsaw" Al Dunlap in the two years that he led Sunbeam, the manufacturer of small kitchen appliances. From mid 1996 to mid 1998 Sunbeam saw its stock jump from under $12 per share to over $53 at it highest, almost totally on Wall Street expectations. Earning the name "Chainsaw," the company's 1998 10-K outlined the damage of Mr. Dunlap's first full year.

> *The Company's restructuring included the closure of eighteen factories, forty-three warehouses and five headquarters, resulting in the consolidation of all corporate offices into a single headquarters office located in Delray Beach, Florida, and an operations center at its Hattiesburg manufacturing and distribution facility. The number of manufacturing facilities was reduced from twenty-six to eight (four in the US and four international.)*

What type of financial results did this carnage cause? Property, plant and equipment reduced from $287 million in 1995 – pre "Chainsaw" – to $249 million by the end of 1997. Overhead was reduced from 22.5 percent of sales to just over 14 percent, a savings of about $70 million. EBIT increased over $350 million from a loss of $261 million to a profit of just under $93 million, but this is a bit deceiving as prior to "Chainsaw" arriving, the EBIT, still was over $60 million (although to be fair, this fell from about $145 the year before.) The company took a restructuring charge against earnings of over $300 million and cash provided by operations dropped $20 million, and the Cash2Cash cycle increased fourteen days to 145 days. "Chainsaw improved gross profits from 8.9 percent to over 22.6 percent, but even this proved to be smoke and mirrors, as 1998's gave this back as gross margin dropped to less than 3 percent. The last gasp was the acquisition of three companies that saddled Sunbeam with over $2 billion in debt, over eight times more than equity.

Here are what the financial statements looked like before and after "Chainsaw."

Sunbeam P&L	Who's Al?	All Al	Goodbye, Al
Year end	1995	1997	1998
Revenue	$1,017	$1,073	$1,837
Total COGS	$809	$831	$1,789
Gross Profit	$208	$242	$48
O/H	$138	$138	$718
Operating Profit	$70	$104	$(670)
Interest Expense	$9	$11	$131
Misc. +/-			$5
Pre Tax Net Profit	$61	$93	$(796)
Taxes (benefit)	$24	$41	$(21)
Net Profit	$37	$52	$(775)

Championship Auto Racing – Gentlemen Stop Your Engines

In 1978, a group of open wheel car owners who were racing under the USAC sanctioning banner broke off and began Championship Auto Racing Teams. They went public in 1997, and are a classic example of "going out through the top."

As business boomed, they made the strategic error of trying to grab too much of the proverbial pie, by becoming their own promoter. Rather than work with the television networks to broadcast their races for a fee, they decided to buy airtime from these same networks, and then resell it to the networks themselves, at a profit. This strategy was about as successful as putting a Fox Executive behind the wheel of one of their racecars. This strategy can be uncovered by looking at their financial returns.

Cart P&L				
For year ended 12/31	2003	2002	2001	2000
REVENUES				
Sanction fees	$24,720	$36,607	$47,226	$38,902
Sponsorship revenue	$7,777	$10,150	$12,314	$21,063
Television revenue	$1,889	$4,538	$5,228	$5,501
Race promotion revenue	$10,772	$1,417	$-	$
Other revenue	$4,538	$4,533	$5,495	$9,582
Total Revenues	**$49,696**	**$57,245**	**$70,263**	**$75,048**
EXPENSES				
Race distributions	$60,850	$19,797	$18,599	$15,370
Race Expenses	$8,059	$10,823	$10,618	$9,869
Race promotion expenses	$20,844	$8,687	$	$ -
Television expense	$14,941	$10,975	$-	$ -
Administrative expense	$20,567	$27,756	$35,605	$25,275
Other expenses	$18,034	$3,858	$13,936	$8,324
Total Expenses	**$143,295**	**$81,896**	**$78,758**	**$58,838**
OPERATING INCOME	**$(93,599)**	**$(24,651)**	**$(8,495)**	**$16,210**

What made this strategy even riskier was that CART had been involved in a "life or death" struggle for market share in open wheel racing with the Indy Racing League, and everyone was in a fight for mindshare of the American racing enthusiast. As they were embarking on this catastrophic strategy, NASCAR was executing an Innovate Strategy, leaving the networks to promote the races, as they innovated everything from multiple racing leagues to overseas races.

Merck

When you look at gross profit margins, you can immediately see that Merck's management had to do something to stem the loss of investors from Merck to the more profitable Pfizer, who far from spending management time and effort managing a low margin business, acquired Warner Lambert in 2000, effectively doubling sales while showing minimal impacts to gross margins. See Figure 10-10 on page 258.

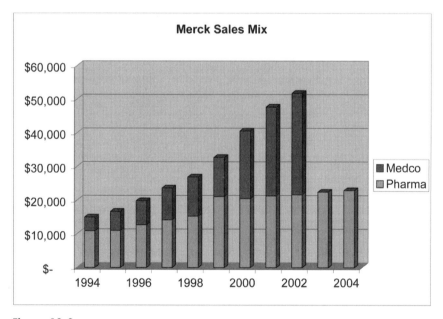

Figure 10-9

A good comparison of different strategies can be seen by comparing two pharmaceutical giants that I was selling into, Pfizer and Merck.

Looking at their 1994 10-K filings, I started by coming up with a market capitalization number to see how the financial markets judged these competitors' strategy over the last ten years. I used their 1994 financial statements to see what type of market capitalization they had. I took the number of shares outstanding as shown on their balance sheet, and multiplied this by the high stock price they showed during the year. While this may not be 100 percent accurate, it does yield a market capitalization number, and in 1994 Merck had a market cap of about $59 billion, while Pfizer had a market cap of just over $27 billion. When I pulled up these companies on the internet to check the recent market capitalization numbers, in the first quarter of 2005, Pfizer's market capitalization had increased over seven times, to just over $191 billion, while Merck's increased just over 20 percent to approximately $71 billion. Clearly, these are two companies going in different directions.

In 1994, Pfizer had sales of approximately $8.3 billion, with sales per employee of $203,000, while Merck had almost twice the sales as they booked just under $15 billion in 1994, with sales per employee a full 55 percent higher than Pfizer's at $315,000. While both these companies competed for pharmaceutical sales, in 1993, Merck implemented a Horizontal Bop Strategy by acquiring Medco Containment Services, Inc., a provider of pharmacy benefit services. The idea was that these programs would help managed care organizations and benefit plan administrators control costs. The problem was that Medco was a different financial model than Merck, so while Merck had pre tax net profit margins of 45 percent in 2002, Medco's were below 2 percent. Taking a look at the sales mix between Medco and Merck's pharmaceutical business as shown in Figure 10-9, one can see how this lower margin business began to dominate the income stream.

Finally, Merck executed the Kill the Dogs Strategy, spinning Medco off as an independent publicly traded company so they could focus on the profitable piece of their business.

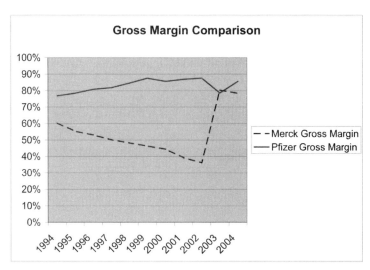

Figure 10.10

*"By all measures, the acquisition of Medco Health by Merck
has been highly successful," said Merck Chairman, President
and Chief Executive Officer Raymond V. Gilmartin. "With
the spin-off, the market now has the ability to value each
entity as 'pure plays' in their respective industries. We believe
that by establishing Merck and Medco Health as two separate
companies, we will enhance the potential for success of both
businesses and, as a result, increase shareholder value."*

Meanwhile, the ten-year financial scorecard shows that in 2004, Pfizer
booked sales of $52.5 billion, while their productivity as measured
by sales per employee zoomed to $457,000, while Merck booked
sales of just under $23 billion, with productivity of $364,000 sales
per employee, just 80 percent of Pfizer's. Of course, the ultimate
scorecard of market capitalization shows Pfizer's multiplying over
seven times versus a 20 percent increase for Merck's.

Wall Street Selling Implications – Profits in the Rearview Mirror

Just as we want to understand what makes a company great, it is also useful to see the other side. Whenever you read an article about a company faltering, pull up their 10-K's to learn how the financial statements demonstrate their problems. See if you can discover what Profit Strategies the company pursued that contributed to their problems. This practice will teach you what "red flags" to look for as you are calling on your prospects, and will come in particularly useful as you are qualifying your prospects.

I once took over a sales team that had built up a tremendous pipeline, but was struggling to close the business. During the first account reviews, I discovered that the team had been following the company's tactical sales methodologies, and were doing a pretty good job on these fundamentals. They were getting agreement to a sales plan, calling high, quantifying the need, uncovering the compelling event, and on top of this, were remaining excited about the sales cycle. The issue became apparent to me as I began to follow the Wall Street Selling Methodology™ in our analysis of their deals, however.

Bill was excited about his prospect. He was able to check off many of the steps that our company's sales process required, including developing a collective sales plan, holding an executive meeting, and achieving the technical architectural review and buy off from the prospect's IT organization. Then we started analyzing the current situation.

The prospect was fourth in their market, and although they had several hundred million dollars of revenue, their revenue was flat while their competitors were growing their top lines. Much of the sales they were garnering were due to discounting, which showed up in their shrinking gross profit margins. The market leaders were showing gross profit levels even, or growing slightly. While not bleeding working capital, the company was showing less and less working capital year over for several years running. A low stock price did not provide the option of raising more equity capital. The balance sheet had no debt and some cash, so at the outside, they could have been an acquisition ion candidate. If they had product differentials. (this is a fragment; suggest getting rid of the period after "candidate" and replacing it with a comma, then appending the above fragment after the comma.)

When I recommended disengaging, my salesperson looked at me as it I had just stepped off of a spaceship.

"But I am at the C-Level," he complained. "The user community is on board, and if we can just make the price right, we can sweep the deal."

"Bill, they wouldn't be able to go with us if we *gave* them the software," I said. "They couldn't afford a few years of maintenance & support."

We disengaged, and moved on to deals that we could win. We began to use the methodology that you are reading about to help qualify deals, and began to focus on prospects with true potential.

As you look at faltering companies, ask yourself if they are hurting due to the competitive environment, or strategic miscues. Have they expanded into markets they didn't belong in? Are they too conservative by not taking advantage of opportunities that are presenting themselves?

This concept of looking for losers will be even more valuable as you focus on companies in the industry that you are selling into.

PART FOUR

Value Integration

"Missed 'your number' again, huh Bill?"

The Ultimate Scorecard–
Financial Markets

FINANCIAL MARKETS PROVIDE HUGE BENEFITS to everyone, regardless of whether or not you invest in stocks. For example, let's look at housing, and the importance that access to capital provided by open financial markets provide. The US government has guaranteed that mortgages written to certain strict standards will not default. Backed by this guarantee, these mortgages are bundled and sold in, you guessed it, an open financial market. This provides for more capital focused to homebuyers. Being publicly traded also allows both Fannie Mae and Freddie Mac to raise equity capital through stock offerings on the New York Stock Exchange, the granddaddy of open financial markets. Finally, they can raise debt capital by issuing unsecured commercial paper, which is traded on – yet another – open financial market for commercial paper. This access to capital is the main reason that the USA has one of the highest home ownership societies in the world.

B-School for me didn't summarize the importance of what financial markets meant to me personally as well as one of the senior partners in the management consulting firm that I worked for after graduating. "You have labor, and you have capital," he'd say trying to look like Clint Eastwood – that is if Clint would ever be caught dead in khakis and a pink Polo shirt. *"You're labor."* After a while, I started looking for a way to be capital.

This chapter is not a detailed discussion of the stock market, but rather is an overview of how financial markets impact executive decision-making. If you understand this, you can use these concepts to drive your sales when dealing with senior level executives.

Concentration of capital allows for expanded opportunity. An access to capital can be an argument as to why many major innovations were either discovered or brought to market by US based individuals. From the automobile, to the airplane, to medical equipment, to software, US innovation leads the way. Without access to capital, an entrepreneur's good idea will last about as long in the market as Pepsi Clear did.

In addition to the equities markets, commonly referred to as the "stock market," there are many other markets that impact an organization's ability to raise capital. For example, if an organization wants to raise debt capital, it can either go to a bank, or issue what is known as commercial paper. A bank has excess funds to loan because it has a concentration of its client's capital.

Likewise, a market for commercial IOU's, called commercial paper, is depended on the ability of a company to issue these IOU's. A broad secondary market that allows the purchased IOU's to in turn resell them, allows this to happen. Like we learned earlier in the book, many companies raise capital by issuing commercial paper. Without these capital markets, CEO's would have one less avenue to raise capital.

The Stock Market

You won't find discussions on "straddle strategies" in this book. In fact, we will use the term stock market in a generic manner, as the differences between the execution of stock trades on the NASDAQ, American Stock Exchange, and the New York Stock Exchange (NYSE) are immaterial to the underlying concepts that we will address.

The first thing to remember about the stock market is that when you as an individual investor purchase stock, the money you spend doesn't go to the company itself, but rather to somebody else who had that stock, and decided to sell it to you. Companies only make money from the stock market when they issue new shares of stock.

Stock Prices

While many financial theorists will happily explain the impacts of the discounted cash flow of future earnings, and how this impacts stock prices, the reality is that that stock price is decided no differently than the price that you might decide to put on that classic '93 Saturn. It's what the market will bear, and abides by the simple rules of supply and demand. That's why a company can see a jump in stock price after a favorable article on them on television, print, or the internet. (This impacts the price earnings ratio, or P/E ratio that we discuss below.) Additionally, the amount of shares offered will increase the supply and therefore put price pressures on the price of the stock. This leads us to the idea of the price to earnings ratio, commonly called the P/E Ratio.

Earnings Management

CFO Magazine ran an article addressing earnings management as an art form, and called it "Earnings Management, The Magic Penny" because as companies got better at managing their earnings, Wall Street began to expect this. Have you ever seen a stock drop because they missed their earnings by that proverbial penny? That's what happened to Network Appliance in February of 2005, when their earnings for the third quarter of fiscal 2005 came in 38.8 percent greater than the year prior. Their gross margins increased from 60.6 percent to 61.1 percent, with most of this increase falling right to the bottom line. However, their EPS came in at $.16 versus the $.17 that was expected, and the stock dived 8 percent from $34.36 to under $32 on a day that saw ten times the average number of shares traded. Unfortunately, the better one gets at setting earnings targets for Wall Street, the higher the expectations. The shift among public companies these days is to give very little guidance to the market to try to lessen the impacts of expectations on the company's stock.

Jack Welch was an "Earnings Management All Star" for the skills he portrayed.

Price to Earnings Ratio (P/E Ratio)

The P/E Ratio is the price of the stock divided by the earnings per share, almost always using the last four quarters. If that stock that we described above had EPS of $1, and was trading at a stock price of $10, the P/E would be ten (price of the stock $10, divided by the EPS of $1.) That's the mathematical explanation. Keep in mind that the P/E Ratio is an indicator of the enthusiasm the market has for that individual stock. If some good publicity comes out on the company, it could drive the stock price up some, and if it went to, say, $12.50, well the P/E Ratio now jumped to 12.5. Same stock, same outlook yesterday as it has today, except more people want to buy it. By the way, the same thing works in reverse, and that advertising executive who said that there is no such thing as bad PR never worked in the stock market!

Looking at a company's P/E Ratio and how it has changed over time is a good indicator of how the market has felt about the stock. Comparisons to its competitors will also yield some insight as to what market expectations are. GE has almost always traded at a premium to its competitors, when you look at its P/E Ratio, so if people are willing to pay more for GE stock than for its direct competitors, you can assume that the expectations for the stock, and the company, are higher. If a company can increase not only its earnings, but also it's P/E Ratio (in effect the demand for its stock) its stock can really see a boost.

A similar measurement that stock analysts are looking at that is very similar to this is the Price to Cash Flow. It generally uses operating cash flow, and uses this to generate a ratio. This is a good measurement, but since most followers of this method are stock analysts and not general market followers, it is probably of less influential value than the P/E ratio. Still, this might come in handy to outline possible impacts to projects that generate cash.

Remember that C-Level executives focus not only on EPS but on their P/E ratio.

Yield

Another key measurement that you will want to understand is called yield. Like The P/E ratio, it is also uses a stock's price in its calculation, and as such, will change with the stock price changes. Yield refers to the rate of dividend divided by the stock price. Note that this is always looked at in full year, or quarterly increments, and like the P/E ratio, is often based on the past 4 quarters dividends. One of the responsibilities of a board member is to vote on the dividend that the organization will pay out. This is almost always stated in per share amounts, for example, $ .25 per share. If we assume that the past three quarters paid out $ .25 per share in dividends also, this offers a dividend of $1 per share of stock. If the stock is trading at $50, this is a 2 percent dividend yield ($1/$50.) What is important in this number, in addition to the absolute amount, is that companies are focused on growing this number.

Boards spend a lot of time thinking about the dividend payout, and establish policies around "payout ratios" to try to put a certain amount of company earnings back into the hands of the shareholders. Although dividend payments are at the discretion of the company whenever they are declared, they can greatly influence a stock price if they are decreased. Just as companies can use a dividend to help support a price floor for the stock, when it is reduced to increase cash flow, the stock often falls right through that floor.

CEO's that pay dividends spend a lot of cash doing it. Even if that dividend yield is measured in decimals, that is still cash going out of the company coffers.

Market Capitalization

Market capitalization, or market cap as it is sometimes called, is another measurement based on the stock price, this time, the stock price multiplied by all the outstanding shares. If a company has 100 million shares outstanding, and the stock is trading at $10 per share, the company has a market cap of $1 billion. This number is oftentimes calculated by financial press as well as internet sites, and is an excellent measurement of how much value a company is producing.

You should also include market capitalization in the analysis that you do to address a project's earnings potential. We have seen how different Profit Strategies will impact the financial statements, and these will directly impact the share price.

I was once selling a major technology deal that was projected to generate a solid $10 million to the bottom line. While that number will get the attention of most people, the executive staff I was selling to must have considered it a rounding error on their P&L. Their P/E ratio was 30 to 1, so I convinced them that the number they should have been focusing on was the impact that the project would have on their market cap, and that was $10 million X 30, or $300 million. I also presented a multiple for their cash flow and ended up getting the deal.

While I would be extremely careful in signing up for an increase in market cap, citing numbers like this certainly can get the visibility that you may want for your project.

Bonds & Commercial Paper

We talked earlier about how financial markets let companies sell their IOU's as commercial paper. In order to do this, two credit rating agencies, Moody's and Standard & Poor's, grade these instruments, helping the market to determine risk and the company to set the price. Once someone buys these instruments, they are still negotiable, so they can be resold to others. This liquidity of the open and efficient financial markets is one of the things that makes America great.

A CEO will want to keep his credit rating the highest that he possibly can, because this lowers his costs of selling these IOU's, and provides him with more flexibility for his company. Looking at Ford in September of 2005 yields the following information from Standard & Poor's with respect to some of the credit instruments they had in the market at this time:

22.	Ford Credit Auto Owner Trust 2003-1
23.	Ford Credit Auto Owner Trust 2003-2
24.	Ford Credit Auto Owner Trust 2003-A
25.	Ford Credit Auto Owner Trust 2003-B
36.	Ford Credit Canada Ltd.
37.	Ford Credit Floor plan Master Owner Trust A
38.	Ford Credit Receivables Trust 2001-1
39.	Ford Credit de Mexico, S.A. de C.V.
40.	Ford Holdings Inc.

Standard & Poor's and Moody's rate both long term and short term credit, and use scales that show the credit worthiness. Standard & Poor's scale goes from AAA to C. Moody's rates credit instruments from Aaa to C, which is the lowest class. It's important to keep in mind that these ratings are for the specific instruments in question, not necessarily the company that they are rating.

Both agencies also rate risk by country. We can see from the example below that Italy will be able to sell its bonds to international investors at a lower rate than Brazil or Russia. For countries that need to raise funds in the international bond market (virtually every country) having and keeping a strong rating is extremely important.

Brazil	BB/Stable/B
Italy	AA-/Negative/ A-1+
Russia	BBB/Stable/ A-3

Bonds & interest rates

Bonds and interest rates move in opposite directions. While many people have difficulty understanding this, if you take a moment to think it through, it makes sense. Bonds are negotiable instruments that you can sell at any time. The bond market is extremely liquid, and it is no harder to sell a bond than it is to pick up a phone and sell shares in a stock. Now, understanding this, imagine purchasing a bond that pays 5 percent interest when this is the going rate for interest for that term of a bond. If interest rates stay at 5 percent, you can sell that bond at any time to someone who wants to get that 5 percent interest. If the interest rate increases to 10 percent, who will buy that bond paying 5 percent? Nobody would buy it unless you discount the price of the bond to match that 10 percent rate. The interest rate increased, and the price of the bond dropped. This works in the opposite manner, too. If interest rates dropped to 2 percent, that 5 percent bond would command a premium. There are mathematical formulas to figure out the new price of the bond, but this goes beyond the scope of what this book is geared to. Just remember that bonds move in the opposite direction of interest rates.

The Financial Press

Many people buy stock based on the articles published in the financial press. A broker once told me that people spend more time trying to save pennies on their canned vegetables than they do when purchasing stock. Now that you have almost finished this book, don't be one of those people! The process of canning the vegetables removes most of the nutrients, which is why you eat vegetables in the first place. If you have the choice, always buy fresh vegetables over canned. Oh yes, and also, the financial press should never be the place you use to make a decision on what strategies a company is undertaking, how strong their financial returns are, or whether they are executing certain strategies.

First of all, the financial press almost always presents company results in a year over year format. Second of all, the financial press is written by members of the press, trained in journalism so that they can be smarter than us, and show us the true meaning behind stories. As you understand by now, a single year over year comparison is no way to understand how an organization is functioning, particularly if you are looking to invest in it! A headline that screams that a company lost billions may mean that the company overpaid for some assets, in effect paying $200,000 for that $100,000 house, resulting in spectacular headlines. If you were looking at that company's financial statements after reading this book, you would have seen this big red flag called goodwill. Then, you would have asked pertinent questions as to why the company embarked on this strategy in the first place, and why did they have to overpay for these assets?

The Issue: Rather than look at Wall Street within the parameters of your 401(K) think about how your prospect's CEO is addressing it.

The Work Involved: You can get most of these metrics right off of just about any fiancial website, or newspaper.

The Bottom Line: Always remember to frame your value propostion around the impacts to Wall Street.

Oftentimes, the financial analysts that follow companies can't even agree on where a company is headed. A financial analyst who doesn't understand manufacturing might not catch all the cash generated by a company implementing Lean Manufacturing, but they will certainly catch the initial drop in gross profit that goes with that strategy. If the company can't manage this to the analyst's satisfaction, they run the risk of missing their expected earnings number. Miss those expectations, and the company stock can be crushed.

For example, on February 16, 2005, Market Watch reported that Network Appliance's shares dropped after the company issued a sales outlook for the fourth quarter that was less than "Wall Street's" consensus estimate. How did they do, you ask? On January 28th, they reported net income of over $60 million, compared to just over $40 million in the same quarter the year before. For the nine-month period their net income increased from approximately $116 million to over $162 million. And they accomplished this without any increase in goodwill. They grew the business organically. The stock market was apparently factoring in a greater increase in earnings. The result was that the stock fell over 7 percent. About a week later, on February 24th, 2005, NetAp's stock was upgraded by Bear Stearns, who more than likely had an analyst who could read financial statements and understand how the company was executing on its business strategy.

Wall Street Selling Implications –
The ultimate Scorecard

Incentive is everything. Even Che Guevara, as economic architect of that workers paradise, Cuba, realized this and began a program to reward the best workers in each branch of industry with a house. He also believed in not just material, but "moral" incentives, so he instituted another program to reward workers who had exceeded production goals. Their reward was to be removed from their current job responsibilities so that they could help to build a new child care center, or lunch-room, or something else that the Cuban central planners felt would benefit their society. (That's kind of like the story of the sales contest where the winner gets a one week all expense paid trip to Philadelphia. The second place finisher gets a two week all expense paid trip to Philadelphia…)

Here in the USA, we have a different view of incentives. The main objective of every for profit company is to raise the value of the company to its shareholders. Because of this incentive, companies are able to raise capital, and we as consumers enjoy everything from hundreds of channels of television to hundreds of different kinds of coffees. Open financial markets allow shareholders, the risk bearers, to earn significant returns.

Innovation takes shape in risk takers of all nationalities, but those lucky enough to find themselves taking this risk in the USA have an opportunity to tap unparalleled amounts of capital. This concentration of capital the American financial markets attract benefits everyone.

The moniker "Wall Street" is really a synonym for financial markets. Now that you understand how to analyze any company, their industry competitors and the industry itself, you must tie it all together by driving these results back into Wall Street. You must know how your value proposition will impact company value, not just their financials.

These are the concepts that senior executives focus on, and your sales focus will not be complete until you do the same.

"Gentlemen, the decision is obvious."

How to Develop & Deliver a Value Proposition that Works

BACK WHEN MTV WAS STILL SHOWING VIDEOS, you could sell your deal by showing a strong ROI. In today's environment, you have to address not just the value, but the risk involved in making the decision. While most sales teams have an understanding of how their product or service will impact value in their clients in most cases, their presentation of their value proposition often is so poor that it actually takes away from the message that your C-Level executive needs to hear. This chapter will outline some basics that will allow you to present your value proposition answering the main questions that executive has on his mind.

We are going to outline some simple techniques and analysis that you will want to include in your value proposition. We will also discuss some strategies that you can use when you are in front of the C-Level executive of your prospective company.

This chapter is not only for sales professionals. For those of you not in sales, ask yourself if you have ever made an appointment with your executive to discuss a project? I can guess how you did it, walking into his office and before he even had a chance to raise a question, you gave him your analysis of your Division, its financial performance, key opportunities to increase the performance, and how much return there would be for the company if you were able to implement your project. Then you made the case for what specific budget and FTE resources you wanted, and showed him a sensitivity analysis demonstrating why he should back the project. Finally, after going through the value proposition and risk analysis in detail, you got most…no, *all* of what you wanted. I did just such an analysis in the early 90's for a manufacturer of capital equipment for the insulation industry.

I did business at one time with a major Department of Defense contractor, where my main contact was a project manager. I worked with her to develop not just a value proposition, but to put that analysis into the overall picture of the company's strategy, as set by the CEO. The project we were working on was going to produce a return in the $5-6 million range, not significant at all in the big picture of the multibillion dollar defense contractor. However, the project would provide a return significantly in excess of the company's cost of capital. That meant that it would help drive divisional profits. Armed with a thorough analysis of the project and an understanding about how the corporation was performing towards its stated metrics, the project manager flew to corporate headquarters to give the presentation and make the pitch for the project. Like most companies, there was no shortage of projects proposed for the limited capital that was available. Using her ability to outline how the project's value proposition fit with the strategic direction set by the CEO, she won approval of her project. The division president was impressed, and she ended up getting a promotion.

My work, developing and presenting investment decisions, as well as working closely with literally hundreds of individuals, has led me to uncover two truths that you will want to keep in mind.

Truth # 1 – Every deal (or project) requires the same overhead.

By "overhead", I mean the team effort of those involved in defining the project. This would include the analysis of the current situation and the value proposition, which can be summarized by the audience in three questions. Why do something? Why do something now? Why implement the project that you are pitching? Executives will dive into these questions the same whether the project is for $1 million of capital investment, or $200,000.

Truth # 2 – The bigger the deal (or project) the higher the likelihood of success.

Projects that have a high level of investment will generate more visibility and much more commitment to success. A smaller project always runs the risk of being "thrown out" when it runs into roadblocks, or chalked up to bad timing, a loss of resources, or any number of other reasons. It seems like economic theory that states "sunk costs are no costs" works better in smaller projects than larger ones!

What executives are like

If you are a top executive reading this, congratulations. (And please pass this book on!) You have worked and scratched and made it to the top of your field. You have proven that you can deliver.

If you are reading this book and are more likely to be pitching your ideas via a presentation to an executive, I'll try to outline what they are like in the next few pages. This, along with the new skills you are developing in looking at an organization and its strategy in terms of its impact to its financial returns, will hopefully help you get there!

Most C-Level executives, like successful individuals in every field, have a healthy ego. Their direct staff may not be of the same stuff, but you can safely assume that in any event, they are concerned about what their boss is thinking of them. If you are going to deal with them, you have to use this to your advantage. You will have the knowledge to think like them, and with a little homework, outthink them. I've found that most executives share similar concerns that can be summarized in three basic buckets. The first thing that the executive is going to be concerned about is the metrics that his boss is focused on. Every executive has a boss. The COO has the CEO, the controller has the CFO, who reports to the CEO, who of course has the board of directors. What is the group of

> Remember that no matter what it is you are selling, there are competitors and substitutes for your solution. You are in a "sales horserace." Your objective, utilizing the tools outlined here, is to make your competitors' projects look like Mr. Ed, while making yours look like Secretariat.

metrics that the executive's boss sees on a regular basis, and what is the first thing they point to when they are looking at this report? As a board member of a large multiple branch financial institution, I see a board packet monthly. The first thing that I look at is return on assets. Now, there are other metrics that are important (earnings, customer service metrics, etc.) but the CEO knows that he needs to be able to address the ROA numbers at our monthly board meeting. Find The Bottom Line for the executive you are dealing with, and you'll get his attention.

The second thing that seasoned executives are interested in, and aware of, is their competitors. Many execs that I have known get some type of information daily on their key competitors. While they are getting all the public information that is available, what would be of value is additional information. Do analyses of the industry, talk to your competitors, and see what they are doing. Then try to fit your project into this space and educate your executive.

Finally, executives are focused to customers, and worry about how their supply chain will impact them. Talk to the key suppliers in the supply chain, and understand the issues and difficulties they face. Understand *their* customer base. This secondary type of information is what will get you listened to, and if you do some of the basic analysis that we have taught you in this book, you will be able to bring significant insight to those discussions.

Getting a Meeting with an Executive

The absolute best way to ensure a meeting with a C-Level executive is to be sponsored in. Often, your sponsor can be someone inside the company who is a Line of Business (LOB) manager in the CEO's organization. Unfortunately, not everyone has a sponsor to get into the corner office. In that case, you need to do the sales fundamentals to get in front of the executive. Whether you are using board level contacts, suppliers, or admin assistants, you have to understand the company's business problem and Profit Strategies.

Executive Meetings

The objective of your first meeting with the CEO or high level executive is simple: gain enough credibility to gain additional contacts and meetings. Don't pitch PowerPoint slides, and don't simply keep the conversation focused to pain. Use the tools in this book to understand the root causes, not simply the symptoms. Bring information about his competitors, suppliers, or business environment to get his attention.

Let him know that you understand his Profit Strategies, and frame your conversation around them.

I had been with the company for a couple of months, and had talked my way into a meeting with a senior level executive by dropping quotes from the annual report, dropping names of his Board Members and talking about his competitors' Profit Strategies. I knew that the executive that I was meeting with was high enough that he wouldn't want to get in the weeds, but I still needed some help in pitching our message.

The help I needed came in the manner of a young, athletic presales consultant dressed in a sport coat and standard industry issue black mock turtleneck. He had seen his stock options soar due to the once in a (consultant) lifetime of Y2K and acted as if he had, in fact, just invented the internet.

He got frustrated with me for the way I was lining out the company's organization, divisional sales and executives, and using their Profit Strategies to craft an account strategy to penetrate them prior to our meeting.

"Look," he said. "Let's just have Reagan (our President) call David Cote (their CEO) direct. He knows him and can tell him our software will take care of his problems."

"How can we do this if we don't understand their pains, or our value prop?" I asked.

He lost his temper and said that that was the way it was going to be if I wanted his help.

Fighting the urge to think I had - finally - hit the golden goose, I fired him from the team and continued to work the company at the division executive level. Nine months later, I closed the first of several deals after being sponsored into the C-Level by the division president whose trust I had earned. He became my sponsor, and after I aligned the value proposition to his Profit Strategy, he understood how my software could solve it. Oh, the other guy – he ended up getting let go.

Getting Action Out of an Executive

Now that you understand how executives think, you need to focus on getting action out of them. Just like you, virtually every executive has more work than hours in the day, so they focus on key initiatives, and eliminate all the other noise. To get your project visible you must get them interested in the project, and not let them push you off on someone else. You want them to say, "This is

Most people come out of their meeting with a C-Level executive with lots of B.S. (That's Blue Sky.)

interesting, and this is worth following up on." To keep them from sending you to others in the organization, make them the owners of what you are working on. There is no better way to do this than to *integrate* the value that your product or solution brings to their Profit Strategies.

A key decision for you will be which executive you want to work with. I have had great success starting high, with the caveat that they will see the value in the discussion. For example, a CEO might not be interested in the integration software that ties in his asset management programs. You need to get to the highest level that feels the pain. For the above-mentioned software, it might be the CFO, or perhaps the controller. So, you want to start high, provided there is some action. Get to the highest level that feels the pain. The techniques that you are learning in this book should allow you to drive your project "up the food chain." The CFO might not be interested in how his customer service organization is planning spare parts, but bring the right value proposition integrated into his CEO's Profit Strategies, and he will indeed question why the organization is leaving that money on the table.

> I once called the administrative assistant to the Chief Operating Officer of a smaller manufacturer looking for an appointment. Not sure if they were a match, I told her so.
>
> "I'm not sure that you are a good fit for our solution, but I would like to see if you could put some information in front of Mr. Executive."
>
> When she inquired as to why they might not be a fit, I told her that although some of their competitors use our solution, they may not be a good fit because they were only about $350 million in sales, with the majority of that domestic.
>
> My answer must have startled her, based on her response.
>
> "Wow. Most of the sales people that get through to me have to ask me what we do. Why don't you send that to me and I'll make sure Mr. Executive looks at it, and if we are a fit, I'll get you on his calendar."
>
> I ended up getting the deal a few quarters later. And they were a good fit.

Budget

Companies generally work on a yearly budget cycle. They will start by planning for earnings, and then address the question of how they are going to hit that number. This may include acquisitions as well as internal program planning. Since many companies have their yearly budget approved by the board up to two months prior to their next fiscal year, the next level of budgets often happen even sooner. In order to get your project approved, you have to understand your company's budgeting process, and get it into the budgeting cycle.

If you don't get your project into the budgeting cycle, there is still a chance that you can get it accepted, but it is much more difficult.. The single best way to work a project through the budgeting cycle and get it budgeted is to have a "pound the table" executive sponsor. The remainder of this chapter will outline how you can put together a clear, concise and C-Level project proposal that will give your project the absolute best chance to get capital approval.

The Value Proposition - Elvis is Dead, Cash is King

The first thing to keep in mind about developing a value proposition is that of all the metrics in a company, the one that gets more attention than any other is cash. Given this fact, your analysis should always start with and focus on cash. You can move to other metrics from there, but you must cover the cash generation angle. In fact, the financial analysis methods that the finance textbooks use, and we will cover here, are all based on cash flow. How much cash does the project require, and how much cash does it generate? Some companies like to do analysis on business projects to estimate how much profit they will bring. In my experience developing value propositions, there is generally always a profit that can be demonstrated. This may or may not be larger than the cash flow impacts, but you have to be able to address and deal withthis.

An example of a project that has a much more significant impact on cash flow than profits would be the types of value proposition that one would get from implementing a Lean Manufacturing program. These types of programs generally have a huge impact on inventory, in effect helping companies turn that inventory into cash. It wasn't unusual to see inventory savings of $10 million. It costs money to hold inventory, because you have to count it, employ labor to move it, hold forklift machines to help stack it, pay for space to store it, pay taxes on it, etc. When you use money to purchase inventory, that is capital that isn't earning interest or providing a return that the business normally gets from its invested capital, and this must also be classified as a cost of holding inventory.

When you add these costs up, you get what is referred to as an "inventory carrying cost." While I have seen studies that suggest this cost can be as high as 25 to 30 percent of the value of the inventory, it probably varies for each company. The concept to keep in mind is that when you don't have as much inventory, you save on some of these costs. Some of this savings in turn goes to the bottom line. If we assume that inventory carrying costs are a 20 to 30 percent number at face value, if a company could lower inventory by $10 million, there would be an additional $2-3 million in savings from this inventory carrying costs.

Building a project plan focusing on the P&L impacts of a Lean Manufacturing project would yield a return in the $2-3 million dollar range, as measured by the inventory carrying costs. The $10 million of inventory that becomes cash does not enter into the equation. Remember what I said above about financial analysis focusing on cash generation, not profits? You must make this your mantra throughout the proposal, and insist that the organization use sophisticated financial metrics. Although these may not be the primary decision points, you will be heard and you will get your project moved forward. If you don't focus on cash, someone trained in finance along the decision flow will shoot holes in your project.

I was working on one project for TRW when the executive insisted that we show hard savings that could be quantified, not soft savings that one might normally throw into the analysis. He didn't want an analysis that was the financial equivalent of "blowing the leaves around." He had a group within his organization that had twenty individuals working in it, and the software that we were proposing was estimated to save each employee just over an hour and a half per day, which worked out to roughly 20 percent. Each of these employees had a cost of about $100,000, including labor burden. Our 20 percent savings added up to about $400,000 per year. Yet, if he wouldn't reduce headcount, this value was really just "blowing the leaves around."

Our normal value proposition used several items that this executive would only see as leaves blowing in the wind. So we took out the "soft savings" that revolved around increasing value added activities, freeing up factory space, etc. The result worked and we got the deal. The key here is to understand what they are, and classify them separately from the hard costs.

Hard and Soft Savings

Because one of the most difficult things to do when looking at a capital project is estimating the returns, the team needs to be complete – yet conservative – in developing your value proposition. Focus on those items that will directly impact the financial returns of the business. The cost to carry inventory that we discussed above is real, but should only be stated as to the direct impacts in the P&L statement. The last P&L statement that I saw did not have an account called, "cost to carry inventory." The savings would come out of warehouse overhead, taxes, etc. Find out what these cost buckets are, and estimate the impact of these on the cash flow of the organization.

Headcount

Some organizations that I have worked with make the decision on projects almost solely on the impacts to headcount. I'll bet that this is because of all the projects that got funded with elaborate analysis of savings, increased revenues, etc, and ended up not showing these at all. Headcount is something that an executive can look at and understand the value prop quickly. Let's say he has an average cost per employee of $100,000, which included base salary and what is referred to as labor burden. Labor burden is simply all the mandated labor costs associated with that employee. FICA, or Social Security taxes, state taxes, unemployment taxes, etc. generally add up to a percentage of the base salary. Although these costs vary by state and location, if you use 30-40 percent you will generally capture these, as well as health insurance costs. So, getting back to our example, if the total labor costs per employee, including labor burden, are $100,000, and the new project can achieve a headcount reduction of ten employees that means a return of $1 million. Because today's managers are so focused to headcount reductions, this will generally always be a part of our value proposition analysis. Saving headcount, or its more politically correct name, FTE (Full Time Equivalent) saves cash, and is probably the major contributor of value in many company decisions.

Cost of Capital

Any Profit Strategy has a cost associated with it, so the planning will try to quantify the return versus the opportunity cost, defined as the cost of capital. Each company will have its own cost of capital, and management's objective is to take on projects that return more than the opportunity cost of the capital. If an organization's cost of capital is 15 percent, referred to as a "hurdle rate," then they must take on projects that will return at least 15 percent, or the project will not bring value to the organization. Looking at three different projects, a company should choose that project with the highest discounted rate of return. Whenever you present a project, you should compare the company's "hurdle rate" with the project discounted return rate. This makes a strong argument for acceptance, as we will show below.

Time Value of Money

In addition to looking at the cash flow that a project will bring in, you have to look at the timing of those cash flows. A dollar today is worth more than a dollar a year from today. Companies can invest a dollar today, and based on their investment returns, they can "discount" future dollars to let them know how these projects compare to today's dollars. This concept is an example of a concept called time value of money.

For example: if a company can invest $1 today and have $1.10 a year from now, today's dollar is only worth $.91 ($1 / $1.10). When you have several years of cash to discount, the math can get more complicated, and you can use financial tables in finance texts, or Excel to discount these future dollars. In order to execute this, we need to know what discount rate to use for your analysis. Each company has its own number to discount future cash flows with called the cost of capital.

The Issue: There are many ways to demonstrate an ROI.

The Work Involved: Find out which measure of return your prospect uses, and then use it – along with whichever one makes the most sense for the business.

The Bottom Line: Always base your analysis on cash flow, and get it down to one number.

Capital has a cost to it and being able to compare your project's returns to how much capital costs the company is key to getting your project funded. There are several different ways to come up with this exact number, and while financial theorists have studied this for years and attempt to get the number down to an exact measurement, it's best to find out what rate your executive uses, because there is a high likelihood that he will require a different – and higher – rate than the company's financial analysts will.

If your project can bring in more than it costs in capital, you can make the argument that it should increase the value of the company. The practice of allocating where the funds will go in a business is called capital budgeting, and requires not just developing the hurdle rate but the evaluation of projects. So, the sooner your project can deliver the cash, the greater the returns will be, and the higher the likelihood of getting it funded.

The value of receiving cash earlier is shown in Figure 15-1, where the same amount of returns are generated, $1,250 for two projects that require a $1,000 investment. On one project, the returns are a constant $250 per year, but in the second project, the first two years returns have increased, and the last three years show diminishing returns. The totals are still the same. This faster cash return shows that the Internal Rate of Return, or the discount rate required to bring the project to $0 in today's dollars, rose from 13 percent to 17 percent. Given the choice between the two projects, on a financial basis, the second project is the one that should be chosen because it provides the highest return.

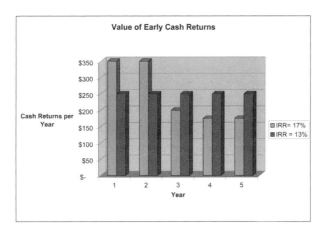

Figure 15.1

Note that if we used a simple ROI on this investment, both investment projects would show the same ROI of 25 percent (return of $250 / investment of $1,000.) This would not give us the information needed to make the best decision on this project, and if the company hurdle rate was actually 15 percent, using a simple ROI we would invest in the project, while if we looked at the discounted analysis, we would reject both, because the discounted return is less than our hurdle rate (10 percent discounted IRR < 25 percent Hurdle Rate.)

Financial Analysis

Based on the example above, we know that we need to develop a value proposition that takes into account when cash is used, and when cash is earned. A good starting point is to demonstrate either a Net Present Value or an Internal Rate of Return in your value proposition to ensure that your executive will get a complete understanding of your project. With the formulas already imbedded in Microsoft Excel, you don't have to worry about finding a finance text to help you do this.

Net Present Value (NPV)

The Net Present Value will provide an analysis in discounted dollars for the executive to see. If the project's NPV is $0, that means that the returns are going to be exactly equal to the required investment plus cost factor. *The company will still be covering its cost of capital, and the return to shareholders is implied in this number.* When executives are looking at several projects, they sometimes use NPV to rank the projects as to total returns. While both of these projects should increase the value of the company to its shareholders, the project that brings in the most NPV dollars will add the most value to the shareholders. A chart showing several projects and their NPV might look like the one below.

Project	Initial Investment (in thousands)	NPV @ 25% Discount (in thousands)
XYZ	$1,500	$2.5
ABC	$1,500	$8.2

Based on this chart, the decision would be to choose Project ABC.

Now let's take a look at how you can present this in a Microsoft Excel format. We are looking at implementing a Lean Manufacturing Project, which we will call Lean Project, which requires an initial investment of $1,500. The company's hurdle rate is 12.5 percent, so all future cash flows must be discounted by this amount. This simple table below shows that the company's discount rate is 12.5 percent, and the project requires an initial investment of $1,500. Anticipated returns that the project will generate are estimated to be $500 per year for five years. While in actual dollars this project will realize $1,000 of returns ($2,500 in returns less the $1,500 investment) when this is discounted by the discount rate, the total return in today's dollars is $249. The formula that you use to get this NPV in cell B5 is in Excel is =NPV (C2, C4:H4).

	A	B	C	D	E	F	G	H
1	LEAN PROJECT			1	2	3	4	5
2		Discount Rate	12.50%					
3		Initial Investment	($1,500)					
4		Anticipated returns	($1,500)	$500	$500	$500	$500	$500
5	NPV	$249.14						

Internal Rate of Return (IRR)

The Internal Rate of Return, or IRR, is the discount rate that would bring the project to $0. Rather than judge various projects by the amount of discounted dollars they are anticipated to bring in, this allows executives to look at the different rates of returns. A table outlining projects that the executive might look to for guidance from the IRR might look like this.

Project	Initial Investment (in thousands)	IRR
XYZ	$1,500	17%
ABC	$1,500	28%

Based on this information, Project ABC should be chosen. Since these two projects are the same ones that we discussed above, this is no surprise. However, note that the decision this time was made on a return rate rather than discounted dollars.

Now let's look at the same Lean Project that was shown above to see what the NPV of $249 discounts to, and compare this to our hurdle rate. Utilizing an IRR, we would immediately anticipate that the IRR is greater than the discount rate of 12.5 percent, because the NPV is greater than zero. Using the IRR formula in Excel yields an IRR of 19.86 percent, which tells us that if our discount rate was 19.86 percent, the NPV would be $0. The formula for IRR in cell B5 is =IRR (C4:H4).

	A	B	C	D	E	F	G	H
1	LEAN PROJECT			1	2	3	4	5
2		Discount Rate	12.50%					
3		Initial Investment	($1,500)					
4		Anticipated returns	($1,500)	$500	$500	$500	$500	$500
5	IRR	19.86%						

This makes it easy to describe the Lean Project to our executives as returning 19 percent, which is significantly above the company's hurdle rate of 12.5 percent.

Unfortunately, the decisions that managers face are seldom as cut and dried as those shown above. In addition to the NPV and IRR's, there are different investment amounts, and different types and amounts of risks to anticipate and analyze. We'll discuss these in a following section when we discuss running a sensitivity analysis on the project.

Break Even Point

New business startups, new product introductions, and additional facility expansions are just a few of the business decisions where the analysis will include the Break Even Point. As we learned earlier, the BEP is a formula that demonstrates how much you need to sell to cover the fixed investment in the project, and is derived by dividing the fixed cost by the contribution margin. In practice, this fixed cost will probably be the investment funds that you are asking for, and the contribution margin can be represented by the gross profit. For example,

Estimated Gross Profit Margin	40%	
Fixed cost of project	$500,000	
Required sales to BEP	$1,250,000.00	$500,000 / .40
Gross profit per unit	$8.50	
Number of units to BEP	58,824	$ 500,000 / $ 8.5

I once worked eighteen months to close a very large deal with one of the Big Three Automotive companies. While there was never any doubt about the value proposition that we collectively worked on, once I put it into a discussion around market share points, how many billions each market share point was worth, and the projected impact our project would have, I got the attention of the executives and ended up getting the deal.

an estimated 40 percent gross profit margin on a fixed investment of $500,000 would yield required sales of $1.25 million to break even, as the chart on page 286 demonstrates.

Likewise, you can estimate how much sales a given return can save, as shown below. Sales are difficult to earn, and because of this many companies use the acquisition strategy to increase them. If you can make the case that your project can generate the same profits as the gross profit generated by increasing sales $25 million, you will get executives' attention.

P&L Statement	
Sales	$250,000,000
COGS	$150,000,000
Gross Profit	$100,000,000
Gross Profit Margin	40%
Projected savings	$10,000,000
Amount of sales required	$25,000,000
Sales % increase	10%

Markup

When building a budget you may have to add a markup to the estimated costs. This is often a confusing proposition that one's common sense does not help solve. For example, consider a part that has a direct cost of $50. The company requires a 40 percent gross profit margin and your job is to price the selling price of the part. Most people would multiply the $50 by 1.4 to come up with a sales price of $70. While this seems intuitively correct, when we look at the gross margin this produces, we find it is only 29 percent.

Sales Price	$70
COGS	$50
Gross Profit	$20
$20/$70 = Gross Margin	29%

In order to price the part to achieve a 40 percent gross profit margin, you have to divide the cost by 1, less the required margin.

$$\$50 / (1-.4) = \$50 / .6 = \$83.33$$

Sales Price	$83.33
COGS	$50.00
Gross Profit	$33.33
$33.33/$83.33 = Gross Margin	40%

Sensitivity Analysis

Making an investment in capital equipment or software, or just about anything that costs hundreds of thousands or millions of dollars, holds risk. One of your goals in presenting your value proposition is to address this issue of risk, and take it off the table. We will do this by focusing on how sensitive the decision is to the risk associated with the project.

For example, what if the returns are half of what is anticipated, or if the costs escalate? There are many different ways to analyze the projected returns in this manner. I have run the various scenarios and increased the costs, reduced the returns, and then showed the IRR. Since there is always some amount of a value perception gap between the buyer and seller, an analysis like this allows the decision makers to see the effects of various cash scenarios.

Another way that has proven effective is to estimate the various scenarios, and put a percentage of occurrence to them. By estimating three scenarios, say, a best guess, a pessimistic, and an optimistic scenario, you can apply percentages of occurrence to each. Weighing these percentages will give you the project's final return. Note the chart below that shows three projected IRR from the Lean Project, ranging from 12.4 percent to 51.4 percent. Let's say that the most likely scenario will have a 20 percent likelihood of occurrence, and the optimistic a 10

		1	2	3	4	5
LEAN PROJECT SENSITIVITY ANALYSIS						
	Initial Investment					
Most Likely	$(1,000)	$400	$400	$400	$400	$400
Optimistic	$(850)	$500	$500	$500	$500	$500
Pessimistic	$(1,250)	$350	$350	$350	$350	$350
Projected IRR						
IRR Most Likely	28.6%					
IRR Optimistic	51.4%					
IRR Pessimistic	12.4%					
% of Occurrence						
Most Likely	20%					
Optimistic	10%					
Pessimistic	70%					
Weighted Average IRR	**18.5%**					
Net Cash Flows						
Most Likely	$(200)	$80	$80	$ 80	$80	$80
Optimistic	$(85)	$50	$50	$50	$50	$50
Pessimistic	$(875)	$245	$245	$245	$245	$245
Sum of % of Occurrence	$(1,160)	$375	$375	$375	$375	$375
Weighted Average IRR	**18.5%**					

percent likelihood and the pessimistic a 70 percent likelihood of occurrence. Using these numbers (which we completely made up) yields a weighted average IRR of 18.5 percent.

Doing an analysis like this with the spreadsheet tools available today allows you to change the percentages and immediately show your prospects of the impacts of your assumptions. If you can get that weighted average above their hurdle rate, you are closer to getting that deal.

As you are doing your analysis, remember the basic tenants that we discussed early in this chapter. Doing the value proposition and analysis is the same whether the sale you are seeking is $200,000 or $2 million. Even though economists like to say that "sunk costs are no costs" companies will chase those sunk costs to the ends of the earth (or at least someone's career) to make sure that the project is successful.

Finally, it is still important to note that you cannot just multiply the Projected IRR to the percent of Occurrence and get the true weighted average. For example, IRR Most Likely of 28.6 percent * 20 percent occurrence + IRR Optimistic of 51.4 percent * 10 percent Occurrence + IRR Pessimistic of 12.4 percent * Pessimistic Occurrence of 70 percent yields 19.54 percent, NOT the true Weighted Average IRR.

Paint the Picture

Another way to drive a decision is to demonstrate the financial results the company might look like once your product or service is implemented. The driving factor should be painting a 3 to 5 year picture of what using your product

Financial Analysis Topic	2006 Current State	2007 Projection	2008 Projection	2009 Projection
Total Revenue-X% Growth				
Costs of Goods Sold-Y% per year reduction				
COGS as Percentage of Revenue				
SG&A				
SG&A as Percent of revenue				
Transportation Spend				
Transportation Spend as % of COGS				
Inventory X% with Y% reduction				
Inventory Turns				
Days sales in inventory				
Inventory as % of COGS				
Supply Chain Carrying Costs				
Supply Chain Costs Reduction Goals				

or services could do if both you and the prospect measure the program together. This presentation method can be very powerful, because many companies are so tied up in fire fighting they have no idea of what they can look like down the road. Show it to them in a chart or graph using their current fundamentals and the impacts your solution will be reflecting the future state. You can either do this by building complete financial statements, or summarize this with a chart demonstrating their key goals, as demonstrated above.

The Board Meeting

Almost all roads for your project lead to the boardroom. If your solution will be taken out of the current, approved capital budget, the CEO will simply apprise the board of the decision that will be made. If it isn't budgeted, your executive will try to get it passed as an exception to the capital budget, which means the board must approve additional capital budget. Finally, the CEO may put it in the capital budgeting process to get funds to pay for it. This final option might be acceptable if you are pitching your project during the company's budget cycle. Otherwise, you had better sell the concepts in this book to gt that project advanced and paid for with one of the first two options discussed above. Either way, the board members will hear about it. And when the presentation goes to the board, they will expect to hear the answer to one question:

How does this project fit in strategically?

It is at this point where all of the work you and your sponsors have done will seal the deal. The CEO's presentation will almost certainly include background for the board members, and then a discussion as to why the deal makes strategic sense. This is where he will reiterate the strategy that the board is focused on. Only after this will the financial impact be addressed, with maybe a quick discussion as to the anticipated risks involved.

"So in summary," your C-Level prospect says, "this investment fits in with our growth strategy, and the IRR is an impressive 22 percent, with a worst case projection – if we just fall on our face – of 16 percent, which is still above our minimum hurdle rate. Our team has even shown me projections where the return could be as high as 40 percent."

If you have done your job, and as a trusted advisor worked to align your product or service and its value proposition to the CEO's Profit Strategies, that summary is usually followed by, in order, a motion, a second, a vote, and then drinks. (For you, that is.)

This book has outlined some specific tools that will allow you to sell high in your prospects organization, and increase your closing percentages, margins, and ASP's. I am so confident of the tools outlined in this book that I have set a goal for the Wall Street Selling Methodology™ to generate $100 million in new sales by the year 2013.

Enjoy the steak.

Wall Street Selling Implications – The Value Proposition

While the concepts that we outlined in this chapter could probably be considered "fundamental football" themselves, I am continually surprised by the sales teams that don't execute on them. Something as basic as discounting a cash flow or speaking in terms of a "hurdle rate" are things that while they should bed second nature, are often not consistently used by sales teams.

With the tools outlined above, you will be able to analyze every decision that you are going to be involved in quicker and more effectively than just about anyone. You will be able to present this as a compelling case to the decision-making authorities so that you can present your project in the best possible light. This knowledge will prove a valuable addition to both your career and the organization that you work for. Master these simple concepts, and you will find yourself booking more deals at a larger profit for you and your company.

"En que hambre tiene, en tortilla piensa."
A widely used saying in Mexico.
(Learn Spanish.)

About the Author

MARK KUTA HAS SOLD over $88 million in technology solutions to C-Level executives. A significant number of these sales were at greater than list price – an unheard of feat in the software industry. Mark has closed deals in a variety of different industries, as demonstrated by his client list which includes General Motors, TRW, General Electric, Honeywell, NACCO, Juniper Networks, Delphi, Steelcase, Ingersoll Rand, Emerson Electric, Harris Industries, Grupo Industrial de Saltillo, Cisco Systems, Qualcomm, Agilent and Vitro, SA.

Since formalizing the Wall Street Selling Methodology™ in the book *Think Like a CEO*, he's become a highly sought-after speaker for national conferences, as well as an advisor to senior executives from companies throughout the world. Mark holds a Master of Business Administration degree from the University of Colorado and a Bachelor of Science degree from the University of Arizona. He is fluent in Spanish and Portuguese and has served on numerous boards.

Always looking for adventure, he has scaled Colorado 14ers, hiked the Grand Canyon, backpacked around the world, and *raised children*. When he's not helping companies increase their top line sales and profitability, Mark is spending time with his family, snowboarding, competing in triathlons, and playing the electric guitar.

Bibliography

Abell, D.F., Hammond, J.S. (1979). *Strategic Market Planning.* Englewood Cliffs, NJ. Prentice-Hall, Inc.

Brigham, E., Gapenski, L. (1985). *Financial Management Theory and Practice.* Fourth Edition. New York. The Dryden Press

Galpin, T.J., Herndon, M. (2000). *The Complete Guide to Mergers and Acquisitions.* San Francisco. Jossey-Bass Publishers

Goodman, R.A. Lawless, M.W. *Technology and Strategy.* (1994). New York. Oxford University Press

Kolb, B.A. (1983). *Principles of Financial Management.* Plano, TX: Business Publications Inc.

Odebrecht, N. (1985). *Survival, Growth and Perpetuity: The Odebrecht Entrepreneurial Technology.* Salvador, Brazil. Odebrecht Foundation.

Tablada, C. (1989) *Che Guevara; Economics and Politics in the Transition to Socialism,* Sydney, Pathfinder.

Index

Toyota, 182, 209-211
Treasury Stock, 117, 118
Trend Analysis, 66, 107
Trump Hotels, 217-219

Ultratech, Inc, 169-171
Under billing, 126-128
United Airlines, 211-213
US Securities and Exchange Commission, (SEC), 74
Utah Correctional Institute, 222

Value Indicators, 143
Value Integration, 68

Value Proposition, 68, 69, 181, 190, 273, 274, 288, 289
Vatican, 223-226
Vertical Analysis, 212

Wall Street Selling Methodology™, 91
Wall Street Selling Methodology™, xvi, 59-70, 79, 130, 138, 186, 259, 292
Wal-Mart, 163, 164, 180, 181, 229, 230
Washington Mutual, 206, 207, 208, 209
www.edgarscan.pwcglobal.com, 74
www.sec.gov., 74, 79, 81

Yield, 266-268

Index to
Company Examples